New Casebooks

SENSE AND SENSIBILITY

and

PRIDE AND PREJUDICE

NEW CASEBOOKS

Further titles are in preparation

New Casebooks Series
Series Standing Order
ISBN 0–333–71702–3 hardcover
ISBN 0–333–69345–0 paperback
(outside North America only)

You can receive future titles in this series as they are published by placing a standing order. Please contact your bookseller or, in case of difficulty, write to us at the address below with your name and address, the title of the series and the ISBN quoted above.

Customer Services Department, Macmillan Distribution Ltd
Houndmills, Basingstoke, Hampshire RG21 6XS, England

New Casebooks

SENSE AND SENSIBILITY

and

PRIDE AND PREJUDICE

JANE AUSTEN

EDITED BY ROBERT CLARK

First published 1994 by
MACMILLAN PRESS LTD
Houndmills, Basingstoke, Hampshire RG21 6XS
and London
Companies and representatives
throughout the world

ISBN 0–333–55016–1 hardcover
ISBN 0–333–55017–X paperback

A catalogue record for this book is available
from the British Library.

10   9   8   7   6   5   4   3
04   03   02   01   00   99   98

Printed in Hong Kong

Contents

v

Acknowledgements

The editor and publishers wish to thank the following for permission to use copyright material:

Isobel Armstrong, for excerpts from her Introduction to the Oxford Classics edition of *Pride and Prejudice*, ed. James Kingsley (1990), pp. vii–xxiv, by permission of Oxford University Press and the author; Julia Prewitt Brown, for an excerpt from *Jane Austen's Novels* (1979), pp. 65–79. Copyright © 1979 by the President and Fellows of Harvard College, by permission of Harvard University Press; Marilyn Butler, for 'Sense and Sensibility', from *Jane Austen and the War of Ideas* (1975), pp. 182–96. Copyright © Oxford University Press (1975), by permission of Oxford University Press; Rachel Brownstein, for Jane Austen: Irony and Authority', *Women Studies*, 15 (1988), pp. 57–70, by permission of Gordon and Breach Science Publishers;Alastair Duckworth, for 'Aspects of Sense and Sensibility' from *The Improvement of the Estate* (1971), pp. 104–14, by permission of the Johns Hopkins University Press; Angela Leighton, for excerpts from 'Sense and Silences: Reading Jane Austen Again' from *Jane Austen: New Perspectives*, ed. Janet Todd (1983), pp. 129–41, Women and Literature Series. Copyright © 1983 by Holmes & Meier, by permission of Holmes & Meier Publishers, Inc.; D. A. Miller, for excerpts from *Narrative and its Discontents: Problems of Closure in the Traditional Novel* (1981), pp. 3–5, 51–5, 63–76. Copyright © 1981 by Princeton University Press, by permission of Princeton University Press; Karen Newman, for 'Can this Marriage be Saved: Jane Austen Makes Sense of an Ending', *Journal of English Literary History*, 50 (1983), 693–708, by permission of the Johns Hopkins University Press; Judith Lowder Newton, for 'Pride and Prejudice' from *Women, Power and Subversion: Social Strategies in British Fiction, 1778–1860* (1981), pp. 55–85, Methuen and Co., by permission of Routledge; Mary Poovey, for 'Ideological Contradictions and the Consolation of Form', from *The Proper Lady and the Woman Writer: Ideology as Style in the Works of Mary Wollstonecraft, Mary Shelley and Jane Austen* (1984), pp. 194–207, by permission of The University of Chicago Press.

Every effort has been made to trace all the copyright holders but if any have been inadvertently overlooked the publishers will be pleased to make the necessary arrangement at the first opportunity.

General Editors' Preface

The purpose of this series of New Casebooks is to reveal some of the ways in which contemporary criticism has changed our understanding of commonly studied texts and writers and, indeed, of the nature of criticism itself. Central to the series is a concern with modern critical theory and its effect on current approaches to the study of literature. Each New Casebook editor has been asked to select a sequence of essays which will introduce the reader to the new critical approaches to the text or texts being discussed in the volume and also illuminate the rich interchange between critical theory and critical practice that characterises so much current writing about literature.

In this focus on modern critical thinking New Casebooks aim not only to inform but also to stimulate, with volumes seeking to reflect both the controversy and the excitement of current criticism. Because much of this criticism is difficult and often employs an unfamiliar critical language, editors have been asked to give the reader as much help as they feel is appropriate, but without simplifying the essays or the issues they raise. Again, editors have been asked to supply a list of further reading which will enable readers to follow up issues raised by the essays in the volume.

The project of New Casebooks, then, is to bring together in an illuminating way those critics who best illustrate the ways in which contemporary criticism has established new methods of analysing texts and who have reinvigorated the important debate about how we 'read' literature. The hope is, of course, that New Casebooks will not only open up this debate to a wider audience, but will also encourage students to extend their own ideas, and think afresh about their responses to the texts they are studying.

John Peck and Martin Coyle
University of Wales, Cardiff

Introduction: Closing (with) Jane Austen

ROBERT CLARK

The act of criticism is an attempt to close with a text and find out more, to open up the ways in which it seems problematic, incomplete, and hence perpetually shifting, different from what it at first seemed to be.[1] Yet this desire is also in part a desire to close the text, to put an end to the play of ambiguity which initially prompted the critical engagement, to produce an illusion that all is understood. To survey the criticism of Austen of recent years is to raise the question of how readers of our day open and close Jane Austen, but also how Austen closes herself, how she brings her own processes of interrogation to an end, for the question of how critics have opened a text and displayed its differences is not a matter only of their personal predilections, but also of the possibilities that the original text affords them.[2]

In the last twenty years critics have typically closed with Jane Austen by reading into and out of her work a history of her times, either from a feminist or from a political historical perspective, or sometimes from both, an activity which has been the local instance of the more general movement known as 'New Historicism'. This widespread critical movement unites a variety of persuasions – mainly feminist, historical materialist and Foucauldian – in the desire to replace the New Critical readings of the 1950s and early 1960s which taught students to read the text as an aesthetic object relatively immune from the pressures both of its moment of original creation and of the politics of later re-reading. New Historical understanding is based upon more sophisticated consideration of how and why texts were initially produced, and what interests are served by their being re-read today. Thus, whereas the high points of Austen criticism in the 1950s and 1960s were works which focused on style and form,[3] the high points of recent work have been concerned with Jane Austen's relationship to her contemporary social and political situation. In 1971 Alastair Duckworth's *The Improvement of the Estate*[4] provided students of Austen with a work which benefits both from the formal textual analysis practised by New Critics, and from the desire to inform interpretation with a greater awareness of the writer's social and historical context. Duckworth's approach to Jane Austen, illustrated in this collection (essay 1) by part of his treatment of *Sense and Sensibility*, moves beyond the aesthetic and moral concerns typical of criticism in the 1960s to analyse the relationship of Austen's novels to the ideological needs of the contemporary gentry. Duckworth's concept of ideology is liberal, which is to say he has no explicit theory of its structure or social motivations, and unlike many other socially oriented critics, he ultimately seems to be on Austen's side. But he recognises that Austen invests in moral and literary order not because it is essentially and always good so to do, but because decorum contains the radically perturbing forces of individualism that have been unleashed by expanding capitalism. Estates must be improved if the gentry are to survive, but Austen urges that they be improved moderately and with due respect for established orders, moral and political, as well as horticultural and architectural. Individuals must recognise the need for objective understanding of themselves and others if the fabric of society is to be preserved.

Duckworth's reading of Jane Austen is in many ways endorsed by a very influential work which was published a few years later, Marilyn Butler's *Jane Austen and the War of Ideas*,[5] an extract from which forms the second essay in this collection. In her book Butler explores Austen's espousal of Tory ideology in the context of the national struggle for ideological control which marked British politics during the years of the three revolutions: between 1780 and 1820 Britain experienced the last spate of agricultural enclosures necessitated by the capitalisation of agricultural production, the beginnings of massive industrialisation and urbanisation, and the political threat posed by the French Revolution and the Napoleonic wars. When published in 1975, Butler's work indicated the new direction in which Austen criticism would evolve, and there has since been an almost continuous flow of historical study and re-interpretation which has greatly expanded our understanding of the links between Austen's fiction and the context of its production: there have been useful biographies by John Halperin, Park Honan and Oliver McDonagh; there has been Warren Roberts's *Jane Austen and the French Revolution*; and, starting with the remarks of Sandra Gilbert and Susan Gubar in their highly influential *The Madwoman in the Attic*,[6] there have been numerous reappraisals of

Jane Austen in relationship to contemporary and modern feminism. In her Introduction to the 1987 edition of *Jane Austen and the War of Ideas*, Marilyn Butler gives a fascinating account of the critical situation that shaped her thinking in the early 1970s, and how this situation was formed by the ways of reading Austen that were current in 1956 when Butler first began to think of her book. In that year, when Soviet tanks crushed the Hungarian uprising and Egypt was invaded by Franco-British imperial forces, Butler's generation were told that Austen was to be considered eternally modern for her ability to teach heightened subjectivity and moral discrimination. Critics such as Lionel Trilling and F. R. Leavis[7] were confident of their ability to discern in Austen a person very much like themselves, someone who believed that a 'moral life should be led privately or domestically behind closed doors', someone whose work evidenced all the tense ambiguity of a refined Modern intellect grappling with the intractable stuff of human experience.[8] If Jane Austen concerned herself with social experience, it was axiomatic that this experience had been so acutely understood as to make her representations timelessly relevant: her fictitious communities were essential communities against which actual communities could be measured.

It was the discrepancy between this refined ahistorical view of Austen, and Butler's sense that the works were deeply engaged in political argument with her contemporaries, that led Butler to embark on research that would lead, by way of her study of Maria Edgeworth,[9] to the writing of *Jane Austen and the War of Ideas*, a book that for all its calm ironic wit and patient scholarship piqued the Leavisite critical community. The 'Janeites' (as Kipling had called Austen's devotees) resented the ivory tower of ambiguity and discrimination being unveiled as a Martello tower standing guard against Napoleonic invasion from without and revolutionary subversion from within. Barbara Hardy, for example, fulminated against a work that discovered politics in a realm naturally free of such sordid matter.[10] All that Butler had sought to achieve was to display the ways in which Austen's texts were full of signs which conveyed political opinions. In the main, these signs implied a deliberate campaign against the social reforms adumbrated by Bage, Godwin, Holcroft, Hays and Wollstonecraft,[11] and a literary campaign against the sensationalist fiction that endorsed conduct subversive of respect for established morals. Butler saw, for example, Elizabeth Bennet and Marianne Dashwood as symbols of a dangerously iconoclastic individualism that would have been read by contemporaries as the moral equivalent of political Jacobinism. The work of Austen's narratives, guided by her ironic commentary, was to recuperate such creatures for a conservative social order.

To understand why Butler's eminently scholarly arguments touched off a modest earthquake it is perhaps necessary to remind ourselves how 'Jane Austen' had been constructed in the earlier years of this century. Austen's rise to prominence occurred not so much in her own time but in the late nineteenth century when a literary canon was being constructed around the inherently unstable configuration of moral seriousness and political disengagement. This configuration, championed by Matthew Arnold in *Culture and Anarchy* (1869), rather reflects the peculiar situation of the Anglican church which was supposed to guard the nation's morals without being political (even though bishops sit in the House of Lords and in Austen's time every ruling-class family had its relations in the clergy). It was because the power of the church was beginning to decline under the secularising impact of Darwin and urbanisation that Arnold suggested literary studies as a spiritual and ideological replacement for waning religious faith. As B. C. Southam makes clear in his Introduction to *Jane Austen: The Critical Heritage*,[12] Austen had only a minor if highly distinguished critical following in her own lifetime and for fifty years afterwards. It was after the publication of J. E. Austen-Leigh's memoir of his aunt in 1870 that Jane Austen decisively entered the list of great British writers. Before 1870 the only significant appreciative voice, apart from the praise of her contemporaries Sir Walter Scott and George Whateley, was that of George Eliot's companion, the critic George Henry Lewes, whose essays in 1849 and 1852 put Austen on a par with Shakespeare. However, after the publication of the Austen-Leigh memoir and Richard Simpson's detailed praise of her work in 1870, Jane Austen became established as a major writer and she did so in ways and for reasons we should explore if we want to read her work with deeper understanding of how it has been constructed.

One feature to which Brian Southam draws attention, and which establishes continuity between critics ancient and modern, is the aesthetic elitism associated with the ability to take pleasure in reading Jane Austen. Oddly perhaps, Austen became an early example of the modernist cult writer whose inner significance can only be got at by the *cognoscenti*. The turning point in Austen's fortunes can thus be seen to be linked to a change in the status of the novel, and indeed of the arts in general, a shift from a sense that serious novels were engaged in what Scott called the 'big-bow-wow' – representing history, passion, and dramatic event in a popularly available way – to a sense that the novel was quintessentially able to provide a refined meditation on the social life of cultivated people. Henry James's novels and essays were as crucial to this redefinition as were Matthew Arnold's reflections on the values of literary education, and the manner of James's recognition of Austen's merits becomes revealing of the motives behind the aestheticist and depoliticising construction of her value. Indeed, it is with James's recognition of Austen's merits that F. R. Leavis begins *The Great Tradition*, a work that refurbished the critical values of the 1870s for the post-war generation against whom modern critics have revolted. A closer examination of the values of this tradition therefore seems particularly necessary.

In his essay on Emerson (1887), James disagrees with Emerson's dismissal of Austen as narrow and vulgar and puts her in the company of Aristophanes, Dickens, Shelley and Cervantes. Emerson's critique is worth quoting because, despite James's view that it was insensitive, its evaluation is quite likely to be shared by some modern readers. Emerson says:

> I am at a loss to understand why people hold Miss Austen's novels at so high a rate, which seem to me vulgar in tone, sterile in artistic invention, imprisoned in the wretched conventions of English society, without genius, wit, or knowledge of the world. Never was life so pinched and narrow. ... All that interests in any character introduced is still this one, Has he or [she] the money to marry with, and conditions conforming? Tis the 'nympholepsy of a fond despair', say, rather, of an English boarding house. Suicide is more respectable.[13]

Emerson seems unable to hear the irony in Austen's representation of the vulgar, but his critique is in other ways germane: he catches the narrowness of the horizons and values, the obsession with money and social competition, the desperate situation of unportioned gentry womanhood, and the contradictory desires, evidenced by so many of Austen's young women, either to accommodate their life to what is practically necessary, or to rebel, run away, or die. This bleak rather than fond despair has received much more attention from recent critics than it did in the nineteenth or early twentieth centuries because as readers learned to admire Austen's ironic tone, so they learned to ignore the social pressures which drove it. In 1902, in his essay on Flaubert, James repeated his praise of Austen in a modest parenthesis which develops more meaning from its context than from what it actually says about Austen. Flaubert was the first novelist to treat each sentence with the aesthetic care previously reserved for poetry and spent five years writing *Madame Bovary* (1857), an unheard of investment of labour at a time when writing a novel usually took less than a year – Balzac, for example, produced both *La Cousine Bette* and *Le Cousin Poins* between 1846 and 1847. In praising Flaubert, James is concerned to thank him for releasing the novel from the obligation to represent grand visions of history, and to announce as a sufficient end in itself the pursuit by the novelist of a satisfactory aesthetic form. In metaphors that locate novel-writing within industrial commodity production, he says,

> may it not be said that we practise our industry ... at relatively little cost just *because* poor Flaubert, producing the most expensive fictions ever written, so handsomely paid for it? It is as if this put it in our power to produce cheap and sell dear; as if, so expressing it, literary honour being by his example effectively secured for the firm at large, and the general concern, on its aesthetic side, floated once and for all, we find our individual attention free for literary aesthetic indifference.[14]

The striking double-action of this appreciation is to make the novel into a manufactured good, crucially subject to the laws of the capitalist market-place, yet at the same time, just because it is so economically determined, the novel becomes utterly indifferent to utility – a purely aesthetic object. A paraphrase of this argument would be that the novel does not now have to be seen as merely a vulgar entertainment (in the manner of Dickens), nor as a morally engaged representation of history (in the manner of Scott's *Waverley* or Eliot's *Middlemarch*), it can be a token of luxury, and of the elevated civilised consciousness that luxury can afford. In keeping with the concerns of the new consumer elite, James tells us that Flaubert exemplifies the conception of the novelist's task as 'the pursuit of a style, of the ideally right one for its relations'.[15] The mention of Austen which then follows implies James's penetrating recognition that Austen, like Flaubert, was engaged in the pursuit of a style, both of writing and of living. Sadly, however, when James comes to include Austen in the pantheon of great stylists, it is with the assumption that, since she was a woman,

Austen's achievement of style must have been the result of accident and intuition: 'Jane Austen was instinctive and charming', he tells us, and like all women, 'enviably unconscious of the requirements of form.' Jane Austen's years of labour to become a novelist, her steadfastness of purpose, her highly conscious valuation of form, are inconsistent with a patriarchal conception of women. James may in part derive his view from J. E. Austen-Leigh's memoir of his aunt, yet it is a perverse sign of James's discrimination that he none the less set aside patriarchal prejudices and listed Austen with the first rank of (male) world historical authors.

We have noted, then, that from 1870 to 1960 there was a tendency to see Jane Austen as a brilliant ironist engaged in moral and epistemological correction and providing a suitable training in the arts of literary and aesthetic discrimination. In this sense, reading Jane Austen taught us about art, and then about life.

Having established this previously dominant view of Austen, it is now possible to appreciate better the value of what has been written in the last two decades. As I indicated above, most recent work is concerned with Austen's relationship to contemporary politics, and with her relationship to women readers, past and present. This focus has made for the valuable debate which is charted in this volume, and to a style of reading that requires a concern with how history and social relations are mediated in literary representations. There is today little of the apparently artless and direct engagement of one highly tuned critical mind with a text, the skill that made the work of Harding, Mudrick and Tanner so stimulating, even when on re-reading one might question the assumptions on which it depended. Their skill was to attend closely to language and textual strategies, a skill which can never be free of ideology but which, because putting linguistic attention before ideological concern, can draw attention to textual matters that a reading focused on ideas and beliefs will not notice. The highest criticism is of course syncretic: ideally one looks for attention to the form in the content and the content in the form, synthesised with an understanding of both the moment of the text's production and to whom and why the act of criticism is now addressed. But, as ideal, such demands may be impossible to fulfil, and certainly as we have recently learned more about Austen's historical moment, so we have not learned much more about how her texts work at the level of the sentence. One critic, however, who does develop this understanding, and who is for that reason included in this volume (essay 8), is Julia Prewitt Brown whose essay on *Pride and Prejudice* attends to the discrepancy of Jane Austen's narrative and her dialogues, the narrative trying to maintain an orderly, objective and unambiguously moral world, whilst the dialogue registers the press of events, or perhaps of otherness-in-language, the precariousness of life that wrecks, thankfully, a conservative sobriety that would abolish vivacity. In developing this view Brown could be accused of essentialising the struggle of chaos against order, and of not recognising that chaos is the name that political order always gives to otherness, but her reading opens a valuable perspective on why Austen's texts resist attempts to attribute to them the stability of values their author probably held.[16]

Another critic whose work tends in this direction is D. A. Miller (essay 4) whose *Narrative and its Discontents* begins from the deconstructionist assumption that a text's scheme of values produces a hierarchised binary opposition between the 'good' and the 'bad' in order to pretend that the terms it negates (in Austen's case, for example, individual passion) are completely antithetical to its interests. Careful analysis of such oppositions, however, reveals that the separation between them is the fiction that enables the fiction, a frame adopted to render experience narratable. Miller adds to this understanding the recognition that the good is almost by definition not narratable because it is a condition without fault: as Milton discovered, one can write at length about being expelled from paradise but little about life before the fall. Hence the narrator is structurally impelled to dwell upon those very experiences which she wishes to negate and must court the danger of infection by what she is convinced she must expel. Looking at the same feature from a psychoanalytic perspective, one would say that the attraction of negation lies in its bringing back to consciousness that which one deeply wants, but dare not allow oneself to have.

To exemplify what this means in reading Austen, it is clear from the moment they meet that Elizabeth Bennet is drawn to Mr Darcy, just as Marianne is drawn to Willoughby. It is also clear that in some ways Elinor is not as cool about Willoughby as she would like to pretend. In *Sense and Sensibility* one of the heroines nearly ruins herself for love of a handsome aristocrat, in *Pride and Prejudice* the heroine marries him and they live happily ever after. The difference between one narrative and the other is made to appear a matter of moral discrimination and an effect of individual character, but actually it is arbitrary, an authorial loading of the dice. Both characters are the same literary *type* – the self-willed romantic heroine who follows her own inclinations and disregards financial prudence. In *Sense and Sensibility*, Austen splits her inclinations into a rationalist who is always right, and a passionate, emotional woman who can only be wrong, and the antithetical opposition of these inclinations predetermines a conclusion in which the rationalist will repress the romantic. In *Pride and Prejudice*, it is the much more delicate combination of both tendencies into one character that makes for a more pleasing working through. In both novels, marriage brings the play of concerns to a close and retrospectively confers on the evolution of the narrative an apparently natural and beneficent causality which the reader assumes will continue into the future. But this is the most fictitious part of the story since it implies that for the happy couple history has ceased and paradise has been regained. Not only did the happy pair escape the possible narrative disasters that attended their courtship – the elopements, scandals and spiritually ruinous marriages that drag down the other characters – they are projected by marriage into the happy-ever-after where apparently nothing can ever go wrong.

Miller's analysis is a very fine example of the work that has been inspired by the deconstructionist theorists of the 1970s. This orientation encourages critics to examine how texts strive to appear logical and coherent, when in fact they are not, so although the approach is apparently ahistorical and apolitical, it can in certain ways assist a politically engaged critique by increasing the critic's power to unmask the ideological stratagems of representation.[17] As we shall see later, Miller's thinking has been directly influential on at least some of the work that has sought to synthesise historical materialist, deconstructionist and feminist approaches into a general theory of Austen's texts, notably that of Karen Newman. In order to lead up to this work I would like now briefly to consider two important historical materialist accounts of Austen which do not deal specifically with either of the novels which are the subject of this volume and so are not included, but which none the less provide important moments in the development of modern critical understanding.

In Terry Lovell's influential essay 'Jane Austen and Gentry Society'[18] we are offered a succinct description of Austen's economic and political situation which underpins many subsequent attempts to interpret her work. Lovell begins with the obvious bio-graphical facts that Austen was a member of the gentry fraction that faced acute financial difficulties during the years 1780–1820, the last years of the agricultural revolution in Britain and the first years of the industrial revolution. Two of her brothers took a bourgeois route to success by becoming naval officers and rising on their merits to the rank of admiral, one receiving a knighthood. Two took the traditional route for the lesser gentry and entered the church and the modest livings experienced by Mr Elton in *Emma*. One entered the higher aristocracy by becoming the adopted heir of distant relatives, a very wealthy and childless landed couple in Kent. To the daughters a pittance of £450 p.a. was all that could be allowed, leaving them in the pinched situation of Elinor and Marianne Dashwood in *Sense and Sensibility*. The absence of suf-ficient capital to provide adequate dowries was a common situation in the 1790s because the capitalisation of agriculture created the need to invest in enclosures and estate improvement. Competition between neighbouring estates, and the need to produce adequate returns on capital invested, meant that to neglect opportunities for improvement was likely to prove fatal in the long run. However, the situation was still transitional and complex. The great estate was a compromise between a self-sufficient feudal manor and a modern trading company: traditional organicist models of the com-munity persisted but were experienced as being in conflict with the commodification of the land and the imperative to reinvest in production. Because estates could for a time rely upon outmoded practices, and because the class was essentially trained in luxurious self-indulgence, change was delayed. Mr Elliot in *Persuasion* is an example of delay; John Dashwood in *Sense and Sensibility* is an example of the aggressive, prudential capitalist; Robert Martin in *Emma* is an example of the hard-working and reinvesting tenant farmer who is able to increase rental values for his landlord, Mr Knightley, and advance his own social position in consequence. Robert Martin is the force that is in fact squeezing Mr Elliot and John Dashwood: if one does not stay abreast of those with new money, one is soon in their pocket.

The literary consequence of this social situation is that Austen's novels perform a series of negotiations and compromises between residual and progressive elements of the social formation, the aim being to effect a moral regeneration of her class and so keep it in the ascendancy. Evidently, as Alastair Duckworth shows in *The*

Improvement of the Estate, Jane Austen saw the great estate as a fundamentally sound traditional order that should be treated with respect. Like Pope in his *Moral Essays*, she upheld the idea of taste as an amalgam of personal faculties that could never be specified but that could be immediately discerned in the design of a house or garden. Henry Crawford and Mr Rushworth in *Mansfield Park* symbolise the appalling destructiveness of tasteless new-moneyed improvements, just as Mr Darcy and Mr Knightley symbolise not just good taste but the good social order that an intelligent respect for the past ensures. The justice dispensed by Mr Knightley (and presumably by Mr Darcy since most large landowners were also Justices of the Peace), is a justice upon which one can rely because he respects the past, is not rude to socially incompetent young ladies, recognises the value of good tenants, and can be relied upon to chase out of the parish gypsies and chicken thieves and other victims of landlordly enclosures.

Where individuals are concerned, Lovell's view of the ambiguous class predicament of the gentry leads her to see the traditional dichotomies of Austen's writing as much more complex than either Butler or Duckworth. Lovell points out that where Butler sees Austen as essentially rather dull and repressive and argues that modern readers fail to recognise Austen's ironic dislike of Elizabeth Bennet, Butler herself does not notice that the authorial voice has more than a little in common with Elizabeth's pertness, for example in the satirical dismissal of Mrs Bennet. For Lovell, all the text's structures are not polar oppositions indicating an unambiguous commitment to Tory ideology – pride against prejudice, sense against sensibility, reliable old money against subversive new money – but ambiguous progressive/reactionary structures which demand complex arts of discrimination.

David Aers develops and complements these understandings in an essay, largely about *Emma*, which has wider import.[19] The thrust of his essay is hostile to Austen and her admirers for the way that they represent a set of values and way of life that is narrow, privileged, exploitative and socially and sexually repressive as good, natural and normative. Aers bases his reading of Austen in her adherence to those Tory ideologists such as Burke who strove to reconcile two contradictory views of society – a view founded in the organicist idea of the gentry as a morally responsible class worthy of the respect of their inferiors, and a contradictory view of society as a universal free market in land and goods. Austen's representation of social problems as matters of individual failing that can be recuperated by the reinsertion of the erring individual into the corrective embrace of the family, is the expression in fiction of Burke's political philosophy. Her novels do provide abundant evidence that the gentry is involved in 'progressive' capitalism, but the figures who are 'good' are moderate traditionalists rather than vigorous progressives. The satirisation of vulgar new money in such characters as the Steeles and Mrs Elton, and the critique of the prudential John Dashwood, has the effect of concealing the actual engagement of other characters (such as Mr Darcy and Mr Knightley) in activities that are no doubt just as coercive and aggressive as those whose vulgarity is exposed. Jane Austen, in other words, is condemned for having performed a whitewash on gentry capitalism.

To read Aers is to encounter a shocking, salutary view that aligns its sympathies with those who will never have the luxury to enjoy Austen's ironies. He asks us to remember the people dispossessed in the enclosures so that capitalist gentlemen could continue to live in their fine houses, and so that novel readers could indulge in fictitious concern over such comparatively small matters as the relatively ungenerous treatment of a mother and three sisters. Looked at from such a point of view, Austen's keenness on the development of a morally acute vision – for example by Elizabeth Bennet – and the elevation of her ironic discriminations into the shibboleth of cultivated intelligence by such critics as James, Trilling and Leavis, seems but an education in clever autism.

Amongst critics who have dealt explicitly with *Sense and Sensibility* and *Pride and Prejudice*, the closest in spirit to Lovell and Aers are Mary Poovey and Isobel Armstrong, selections from whose work appear in this collection (essays 5 and 6, and essay 9).[20] Neither critic is explicitly Marxist but both are concerned with how Austen's texts mediate between, on the one hand, an established gentry ideology founded in ideas of untransformable hierarchy, organic community and a transcendental view of the value of land, and on the other, the disruptive ideology of a rising, commodifying bourgeoisie that has a much greater respect for individualistic passion and intelligence. For Poovey, Austen's irony stems from the contradictory desire both to reward individual desire and to establish a critical distance from it. Romance has its way, but only within the framework of established hierarchy. For Armstrong, the ideological action is similarly understood as a process of accommodation and reconciliation between the upper aristocracy and those elements of the lesser gentry and new merchant classes who, like Mr Bingley, are buying into land and hereditary status. Armstrong adds to this understanding the important recognition that the text of *Pride and Prejudice* – and the same could be said of *Sense and Sensibility* – was originally written in the late 1790s, and then extensively rewritten in the early 1810s. The texts thus bear the traces of moments fifteen years apart, the first being a period of hysterical show trials as middle-class radicalism was repressed, and the latter being at the height of Napoleonic dictatorship and imperial conquest. The need for curbs on individualism which may have been widely felt in the earlier period, may have been balanced by a greater awareness of the need for libertarian resistance and social transformation as the Napoleonic wars, and British governmental authoritarianism, reached their height. Through exploring the complex contemporary significations of the words 'pride' and 'prejudice', Armstrong reveals the shifting field of semantics and evaluations at the heart of Austen's apparently coherent valuations. Her account thus proceeds through historical awareness and philological attention towards conclusions which other critics arrive at via more explicitly ideological or deconstructionist approaches: a recognition that Austen's meanings are ironically questioned even as they are propounded.

Taken together, the value of the accounts offered by Armstrong, Poovey, Duckworth, Butler, Lovell and Aers is to greatly extend our understanding of the ways in which Austen's work related to its original political and economic context, and thus to reveal ideological aspects that are still potent today, especially the work of conservative ideology in representing problems that are inherently social and economic as individual moral issues, and in making a narrow and partial experience of life appear essential and of general relevance. The limitation of these approaches is that, however valuable the social understanding they bring to the texts, they do not explain the complex fascination that Austen's novels still hold for many non-specialist readers who have little concern with social conditions in the early nineteenth century, and it is surely this that critics need to explore if they are to account not only for Austen's genesis but also for her continuing popularity. Attempts to explain the effects of language and narrative stratagems in constructing the readers' subject positions have rather tended to come from feminists who have sought to decipher Austen's work as radically subversive of male power, an attempt which to some Austen critics has

appeared a fool's errand. Austen's decisive opposition to sentimental radicalism and reform is so evident to many who have
studied the original ideological context of the novels that the re-
reading of Austen as a 'sister under the skin' can only be seen as
evidence of the fallacy that all women, because they are women,
will appreciate feminist arguments. The heat which this debate can
generate is neatly recorded in a recent review article by Julia Prewitt
Brown.[21] However, we must also recognise that feminist arguments
are both well-rooted in the period that saw the first extensive
feminist critique of patriarchy, and well-rooted in their recognition
of the need to explain not just what made Jane Austen an
interesting writer in the early nineteenth century, but what makes
her interesting to readers today.

One critic who provides a persuasive explanation of both phenomena is Judith Lowder Newton. Newton's reading of Austen,
reprinted in this selection (essay 7), creates a variation in the
argument that Elizabeth Bennet is a bourgeois heroine by noticing
that Austen has little respect for bourgeois men such as Mr
Wickham and Mr Collins. Austen's respect, according to Newton, is
not for the bourgeoisie but for the autonomous woman who has a
power founded not in money or status but in her own intrinsic wit.
Newton recognises that Austen's representation of the autonomous
woman is to some extent a compensatory fantasy, but sees it as
nevertheless valuable for suggesting that women do not need to
submit to male ideological domination, even if the economic and
legal structures place most power in male hands. Indeed, Newton
usefully points out that whilst men are represented by Austen as
having the power to move around geographical space, and to
evaluate and to choose, men in her works are frequently vain, pompous, and incompetent. They are also invariably servile before other
witless men of higher social standing. Elizabeth Bennet, on the other
hand, disregards economic self-interest and puts fools firmly in their
places. She anticipates and forestalls each move that Darcy makes
towards her, perhaps to a point of excess, but in so doing she ensures that she maintains her own self-respect and independence of
spirit. Newton recognises that Elizabeth's power is precarious and
provisional, given her lack of financial prospects, but sees the novel
as offering Austen's contemporaries, and indeed women today, a
basis for their own resistance to patriarchal domination. Real power
may be economic, but by redefining power as intellectual ability,
Austen moves the battleground to a more equal terrain.

Newton's reading offers a valuable insight into the complex gratifications that reading Austen can provide. It also offers, somewhat against its own grain, a better explanation than mere presumption of why Elizabeth should be seen as a bourgeois heroine. Elizabeth is a woman in the tradition of Richardson's Pamela and Defoe's Roxana: never mind her gentry origins, she makes her career by being true to her self and saying what she believes. She transforms even aristocratic marriage – quite improbably – into a career open to talent. The energy she captures, like the energy of the novel in which she has her being, is a thrusting middle-class innovation that challenges gentry values and will eventually replace them.

Newton's essay constitutes a stimulating blend of class analysis with feminist politics. Of critics who have been more directly feminist and less historicist, Gilbert and Gubar take pride of place because their *The Madwoman in the Attic* has been so widely influential. In their discussion of Austen, Gilbert and Gubar assume that no woman would be stupid enough to enjoy submission to patriarchy and therefore that Austen's narratives only appear to defer to male authority in order for women to gain limited power. They admit that Austen's narratives usually feature the rejection of inadequate father figures and their replacement by husbands who are ideal daddies to whom the heroine is urged to submit, but then surmount this obstacle by making the process more conscious than their writing elsewhere suggests. In a key passage, which gives them the title for their Austen chapter, they describe how Austen's *cover story* dramatises 'the necessity of female submission for female survival', and is 'especially flattering to male readers because it describes the taming of not just any young woman but specifically of a rebellious, imaginative girl who is amorously mastered by a sensible man. No less than the blotter literally held over the manuscript on her writing desk, Austen's cover story of the necessity for silence and submission reinforces women's subordinate position in patriarchal culture.'[22]

The rhetorical strategy in this passage is very like the strategy it imputes to Jane Austen: it implies that the ostensible values of Austen's typical narrative are a trap for the unwary because this is only the 'cover story', but it ends in a clause which affirms the normal reading of Austen – that her work 'reinforces women's subordinate position'. There is on the one hand a secret, subversive message, but there is also no doubt that the message is so little read that the effects are quite the reverse of subversive.

Gilbert and Gubar's essay follows this suggestive passage with an analysis that draws attention to the way in which imaginative, passionate and rebellious young women are brought to order by the narrative events and morally corrected by an ironising narrator who may sympathise with the rebel but always sides with repression. Thus far, their account reads like that of many other critics. Where Gilbert and Gubar break new ground is in noticing that the work of repression leads not to a triumphant endorsement of the *status quo*, but to a barely contained madness. Catherine Moreland in *Northanger Abbey* and Marianne Dashwood in *Sense and Sensibility* are reduced to 'silence and sadness'; Elizabeth Bennet is reduced to humility and grief, 'though she hardly knew of what'.[23] If these fictions are underwriting Tory orthodoxy and Christian marriage, as Butler and Aers believe, they are doing so in full recognition of the psychic damage that renunciation entails.

Gilbert and Gubar's attention to the bleak side of Austen's comic surface allows them to re-evaluate figures like Aunt Norris in *Mansfield Park* who is normally seen as abhorrent. The typical vixen or shrewish woman, she is often described as silly, nasty, loquacious and manipulative, a woman who appears to acquiesce in her own impotence but who in fact always manages to talk her brother-in-law into her schemes. Aunt Norris is re-read by Gilbert and Gubar as 'quite openly dedicated to the pursuit of pleasures and ... the joy of controlling other people's lives. [She] is a parodic surrogate of the author, a suitable double whose manipulations match those of Aunt Jane.'[24]

Through such reinterpretation Gilbert and Gubar make apparent the doubleness of Austen's writing, using irony to expel the very characters and forces that resist male domination, people such as Lucy Steele who themselves 'become agents of repression, manipulators of conventions, and survivors'.[25] The implicit praise of Lucy Steele in this reading stands Austen's apparent dislike of Lucy's mercenary spirit on its head. Gilbert and Gubar recognise that the characters that have often been thought to attract their author's most intense dislike are those who turn the tables on patriarchy, but see in their vivacity and cunning a tacit admiration for those who can beat men at their own game. Austen thus remains for Gilbert and Gubar a conservative patriarchal writer, but one whose vigorous awareness of patriarchal power makes it possible for women to recognise strategies of resistance, and understand the havoc wreaked by submission.

It is possible to argue that such a way of reading Austen maps modern American feminist values onto a writer who in all probability would have found Gilbert and Gubar's admiration for the amoral female self-seeker as appalling as she found the venial attitudes of many of her contemporaries. However, it is also worth admitting that the fascination of repulsion provides a valuable path into Austen's motivations and our own reasons for reading her novels. Marianne Dashwood and Elizabeth Bennet are attractive because unconventional and rebellious, and the mixed quality of their appeal is perhaps merely writ larger in those characters whom the novels decide to destroy.

Despite its general importance for the development of Austen criticism, and for readings of nineteenth-century fiction in general, Gilbert and Gubar's account is not reprinted in this collection because their discussion has little directly to say about either *Sense and Sensibility* or *Pride and Prejudice*, though their influence is evident on many other critics of these novels. Angela Leighton, for example, develops an account of *Sense and Sensibility* (essay 3) which travels a parallel path to Gilbert and Gubar but which avoids their forced if forceful reading against Austen's grain. Leighton sees Marianne Dashwood as the victim of patriarchal repression but constructs an argument which is the more cogent for proceeding at the level where Austen excels, the use of language. Following modern French feminist thinkers at a discrete remove, Leighton explores the way in which the refusal of women to speak can signify different attitudes to conventions of discourse and conduct. Typically, Elinor does not speak out of consideration for others; whereas Marianne does not speak because she finds her companions not worth speaking to. The one is all good manners, the other all truth. But for Austen, Marianne's silence is a refusal, an act of rebellion that threatens not just social propriety but the fundamentals of her own art. Marianne's rebellious silence must be converted into Elinor's articulate self-repression.

It is interesting to note how Leighton's reading parallels that of D. A. Miller, yet also turns it upside down: Miller argues that Marianne is the more narratable subject because she is the dangerous, the rebellious expression of repressed desire; she is also that which the narrative must eventually close down if it is to reach a happy end and complete its conservative ideological work. Whilst in general agreement with Miller's argument, Leighton, however, implies that the truly radical position is not the threat of

Marianne's conduct, but her ultimate unwritability – the fact that the truly dangerous Marianne, that distant fantasm of fears of the Wollstonecraft feminists, of Jacobites, of social unrest, the fear of poverty and failure or her own sexual desires – is unreachable in Austen's language. She can be re-presented in Marianne, she can be caricatured and figured in an elementary way, but to actually allow this fantasm (or the real itself) to speak would be to tear apart the decorum in which Austen invests. It is therefore only in Marianne's not-said that the real threat lies, and it is therefore in the reconfiguration of what her not-said means that we see the real triumph of conservatism in the battle of *Sense and Sensibility*.

Rachel Brownstein is another feminist critic who explores the implications of Austen's investment in decorum. She begins her analysis (essay 10) by taking up Mary Poovey's argument that Jane Austen gained power for herself, as had generations of late eighteenth-century women, by becoming a 'Proper Lady', a symbol of refinement and taste that empowers even as it imprisons. Brownstein recognises that the power granted by this style is deeply hierarchical: its skill lies in developing a double code within the language of representation which enables the reader to perceive the represented at an ironic distance, indicating the gulf between the petty, vulgar behaviour of grasping and unaware people and the high values of intelligence, wit, decorum and taste. Austen's writing has therefore been used as an exercise in discrimination for snobbish ends, a writing which, as we have seen above, can be used as a conduct book for training superior manners and as an indicator of achieved superiority. As Wayne Booth says in *The Rhetoric of Fiction*, 'we readers of Austen have the illusion of travelling intimately with a hardy little band of readers whose heads are screwed on tight and whose hearts are in the right place.'[26] The implication of such a 'we' is that others have loose heads, and hearts anywhere but in their chests. Austen readers – and there are still those like P. D. James who claim to re-read Austen every year – are a savant elite, a *cognoscenti*. Put another way, in recognising her style as their own, they gain the power to denigrate the style-less.

By writing as 'A Lady', then, Austen removes herself to a high, abstract ground, a ground of superior consciousness and implied social standing she cannot finance, and grants herself a specular, compensatory authority that appears to locate and contain the disruptive forces of new money, the very forces which we have seen are emblem and agency of the changes that are driving many members of Austen's class out of their secure 'traditional' lives. Austen's discourse is a triumphant *novelistic* invention because the function of the genre itself is to offer solitary and usually impotent people (a high proportion of them women) the illusion of comprehending omnipotence. In the process of establishing this illusion Austen fashions a discourse that constitutes an epistemological break in the history of the genre, one which becomes a paradigmatic discourse of novelistic narration from that day to this.

The implication of the work of Lovell, Aers and Butler is that this discourse should be seen as gentry-conservative and as paving the way for an idea of women's fate as best negotiated within the constraints of a modest, repressive bourgeois marriage. The implication of feminist readings is that Austen's discourse should be seen both as patriarchal in its naïve readings, and as in some ways at least subversive of patriarchy in its ironisation of the presumptions of male authority. Following Virginia Woolf, Brownstein, for example, convincingly argues that the opening sentence of *Pride and Prejudice* is a deliberate ironisation of male 'authoritative sentence making',[27] a suggestion that alerts us to the fact that many of Austen's balanced Johnsonian periods – which are usually taken as affirming conservative order – can be read ironically by those who have the will to do so. To some, such a reading can only seem a wilful misreading since, for example, what follows the opening sentence appears to make it clear that it is rather the mind of Mrs Bennet, and the collective wisdom of the rural gentry, that is being ironised, not the speech patterns of Mr Bennet himself. Indeed, Mr Bennet conspicuously distances himself from the 'truths universally acknowledged' by his wife. The evidence of the full context indicates that the undermining of authority is for Jane Austen not an attack on the form of Johnsonian epigrams, or on patriarchal attitudes; it is an attack on simple-mindedness, on socially sanctioned stupidity. The sentence is written ironically in order to display Austen's possession of what might be considered a very 'male' skill: superior authoritative wit.

None the less, it is a valid recognition that Austen's critique, however motivated, opens a space of suspicion between the reader and the discursive instruments of male authority, and in a political sense. The ideological work of any text (and it may be a litmus test for great ones) is not uniform or predictable. Art lives in ideology only to expose or undermine it.[28] Hence the artistic text's openness to re-reading, its refusal to be closed. The space of suspicion which one highly intelligent and economically marginalised woman might open out of the desire to defend her own psychic integrity, can be closed down by ciphering it as snobbism (and then either agreeing snobbery is a good thing, or taking revolutionary measures), or it can be seen as a potentially destabilising tendency that exposes the negative aspects of even the very sentence that it uses.

This is Brownstein's invigorating, deconstructive case, and it finds support in the last essay in this collection, Karen Newman's 'Can this Marriage be Saved: Jane Austen Makes Sense of an Ending'. Newman again takes her starting point from the hermeneutical crux that either we read Austen's novels as romantic love stories in which the 'social and economic realities of women's lives are exposed, but undermined by comedy, irony, and more tellingly marriage, or [we] read marriage as the overcoming of foolish egoism, a sign of social maturity'.[29] In either reading the effect of the ending is apparently to undermine the foreclosure of women's human rights. From a feminist point of view, such endings can only be tragic, and Austen's texts provide abundant evidence that this is indeed the case; but the form of Austen's novels is comic-romance so that for the heroine, wish-fulfilment satisfaction is the case (after the pattern of Cinderella or Snow White).

Admitting this but disturbing it, Newman discovers a fault in our tendency to read back from any ending a teleology that closes down the possible meanings of anything that leads up to it. From 'Aha, so that's how it turns out!' we tend, like poor detectives, to array the evidence into coherent teleological patterns. This habit of reading is constructed in part by the tendency of nineteenth-century novels to point the way forward by authorial interjections or implicit generalisations that give the moral coordinates of the fiction, and indeed of the historical world it purports to represent. Thus, in Jane Austen's narrative all minds are bent upon marriage and it is only a question of when and what kind it will be. However, as we have seen, in Austen's narration the very maxims that point towards marriage are as prone to ironisation as any part of her texts. We thus travel with untrustworthy signposts, and through a landscape of wrecked marriages which have served as the *teloi* of micro-narratives along the way: the mean conspiracies of Mr and Mrs Dashwood, the vanity of Lady Bertram, the emptiness and ironic reserve of the Bennet seniors, the cold calculating manipulations of Charlotte Lucas – the list of moral and psychic wrecks is long. We are therefore confronted with texts which appear to adumbrate as a resolution an institution that is more often represented as no solution at all.

Newman's explanation of this discrepancy is to remind us that in the theory of Pierre Macherey and Louis Althusser literary texts juxtapose contradictory meanings and so display to us the essentially faulty nature of ideology. In Althusser's terms they provide 'an internal distanciation from the very ideology from which [they] emerge]'.[30] One of Newman's specimen lines for displaying this process is this: 'his friend, Mr Darcy drew the attention of the room by his fine, tall person, handsome features, noble mien; and the report which was in general circulation within five minutes after his entrance, of his having ten thousand a year'.

Austen's irony here is produced by the stark juxtaposition of a romantic image and its material base. She exposes the interrelation of fiduciary interest and romantic allure without comment, and indeed it is interesting to reflect that Austen's irony only works here because we habitually keep such perceptions entirely separate. Such compartmentalisation is typical of the work of ideology, and Austen short-circuits the amnesia which power – and especially aristocratic power – tends to draw over the links between noble mien, psychic allure, and cash in the bank. A similar example can be found when Mrs Bennet, lamenting the defection of Bingley, says to her sister-in-law Mrs Gardiner, 'Your coming at this time is the greatest of comforts, and I am very glad to hear what you tell us of long sleeves'. Again the juxtaposition of what one is supposed to do and feel (the ideological *pre-script*, one might say) with Mrs Bennet's primary concern with trivial matters of fashion, establishes an ironic distance merely by deleting the camouflage that usually obscures motivation. Such an example is perhaps too evident, too easy. Austen scores better when representing more complex creatures. For example, when Elizabeth thanks Charlotte Lucas for listening to the tediously moralising Mr Collins: 'Charlotte assured her friend of her satisfaction in being useful, and [said] that it amply repaid her for the little sacrifice of her time. This was very amiable, but Charlotte's kindness extended farther than Elizabeth had any conceptions of; – its object was nothing less than to secure her from any return of Mr Collins's addresses, by engaging them to herself. Such was Miss Lucas's scheme.'

Here the ironic thrust hinges upon the word 'amiable' which Johnson's dictionary of 1755 defines as (i) pleasing and lovely, and (ii) pretending or shewing love. Charlotte's behaviour is pleasing, and pretending. Two chapters later the author remarks: 'After a week spent in professions of love and schemes of felicity, Mr Collins was called from his amiable Charlotte.' Austen's irony consists in harnessing the explosive ambiguous range of each word, providing an amiable surface reading, and a scheming, treacherous deep reading. A 'profession' is an announcement, a declaration, even a calling; it is also an empty sham. A 'scheme' is a plan, and a deceptive stratagem. The language professes an amused pleasure in trivial courtship; it also systematically reveals a world where people invest in sadly thin and duplicitous representations, perhaps knowing, perhaps not knowing what they are doing.

One could illustrate this process almost *ad infinitum*. Newman's point is very well made. Sometimes by no more than calling into play the full potential semantic range of Johnson's dictionary, Jane Austen reveals the gap between sentimental ideals, novelists' conventions, and the actuality of a hypocritical and avaricious world that reduces people to commodities to be brokered in a marriage market. Her texts cannot be said *not* to advocate a conservative view of marriage that closes down all other possibilities of existence and weds women and men to a structure of bourgeois property relations; and they can certainly be said to construct a world which is entirely bourgeois in its discourse, its presumptions of knowledge, its hierarchical rankings, its wilful blindness to the effects of social power on those outside the ruling class. This is certainly Tory fiction and it is right for critics to draw our attention to its ideological investments. At the same time, Austen accedes to power as a writer through the inhabitation of a linguistic-ideological system pre-determining thought in patriarchal lines. Her 'mastery' of this discourse does provide women readers with an empowering possibility; but, more than this, when Austen makes show of her wit to unpack patriarchal sententiousness, she may only consider she is out-mastering men at a very male game, but the effect of her ironisation is to reveal the faults in the very ideology she seems to espouse. Her writing thus may be inspired by a Tory desire to close down the options for women by censoring rebellion and sentimentality and the struggle to live free of bourgeois constraint, but the effect of the work it performs in language is to constantly expose and open up the processes whereby closure is attempted. This leaves modern readers with a questioning space in which to make up their own minds how they want to close with Jane Austen.

NOTES

1. This introduction was first delivered as a plenary lecture at the annual conference of the Portuguese Association for the Study of English, Oporto, March 1992. My thanks to Portuguese colleagues and friends for their helpful comments.

2. Readers who would like to explore this orientation towards critical practice might begin with the classic work by Barbara Johnson, *The Critical Difference: Essays in the Contemporary Rhetoric of Reading* (Baltimore, 1980) or Christopher Norris, *Deconstruction: Theory and Practice* (London, 1982).

3. Marvin Mudrick, *Jane Austen; Irony as Defence and Discovery* (Princeton, NJ, 1952); Tony Tanner's essays and introductions of the 1960s were later revised and collected in his *Jane Austen* (London, 1986).

4. Alastair Duckworth, *The Improvement of the Estate* (Baltimore, 1971).

5. Marilyn Butler, *Jane Austen and the War of Ideas* (Oxford, 1975; reissued with a new introduction, 1987).

6. Warren Roberts, *Jane Austen and the French Revolution* (Basingstoke, 1979); Susan Gilbert and Sandra Gubar, *The Madwoman in the Attic: The Woman Writer and the Nineteenth-Century Literary Imagination* (New Haven, 1979).

7. Lionel Trilling, *The Opposing Self* (New York, 1955); F. R. Leavis, *The Great Tradition* (London, 1948). Whilst anyone who engaged in the critical struggles of the 1960s will understand immediately the ethos which Butler describes, it is important to note in retrospect that Leavis and Trilling sought to provide a moral dimension to a literary criticism which was traditionally aestheticist. To re-read what Leavis says of Austen in *The Great Tradition* is to be reminded that his effort was to read Austen as morally engaged rather than someone who merely achieved formal perfection. Leavis's view of morality was Christian and individual, but his concern with 'life' – a notorious Leavisian word – did begin the movement of criticism towards social and historical engagement, even though those who took up the task two decades later would proclaim its triumphs in opposition to his legacy.

8. Marilyn Butler, *Jane Austen and the War of Ideas*, 1987 edition, p. xiii.

9. Marilyn Butler, *Maria Edgeworth: A Literary Biography* (Oxford, 1972).

10. Barbara Hardy, 'Antidotes to Idolatry,' *The Times Higher Education Supplement*, 9 January 1976, p. 14.

11. Robert Bage (1720–1801), author of *Hermsprong* (1796); William Godwin (1756–1836), author of *Enquiry concerning Political Justice* (1793) and *The Adventures of Caleb Williams* (1794); Thomas Holcroft (1745–1809), a playwright and associate of Godwin, tried for high treason in 1794; Mary Hays (1760–1843), feminist and author of *The Memoirs of Emma Courtney* (1796); Mary Wollstonecraft (1759–97), author of *A Vindication of the Rights of Woman* (1792). The best introduction to writing in this period is Marilyn Butler's *Romantics, Rebels and Reactionaries: English Literature and its Background, 1760–1830* (Oxford, 1981).

12. B. C. Southam, *Jane Austen: The Critical Heritage* (London, 1968).

13. *The Journals of Ralph Waldo Emerson, 1856–1863* (1913) ed. E. W. Emerson and W. E. Forbes, ix, 336–7, quoted by Southam, *The Critical Heritage*, p. 28. The 'nympholepsy of fond despair' is a reference to Byron, *Childe Harold*, IV, cxv.

14. Henry James, 'Gustave Flaubert' (1902), reprinted in *Selected Literary Criticism*, ed. Morris Shapira (Harmondsworth, 1968), p. 268.

15. Ibid., p. 269.

16. Studies of Austen's language in recent years have tended to focus on her development of the free indirect style. Notable among these are Roy Pascal, *The Dual Voice: Free Indirect Speech and its Functions in the Nineteenth Century European Novel* (Manchester, 1977); Ann Banfield, *Unspeakable Sentences: Narration and Representation in the Language of Fiction* (London, 1982). See also Zelda Boyd, 'Jane Austen's "must": the will and the world', *Nineteenth Century Fiction*, 39 (1984), 127–43.

17. Michael Ryan's *Marxism and Deconstruction: A Critical Articulation* (Baltimore, 1982) provides a very intelligent discrimination of how historical materialism and deconstruction can and cannot inform each other.

18. See *Literature, Society and the Sociology of Literature: Proceedings of the Conference held at the University of Essex, 1976*, ed. Francis Barker et al. (Colchester, 1977).

19. David Aers, 'Community and Morality: Towards a Reading of Jane Austen', in David Aers, Jon Cook and David Punter, *Romanticism and Ideology* (London, 1981), pp. 118–87.

20. Mary Poovey, *The Proper Lady and the Woman Writer: Ideology as Style in the Works of Mary Wollstonecraft, Mary Shelley and Jane Austen* (Chicago, 1984); and Isobel Armstrong, 'Introduction,' *Pride and Prejudice* (Oxford, 1990).

21. Julia Prewitt Brown, 'The Feminist Depreciation of Jane Austen,' *Novel*, 23 (1990), 303–13.

22. Gilbert and Gubar, *The Madwoman in the Attic*, p. 154.

23. Ibid., p. 160.

24. Ibid., p. 171.

25. Ibid., p. 172.

26. Wayne Booth, *The Rhetoric of Fiction* (Chicago, 1961), p. 266. See Brownstein's essay, p. 185 below.

27. See p. 186 below.

28. Louis Althusser, 'Letter to André Daspre' (1966); reprinted in *Essays on Ideology* (London, 1984); see also Terry Eagleton, *Criticism and Ideology* (London, 1978); Pierre Macherey, *Pour une théorie de la production littéraire* (Paris, 1966), translated by Geoffrey Wall as *A Theory of Literary Production* (London, 1978); and 'On Literature as an Ideological Form', in Robert Young, *Untying the Text: A Post-Structuralist Reader* (London, 1981), pp. 79–97.

29. See below, p. 194.

30. Althusser, *Essays on Ideology*, p. 175.

1

Improving on Sensibility

ALASTAIR DUCKWORTH

As many scholars have shown, Jane Austen works within inherited terms of aesthetic and ethical debate. Mrs Inchbald's *Art and Nature* (1796) and Maria Edgeworth's *Letters of Julia and Caroline* (1795) are only two of many novels, in the decade in which *Sense and Sensibility* had its genesis as *Elinor and Marianne*, to anticipate Jane Austen's treatment of familiar dualities of prudence and benevolence, reason and passion, discipline and freedom. While Mrs Inchbald is Godwinian in her dislike of institutions and Rousseauesque in her affirmation of the natural virtues, Maria Edgeworth is nearer the norm of the genre and Jane Austen's own position in recognising the potential excesses of sensibility and the need for the temporising effect of reason. Another novel, Mme d'Arblay's *Camilla* (1796), suggests in its description of the heroine a common view of the 'wayward' faculty:

> [Her] every propensity was pure, and, when reflection came to her aid, her conduct was as exemplary as her wishes. But the ardour of her imagination, acted upon by every passing idea, shook her Judgment from its yet unsteady seat, and left her at the mercy of wayward Sensibility – that delicate, but irregular power, which now impels to all that is most disinterested for others, now forgets all mankind, to watch the pulsations of its own fancies.[1]

Jane Austen is listed among the subscribers to the first edition of *Camilla*, and she would, on the whole, subscribe to these reflections.

Her achievement in *Sense and Sensibility* is not, however, to be assessed merely in terms of her ability to reveal the dangers of excessive sensibility, or, for that matter, to modify a strictly rational outlook. Given her awareness of the widespread corruption of traditional moral assumptions, more than a mere accommodation of her inherited – almost hackneyed – terms was needed. The resolution of the novel was intended, I believe, not merely to discover the private happiness of the central characters, but to reconstitute around these unions the grounds of a moral society. It cannot be said that this intention is convincingly achieved – Marianne's marriage to the rheumatic Colonel Brandon is a gross over-compensation for her misguided sensibility – but it is wrong to imply, as Marvin Mudrick does, that the novel's failure reveals bad faith on Jane Austen's part, that Marianne's vitality and enthusiasm are betrayed not by Willoughby, but by an author who has here substituted for a personal commitment to feeling a dull conformity to social conventions.[2]

Marianne is one of the most interesting characters in Jane Austen's fiction. More than Emma even, she anticipates the tragically Quixotic heroines of the nineteenth-century novel, whose visions of existence can find no fulfilment within the limitations of their societies. But while Jane Austen permits Marianne's quixotism to act as an implicit criticism of what is limited and pedestrian in her society, she also, quite convincingly, reveals the deficiencies of her idealism.

Nothing is clearer initially than that we are to view Marianne with a good deal of sympathy: she has 'a life, a spirit, an eagerness which could hardly be seen without delight' (p. 46). At first it seems she is to exhibit 'heroic' qualities, conspicuous by their absence in the young Catherine Morland. Like her mother, she 'can feel no sentiment of approbation inferior to love' (p. 16); she is passionately fond of music and drawing; she objects to Elinor's friend, Edward Ferrars, because 'he has no real taste' (p. 17); and when they leave Norland, she sheds tears for a 'place so much beloved' (p. 27). But although her enthusiasms are occasionally those of the romantic heroines Jane Austen had delighted in burlesquing in her juvenilia, the parodic satire here is not harsh. What vindicates Marianne in the early scenes is the sincerity behind her enthusiasms, the personal quality present even when her sensibility is mediated through her reading. That she is not merely fashionable is shown in her dislike of Gilpinesque 'jargon', indeed of 'jargon of every kind' (p. 97). During her conversation with Edward about landscape scenery she observes: 'sometimes I have kept my feelings to myself, because I could find no language to describe them in but what was worn and hackneyed out of all sense and meaning' (p. 97). And when Sir John Middleton suggests that she 'will be setting [her] cap' at Willoughby, her caustic reply, though somewhat outspoken from a seventeen-year-old, is no less than his use of cliché deserves (p. 45).

Strongly individualistic, Marianne's attitudes are often without egoism, and her disregard of 'every common-place notion of decorum' (p. 48) is on occasions magnificent. When Mrs Ferrars, in the drawing room of her home in Harley Street, ignores the painted screens of Elinor to praise the absent art of the absent Miss Morton, Marianne's reaction is superb:

> 'This is admiration of a very particular kind – what is Miss Morton to us? – who knows, or who cares, for her? – it is Elinor of whom *we* think and speak.'
> And so saying, she took the screens out of her sister-in-law's hands, to admire them herself as they ought to be admired.
> Mrs Ferrars looked exceedingly angry, and drawing herself up more stiffly than ever, pronounced in retort this bitter phillippic: 'Miss Morton is Lord Morton's daughter.'
>
> (pp. 235–6)

Given the mercenary and mediocre world in which she lives, Marianne's responses are often admirable, and one can understand why Mudrick sees in her a 'passionate, discriminating, instantaneous sympathy for worthy people and beautiful things', a 'basic opposition to lying and the forms of lying'.[3] But if one sees Marianne not only as an aspect of her author (which she is, I think) but also as a representative of sensibility, then her outlook is not so unequivocally to be affirmed nor her subsequent chastening wholly deplored. Rather than unconsciously destroying what is authentic in her nature, I would argue that Jane Austen is consciously rejecting a tendency, in herself as in her time, which she sees to be mistaken and, when taken to an extreme, immoral.

Marianne is the legatee of a philosophy of sentiment, which, wherever its roots are exactly to be located, was generally considered to have begun in the *Characteristics of Men, Manners, Opinions, Times* (1711) of the third Earl of Shaftesbury.[4] Happiness for the sentimental philosopher, in opposition to the Calvinist view of man's innate depravity and necessarily troubled life in this world, is possible for the individual who recognises the promptings of virtue and exercises his innate benevolence. Morality is discoverable in the 'heart' rather than the 'head', in feelings rather than in conformity with received precepts. Shaftesbury's thought did not deny a rational access to truth, but his emphasis on an innate moral sense tended in later writers to become a full-fledged sentimentalism, and when his views were joined with the sensationalist epistemology of the empiricists, who were reducing the function of the mind to that of passive receptor of external impressions, ethical rationalism was frequently discredited. In Hume's moral philosophy, for example, morality is 'more properly felt than judged of'.[5] The tendency toward ethical sentimentalism did not go unchallenged; Bishop Butler, for example, opposed it, arguing that any theory of ethics must include judgement as a primary component;[6] but when the rapprochement of Shaftesburian rationalism and Humean empiricism was aided by Adam Smith's theory of sympathy and Rousseau's immense influence as a philosopher of 'natural' goodness, not only was a rational access to moral truth frequently denied, but the validity of all external structures was called into question.

Jane Austen sets herself against these tendencies in *Sense and Sensibility*, insisting on the necessary aid of judgement in the process of moral decision, and requiring, as she will elsewhere in her fiction, that the individual respect and support his cultural heritage. The major limitations of Marianne's sensibility, adequately dramatised as we will see, are that it places excessive faith in the self's inner ability to reach moral decisions intuitively and rejects entirely the need for living within conventional limits.

The dangerous tendencies of Marianne's individualism only become apparent in her relationship with Willoughby, who is, like Anna Karenina's Vronsky, to a large degree an invention of the imaginative mind. This is not to deny that he is handsome and possessed of 'ardour', 'talents', and 'spirit', which put Ferrars and Brandon in the shade, merely to note that from the moment he becomes her 'preserver' (p. 46), Willoughby is defined, and is willing to be defined, in terms of 'the hero of a favourite story' (p. 43). Hearing of his indefatigable dancing powers, Marianne cries: 'That is what I like; that is what a young man ought to be. Whatever be his pursuits, his eagerness in them should know no moderation, and leave him no sense of fatigue' (p. 45) – and his expressed passion for dancing on their first meeting is sufficient to earn him from Marianne 'such a look of approbation' (p. 46). Thereafter, the 'general conformity of judgement' that is discovered between them is not a little due to her enthusiasm and his compliance. It is she who brings forward and rapturously describes her favourite authors, while Willoughby 'acquiesced in all her decisions, caught all her enthusiasm' (p. 47).

In company with Willoughby, Marianne is drawn into increasingly serious acts of impropriety. She accepts from Willoughby the gift of a horse, forgetting that the expense of keeping it will be a burden to the family's reduced income. Faced with the additional charge that it may be improper to accept a gift of this kind from a man so lately known to her, Marianne answers with spirit that 'it is not time or opportunity that is to determine intimacy; – it is disposition alone' (p. 59). Though Marianne is persuaded by Elinor to give up the horse, Willoughby is heard to promise that 'when you leave Barton to form your own establishment in a more lasting home, Queen Mab shall receive you' (p. 59), and this hint, together with his use of Marianne's Christian name, is sufficient to convince Elinor of their being engaged.

Such instances of their disregard of decorum culminate in their unchaperoned visit to Allenham, the home of Mrs Smith, the elderly relative and benefactress of Willoughby. This trip is not only indecorous, it more seriously shows an entire lack of concern for the feelings of others. From the point of view of the present owner, the unannounced visit of her heir and a young female companion can only indicate barely concealed impatience for her death. In her Shaftesburian defence of her conduct on this occasion the weakness of Marianne's position is evident: 'If there had been any real impropriety in what I did, I should have been sensible of it at the time, for we always know when we are acting wrong, and with such a conviction I could have had no pleasure' (p. 68).

In keeping with the tenets of the tradition she represents, propriety and morality in Marianne's definition are innate qualities of the self and not conformity to any set of social rules. She has responded to her experience of seemingly universal selfishness by retiring into a subjective world into which she will allow only a few privileged and manifestly worthy people. When Willoughby comes dramatically into view, Marianne looks to him for the limits of her happiness, and, like Hester Prynne in *The Scarlet Letter*, argues that what she and her lover do together has 'a consecration of its own'. Like Hawthorne, however, Jane Austen refuses to sanction the spiritual autonomy of a relationship.

In rejecting the forms of this world in her passion for Willoughby, Marianne has substituted emotional laws for social laws: 'I felt myself ... to be as solemnly engaged to him, as if the strictest legal covenant had bound us to each other' (p. 188). Willoughby, however is unwilling to obey the unwritten laws of Marianne's private world, and instead prudently adheres to the propriety of society for his own selfish ends. Thus it is that in the climactic scene of their meeting in London, the sincerity of her sensibility is noticeable in her manner of speech and salutation, while the falsity of his sensibility (and its prudent content) is seen in the reserved manner of his response. Marianne, on sighting him across the room,

> started up, and pronouncing his name in a tone of affection, held out her hand to him. He approached, and addressing himself rather to Elinor than Marianne, as if wishing to avoid her eye, and determined not to observe her attitude, inquired in a hurried manner after Mrs Dashwood, and asked how long they had been in town. Elinor was robbed of all presence of mind by such an address, and was unable to say a word. But the feelings of her sister were instantly expressed. Her face was crimsoned over, and she exclaimed in a voice of the greatest emotion, 'Good God! Willoughby, what is the meaning of this? Have you not received my letters? Will you not shake hands with me?
>
> (p. 176)

Whereas at Barton the ancillary features of sensibility – extravagant language, the shaking of hands – had been found in both Willoughby and Marianne, in the London assembly Willoughby is aloof, 'her touch seemed painful to him, and he held her hand only for a moment' (p. 177).

Her relationship to Willoughby has been for Marianne the constitution of a society of two, and when this is lost through the defection of one of its members, Marianne has no rule for living, no motive for action, no 'ground' on which to stand. Misery like hers, she admits, has no pride, and in keeping with the anti-stoical strain of the sentimental philosophy in which tears are considered the evidence of feeling, Marianne's subsequent behaviour is an active soliciting of grief. Her illness at Cleveland is spiritual, and the death to which it might easily have led would have been suicide. We should not discount the solemnity of Marianne's retrospections on her recovery. Recognising that, 'Had I died – it would have been self-destruction' (p. 345), she wonders that she has been allowed to live, 'to have time for atonement to my God' (p. 346).

In Marianne's subjective attitudes Jane Austen has revealed how the self, unaided by the forms of culture and the administration of self-discipline, finds itself alienated from society and friends. By considering her internal inclinations sufficient arbiters of moral action, Marianne has denied external sources of obligation in family, society, and religion. The inevitably negative effects of her extreme, individualistic response are sufficiently clear, but even if they were not so, Elinor's contrasting behaviour in regard to personal grief, no less than in regard to the maintenance of a decorous politeness even in the company of fools, would indicate her author's requirement for a positive and social response. When Elinor discovers that Edward is engaged to Lucy Steele, 'she wept for him, more than for herself' (p. 140), yet when she joins Mrs Jennings and Marianne at dinner, 'no one would have supposed ... that Elinor was mourning in secret over obstacles which must divide her for ever from the object of her love' (p. 141).

Elinor's characterisation in *Sense and Sensibility* is more successful than has generally been recognised in critical discussion. She starts off with the disadvantage of being the single normative representative of 'sense' in the novel. Other characters – the John Dashwoods, Lady Middleton, Mrs Ferrars, Lucy Steele – exhibit 'sense', as well as 'prudence' and 'reserve', only in debased and 'economic' meanings. Added to this, the two possible male representatives of the term fail entirely to provide an effective counterbalance to the selfishness and expedient behaviour everywhere evident. (In later novels, Darcy and Knightley will successfully provide such counterbalance.) Elinor's task of upholding the true moral conception of the word is, therefore, large – too large for her to achieve unaided. Yet Elinor is not quite the bloodless figure of sense she has been considered. It is clear, for example, that Marianne's vital and central position in the novel is in part accounted for by the fact that she is the object of Elinor's observation. If the first volume describes the rise of Marianne's hopes and their temporary disappointment on Willoughby's departure from Devonshire, the second volume her renewed hopes in London and their cruel destruction, and the third volume her near fatal illness and gradual recovery, they describe these events often through Elinor's consciousness. Consequently, while it is Marianne's acts that are described, they are frequently filtered through Elinor's subjective experience of them. Edmund Wilson was perhaps the first to understand the importance of this when he commented upon the scene in which Marianne meets Willoughby in London (the scene which for George Moore revealed the 'burning human heart in English prose fiction for the first and alas the last time'). 'Isn't it rather', Wilson asks, 'the emotion of Elinor as she witnesses her sister's disaster than Marianne's emotion over Willoughby of which the poignancy is communicated to the reader?'[7]

In this partial internalisation of the debate in Elinor's consciousness – as Marianne's actions and Elinor's perception of these actions merge – Jane Austen's technical advance over *Northanger Abbey*, and her movement in the direction of *Pride and Prejudice*, are evident. Elinor may seem to others to be reserved, rational, and cold, but the reader is given access to her continued inner struggle, not only with respect to her own love affair, but vicariously, as she watches Marianne impetuously fall in love, and, her love slighted, no less passionately give way to melancholy. Elinor, much more than Catherine Morland, though less than Emma, has become a centre of consciousness. She is the only character (apart from Mrs Jennings on one occasion ([III, iii] which must be judged a technical lapse) whose mind the reader is allowed to enter. Opaque to the other characters, Elinor is transparent to the reader. By allowing us frequent access to Elinor's observing mind, the narrator reveals that 'sense' need not be cold, nor introspection selfish.

Elinor's sense is neither a Mandevillian self-interest nor an emotionless calculation. In its affirmation of social principles it resembles, rather, the 'early received and uniformly continued sense of mankind',[8] which Burke considered had not only built up the 'august fabric of states' but had continued to preserve it from ruin. Like her lover Edward, Elinor accepts the validity of social institutions and acts within received principles of ethical and social conduct. Against the private instinct of her sister, as against the selfish motivations of those around her, Elinor opposes a stoical fidelity to traditional and basically Christian values. Her withdrawal into a personal reserve is a committed withdrawal.

The theme of profession, so central to *Mansfield Park*, and found in all the mature novels, is relevant here. In the moment of social discontinuity, the responsible individual can only look conscientiously to his duty and actively profess his role. Unlike Willoughby, who is 'of no profession at all' (p. 61), or Mr Palmer, who 'idled away the mornings at billiards, which ought to have been devoted to business' (p. 305), or John Dashwood, who is always 'thinking about writing a letter to his steward in the country' (p. 259), but never does, the responsible characters of the novel, Ferrars and Brandon, are characterised by their commitment to their roles. Edward, indeed, agrees with Mrs Dashwood when she suggests that he would 'be a happier man if [he] had any profession' to engage his time (p. 102). He admits, 'It has been, and is, and probably will always be a heavy misfortune to me, that I have no necessary business to engage me, no profession to give me employment' (p. 102). And, later, looking back on the foolish infatuation which caused him to engage himself to Lucy, he recognises that his error sprang from his ignorance of the world, his 'want of employment', and his lack of an 'active profession' (p. 362). Yet, having made the betrothal, Edward has proved himself willing to take responsibility for his actions, as Willoughby for all his superior appearance and talents has not.

The need for 'employment', 'duty', 'responsibility', is sounded again and again in Jane Austen's novels, as her heroines all learn that the act of living itself is a profession. After Edward has left the Barton cottage, his melancholy over his commitment to Lucy having communicated itself to Elinor, her reaction may be taken as the positive response that is to be affirmed: she '*busily* employed herself the whole day' and addressed herself to the '*business* of self-command' (p. 104; my italics). In comparison with this self-discipline, Marianne's 'indulgence of feeling' and 'nourishment of grief' (p. 83) are hardly admirable.

Only when Marianne's recovery is assured by the attentions of Elinor and the much maligned Mrs Jennings may Elinor's self-discipline be relaxed. At the end of the novel we are given explicit indications of Elinor's sensibility. First she feels for Marianne, who, 'restored to life, health, friends ... was an idea to fill her heart with sensations of exquisite comfort, and expand it in fervent gratitude' (p. 315). Then she responds sympathetically to Willoughby's tempestuous arrival and self-pitying tale, and for a time, 'Willoughby, "poor Willoughby", as she now allowed herself to call him, was constantly in her thoughts' (p. 334). Finally with Edward's arrival the question becomes, 'How are [Elinor's] feelings to be described?' (p. 363), and on news of Edward's freedom from the duty of his engagement to Lucy, we are given the answer:

> Elinor could sit it no longer. She almost ran out of the room, and as soon as the door was closed, burst into tears of joy, which at first she thought would never cease. Edward, who had till then looked any where, rather than at her, saw her hurry away, and perhaps saw – or even heard, her emotion. ...
>
> (p. 360)

Marianne's danger over, her morality now properly directed, Elinor may release the emotional tension thus far contained, and herself give way to a temporary display of feeling. By choosing sense as her point of view over sensibility, Jane Austen has made a statement about the priority of discipline to freedom, and of social principles to individual propensities; but, that statement made, she has also recognised in Elinor's emotion the necessary presence of feeling in the ethical constitution of the individual, if rationality is not to become cold and inhuman.

The novel ends with a union of terms similar to that which will be more successfully achieved in *Pride and Prejudice*. Marianne, like Elizabeth Bennet, comes to the recognition of the need for self-discipline. She promises that '[her] feelings shall be governed and [her] temper improved' (p. 347), and instead of further indulging her grief, she exercises a 'reasonable exertion' (p. 342). Coming to a gradual awareness of Willoughby's false sensibility, his prudent core of self, she compares her conduct to 'what it ought to have been' (p. 345). Her language is characterised now by its ethical vocabulary, and while her sister may show that the individual emotion is a component part of the social response, Marianne determines that, though Willoughby can never be forgotten, his remembrance 'shall be regulated, it shall be checked by religion, by reason, by constant employment' (p. 347). Although her marriage to Colonel Brandon fails to convince, it at least demonstrates the imprudence of her previous arguments that wealth had nothing to do with happiness, for with Brandon's £2,000 a year Marianne gains for herself the 'competence' which Elinor earlier had laughingly considered her own idea of 'wealth' (p. 91).

There is no doubt that the decision to portray two heroines, and the selection of the 'sensible' sister as point of view, led Jane Austen into aesthetic difficulties from which she could not entirely escape. Given the vivacity of Marianne, Elinor's explicitly normative function can only seem didactic on occasions, though this is less often so than is sometimes charged. By looking through the eyes of one of the heroines, Jane Austen has escaped the narrative problem of *Northanger Abbey* without discovering the solutions of *Pride and Prejudice* and *Emma*. She has to some degree dramatised her standards in the psychology of Elinor (as she failed to do in either Henry Tilney or Catherine [in *Northanger Abbey*]) and has thus escaped the problems that arise when judgements remain at the level of the presiding and anonymous narrative consciousness, but she has still left herself with a task of persuasion, of making art and morality coincident. The reader must be made to accept the priority of one sister's moral vision, and the task is complicated by the author's refusal in any way to limit the attractive individualism of the other sister. In *Pride and Prejudice* and *Emma* this problem is successfully avoided by making the individualistic heroines also the central intelligences of their novels, and by allowing these heroines to come to a gradual internal awareness of the insufficiency of their outlooks. Whereas in *Sense and Sensibility* there is a bifurcation of action and reflection, in the later novels the two modes are one in the actions and retrospective reflections of the heroine. In *Sense and Sensibility*, Marianne's moral growth can only be seen externally in her words and actions, frequently as they are observed through Elinor's consciousness of them. Elinor herself does not so much evince a moral growth as a constant internal moral struggle. In *Pride and Prejudice* and *Emma* (though in ways to be distinguished), the movement from an individualistic to a social morality is followed within the psyche of a single heroine.

From Alastair Duckworth, *The Improvement of the Estate* (Baltimore, 1971), pp. 104–14.

NOTES

[Duckworth sees Marianne as the representative of sensibility, a movement in thought, manners and opinion in the late eighteenth century which seemed superior to the mercenary values of many of Austen's contemporaries, yet also dangerously immoral because prioritising individual subjective feelings over objective social conventions. Duckworth notices that rather than Elinor being a rather dull and repressive foil to Marianne's transgressive liveliness, she stands for a very complex and discriminating kind of sense when she is compared with characters whose minds are narrowly concerned with their own economic betterment. Her tendency to self-repression is born of a responsible Christian appreciation of her place in society and of the needs of others. Duckworth's account appears to be a very perceptive reading *along the grain* of Austen's world view and illuminates the sophisticated discriminations to which the contemporary reader of Austen might have been attuned.

References to Jane Austen's work are to *The Works of Jane Austen*, ed. R. W. Chapman, 3rd edn, 5 vols (London, 1933), and vol. 6, *Minor Works,* ed. R. W. Chapman (London, 1954). References to Austen's letters are to *Jane Austen's Letters to her Sister Cassandra and Others*, ed. R. W. Chapman, 2 vols (Oxford, 1932), cited as *Letters*. Ed.]

1. *Camilla* (London, 1796), IV, 399. For studies treating the literary background to *Sense and Sensibility*, see the relevant portions of Henrietta Ten Harmsel, *Jane Austen: A Study in Fictional Conventions* (The Hague, 1934); A. Walton Litz, *Jane Austen: A Study of her Artistic Development* (London, 1965); Kenneth Moler, *Jane Austen's Art of*

Allusion (Lincoln, 1968); also Alan D. McKillop, 'The Context of *Sense and Sensibility*', *The Rice Institute Pamphlet*, 44 (April 1957), 65–78. J. M. S. Tompkins, '"Elinor and Marianne": A Note on Jane Austen', *The Review of English Studies*, 16 (1940), 33–43, suggests Jane West's *A Gossip's Story* (London, 1796) as a single model of *Sense and Sensibility*, but Kenneth Moler, while not denying Jane West's influence, is one of several critics to see affinities with a number of other sentimental novels.

2. For an excellent brief rebuttal to Mudrick's view contained in *Jane Austen: Irony as Defense and Discovery* (Princeton, 1952), see A. Walton Litz, *Artistic Development*, pp. 81–3. Litz argues that 'the alternative to Willoughby is Colonel Brandon not because this was Jane Austen's heritage from life, but because it was her heritage from the broad antitheses of moralistic fiction', and that Jane Austen in *Sense and Sensibility* was 'the victim of conventions, but these were primarily artistic, not social'.

3. Mudrick, *Irony as Defense*, pp. 75, 74.

4. Ronald Crane, 'Suggestions Toward a Genealogy of the "Man of Feeling"', *Journal of English Literary History*, 1 (1934), 205–30, argues for an earlier expression of the sentimental outlook in the latitudinarian preachers of the late seventeenth and early eighteenth centuries. Other critical studies which consider the philosophy of sentiment and its development in the eighteenth century are: A. S. P. Woodhouse, 'Romanticism and the History of Ideas', *English Studies Today* (Oxford, 1951), pp. 120–41, and Walter Jackson Bate, 'The Premise of Feeling', in *From Classic to Romantic: Premises of Taste in Eighteenth Century England* (1946; rpt New York, 1961), pp. 129–60. Perhaps the best treatment of the idea in Jane Austen's novel is found in Ian Watt's Introduction to *Sense and Sensibility* (New York, 1961), reprinted in *Jane Austen: A Collection of Critical Essays*, ed. Ian Watt (Englewood Cliff, N J, 1963).

5. *Treatise on Human Nature*, ed. T. H. Green and T. H. Grose (London, 1874), p. 235.

6. *The Works of Joseph Butler*, ed. W. E. Gladstone (Oxford, 1896), vol. 2, pp. 14–15.

7. 'A Long Talk About Jane Austen', *Classics and Commercials: A Literary Chronicle of the Forties* (New York, 1950), p. 203.

8. Edmund Burke, *Reflections on the Revolution in France*, ed. William B. Todd (New York, 1959), p. 111.

2

Sensibility and Jacobinism

MARILYN BUTLER

Of the novels Jane Austen completed, *Sense and Sensibility* appears to be the earliest in conception. An uncertain family tradition suggests that its original letter-version, 'Elinor and Marianne', may have been written in 1795:[1] before the publication of Mrs West's similar *Gossip's Story*, and in the same year as Maria Edgeworth's *Letters of Julia and Caroline*. The didactic novel which compares the beliefs and conduct of two protagonists – with the object of finding one invariably right and the other invariably wrong – seems to have been particularly fashionable during the years 1795–6. Most novelists, even the most purposeful, afterwards abandon it for a format using a single protagonist, whose experiences can be handled more flexibly and with much less repetition.[2] On the whole, therefore, all Jane Austen's other novels are more sophisticated in conception, and they are capable of more interesting treatment of the central character in relation to her world. But there is a caveat. Catherine in *Northanger Abbey* is dealt with in an inhibited manner. A rather mindless character, of somewhat undefined good principles, she matures in a curiously oblique process that the reader does not quite witness. The format of the contrast-novel, with all its drawbacks, at least obliges Jane Austen to chart the mental processes of her heroines directly, and to locate the drama in their minds.

By its very nature *Sense and Sensibility* is unremittingly didactic. All the novelists who choose the contrast format do so in order to make an explicit ideological point. Essentially they are taking part in the old argument between 'nature' and 'nurture': which is the more virtuous man, the sophisticated, or schooled individual, or the natural one? Obviously there is a total division on the issue between the type of traditional Christian who takes a gloomy view of man's unredeemed nature, and the various schools of eighteenth-century optimists, whether Christian or not. Although a Catholic, Mrs Inchbald is also a progressive: of the two brothers in her *Nature and Art*, the sophisticated one stands for greed, self-seeking, worldly corruption, the 'natural' one for primal simplicity, honesty, sympathy, and innate virtue.[3] Maria Edgeworth, although in a sense favouring 'nurture' in her *Letters of Julia and Caroline*, does so on idiosyncratic terms which take her out of rancorous current controversy. But Mrs West, in preferring her disciplined, self-denying Louisa to her self-indulgent Marianne, is entirely relevant to the contemporary issue and entirely conservative. So, too, is Jane Austen.[4]

Jane Austen conscientiously maintains the principle of a didactic comparison. Her novel advances on the assumption that what happens to one of the central characters must also happen to the other; at every turn the reader cannot avoid the appropriate conclusion. The motif of the first volume is the attitude of each girl towards the man she hopes to marry. When the novel opens Elinor already knows Edward Ferrars. Her views about him are developed in conversation with Mrs Dashwood, and the reader is also given Marianne's rather qualified opinion. When Edward and Elinor have to separate, Mrs Dashwood invites him to visit them at Barton, but Edward seems reluctant. Thereafter Elinor's endurance of uncertainty about Edward's feelings becomes a factor in her character, and in our response to her.

Shortly after the family's arrival at Barton Cottage, Marianne's lover, Willoughby, enters the novel. His dramatic arrival is in keeping with his more flamboyant character; his appearance, too, is contrasted with Edward's; but the manner in which the sequence of his courtship is developed shows Jane Austen's concern to enforce a similarity of situation in order to bring out a dissimilarity of character. Again, Mrs Dashwood gives her enthusiastic approval, while the other sister, in this case Elinor, expresses her reservations. When Willoughby leaves, Mrs Dashwood once more issues her invitation, which is inexplicably not accepted, and Marianne, like Elinor, is left to a period of loneliness and anxiety.

When in the second volume the two heroines go to London they are placed, again, in a similar predicament. Both expect to meet the loved one there, both are obliged uneasily to wait; cards are left by each of the young men; each is lost, or seems lost, to a rival woman. In all the embarrassments and worries of the London visit, the reader's developing knowledge of the sisters is based on a substructure which demands that he adjudicate between them. And they leave London, as they entered it, still similarly placed, travelling towards the county, Somerset, where each believes her lover to be setting up house with his bride.

The parallels can be taken further, for example to the influence first of upbringing, later of idleness, on the characters of the two young men. The entire action is organised to represent Elinor and Marianne in terms of rival value-systems, which are seen directing their behaviour in the most crucial choices of their lives. It is an arrangement which necessarily directs the reader's attention not towards what they experience, but towards how they cope with experience, away from the experiential to the ethical.

In the two contrasted opening sequences the emphasis is on each girl's scale of values as she applies it to both young men. Edward Ferrars's attractions are not external. 'Edward Ferrars was not recommended to their good opinion by any peculiar graces of person or address. He was not handsome, and his manners required intimacy to make them pleasing' (p. 15). But even Marianne, who has reservations about Edward as a lover, has 'the highest opinion in the world of his goodness and sense. I think him everything that is worthy and amiable' (p. 20). For Elinor, this is commendation so high that she does not know what more could be said. As for herself, she admits that she 'greatly esteems' and 'likes' him: words which define the state of her understanding rather than her feelings, and, as such, seem to Marianne inappropriate.

But Marianne hesitates because in addition to Edward's lack of physical grace (what we might call physical attractiveness), he does not act like a lover with Elinor. In Marianne's language, he wants fire and spirit. His passionless temperament is further illustrated in his attitude to literature and to matters of 'taste' generally. When set by Marianne to read Cowper, he was, as she complains to her mother, tame and spiritless:

> 'To hear those beautiful lines which have frequently almost driven me wild, pronounced with such impenetrable coldness, such dreadful indifference! – '

'He would certainly have done more justice to simple and elegant prose. I thought so at the time; but you *would* give him Cowper.'

'Nay, Mama, if he is not to be animated by Cowper! – but we must allow for difference of taste. Elinor has not my feelings, and therefore she may overlook it, and be happy with him. But it would have broke *my* heart had I loved him, to hear him read with so little sensibility!'

(p. 18)

Marianne's objection is that Edward does not give free rein to the intuitive side of his nature. She equates lack of 'taste' with lack of response, an inability to enter subjectively into the emotions of a writer, or to attempt *rapport* with the spirit of a landscape. Again, as in *Northanger Abbey*, the reader is certainly not supposed to draw a moral distinction between characters concerned with literature, and characters concerned with life: for Elinor likes books and drawing, and Edward, who has views about both, and about landscape too, would do justice to 'simple and elegant prose'. But he, like Elinor, approaches the arts differently from Marianne. He would be likely to concern himself more than she with the intellectual content; when he looks at a landscape, he considers questions of utility – such as whether the terrain would be good for farming – and practicality – such as whether a lane would be too muddy for walking.

Edward's tastes can be considered aesthetically, as Augustan and thus in terms of contemporary landscape art old-fashioned: he has more in common with Pope than would please Marianne. But, and this is more to the novel's purposes, they are also the tastes of a self-effacing man, who likes to apply objective criteria, independent of his own prejudices and the limitations of his knowledge. His objective approach to art resembles Elinor's way of evaluating him. She knows enough of his background to see beyond the defects of his manner to the enduring qualities of his mind and spirit, his 'sense' and 'goodness', and both these words imply that Edward's virtues are those of a given code of value, namely the Christian. Edward's character, Edward's aesthetic opinions, and Elinor's method of assessing Edward, all have this much in common – that they are based on prescribed standards, not on subjective impulse.

With all this Marianne's choice of Willoughby is carefully compared. His entrance, like that of the 'preserver' of the heroine in a romantic novel, at once gives him a superficial glamour. He is 'uncommonly handsome' and his manner 'frank and graceful', so that not merely Marianne, but Mrs Dashwood and Elinor,[5] are

struck with admiration on his first appearance. His beauty encourages an intuitive response from Marianne, and receives it. She reacts
to Willoughby with the same whole-hearteded impulsiveness with
which she reacts to books, and indeed before long she is reacting to
books and Willoughby together, in a style that suggests all feeling,
little or no intellectual detachment:

> The same books, the same passages were idolised by each – or, if any
> difference appeared, any objection arose, it lasted no longer than till
> the force of her arguments and the brightness of her eyes could be
> displayed. He acquiesced in all her decisions, caught all her
> enthusiasm; and long before his visit concluded, they conversed with
> the freedom of a long-established acquaintance.
>
> (p. 47)

When Elinor teases Marianne for running so recklessly through
the beauties of Cowper and Scott, Jane Austen clearly means no
criticism of two poets who were among her own favourites. But she
does mean to criticise, through Elinor, the way Willoughby and
Marianne read, and to show that, when they abandon themselves to
their reading together, the result is grossly self-indulgent. Everything they do follows the same pattern of shared selfishness. Wholly
absorbed in one another and in their exclusive pursuits, they rudely
ignore the rest of their social circle, and, on the day of the cancelled
outing, drive off together to Allerton in Willoughby's phaeton. As it
happens, Sir John Middleton and Mrs Jennings cheerfully tolerate
the lovers. They in their turn are less tolerant; indeed, their self-
sufficiency has an unattractive arrogance about it, which is displayed when they mount their unreasonable joint attack on Colonel
Brandon. Willoughby's irrationality is as apparent here – 'he has
threatened me with rain when I wanted it to be fine' (p. 52) – as it is
later, when he begs that no alteration be made to Barton Cottage
because he has pleasant associations with it as it is (p. 73). That
Marianne has gone far along the same subjective path is demonstrated after her visit to Allerton. Elinor argues that she has been
guilty of serious impropriety in going there in Mrs Smith's absence.
Marianne relies on her usual criterion, intuition: 'If there had been
any real impropriety in what I did, I should have been sensible of it
at the time, for we always know when we are acting wrong, and
with such a conviction I could have had no pleasure' (p. 68).

She believes in the innate moral sense; and, since man is naturally
good, his actions when he acts on impulse are likely to be good
also. Just as Marianne has no doubts about herself, so she can have

none about her *alter ego*, Willoughby. Neither can Mrs Dashwood, who, proceeding according to the same intuitional method as her second daughter, is wholly convinced of the goodness of Willoughby. When Elinor tries to argue with her, and to check instinct with the objective test of Willoughby's behaviour, her mother protests. She rightly sees that a broader question is at issue: Elinor's sense (stemming from the Christian tradition that man's nature is fallible) has come into conflict with the sentimentalist's tendency to idealise human nature. From Elinor's caution, Mrs Dashwood draws a universal inference. 'You had rather take evil upon credit than good' (p. 78).

So far, then, the issue between the two contrasted sisters is presented according to the view of the nature–nurture dichotomy usually adopted by conservatives. The contrast, as always, is between two modes of perception. On the one hand, Marianne's way is subjective, intuitive, implying confidence in the natural goodness of human nature when untrammelled by convention. Her view is corrected by the more cautious orthodoxy of Elinor, who mistrusts her own desires, and requires even her reason to seek the support of objective evidence.

It is in keeping with Elinor's objectivity (and also typical of the feminine variant of the anti-Jacobin novel) that she should advocate a doctrine of civility in opposition to Marianne's individualism. Elinor restrains her own sorrow in order to shield her mother and sister. By her politeness to Mrs Jennings she steadily makes up what Marianne has carelessly omitted. She respects Colonel Brandon for his activity in helping his friends long before Mrs Dashwood and Marianne have seen his virtues. Civility is a favourite anti-Jacobin theme, which does not appear in *Northanger Abbey*, although it is present in Jane Austen's later novels. Its objective correlative, the sketch given in *Sense and Sensibility* of society at large, is impoverished compared with the solid worlds of *Mansfield Park*, *Emma* and *Persuasion*: the Middletons and Colonel Brandon, even supported by Mrs Jennings, hardly stand in for a whole community. Yet this is a judgement arrived at by a comparison with Jane Austen's later work. If *Sense and Sensibility* is compared with other novels of the same genre, and originating at the same time, it can be seen to move in innumerable small ways towards fullness and naturalness. A conception of civility illustrated by gratitude to Mrs Jennings is more natural, for example, than portraying a similar concept in terms of prayers beside a dying father, or fidelity to the death-bed advice of an aunt.[6]

In fact, granted the rigidity imposed by the form, the second half of *Sense and Sensibility* is remarkably natural, flexible, and inventive. Both the sisters are presented as plausible individuals as well as professors of two opposing creeds. Another contemporary novelist – Mrs West, Mrs Hamilton, or the young Maria Edgeworth – would almost certainly have had Marianne seduced and killed off, after the errors of which she has been guilty. For during the first half of the novel Marianne has stood for a doctrine of complacency and self-sufficiency which Jane Austen as a Christian deplored:

> Teach us to understand the sinfulness of our own hearts, and bring to our knowledge every fault of temper and every evil habit in which we have indulged to the discomfort of our fellow-creatures, and the danger of our own souls. ... Incline us to ask our hearts these questions oh! God, and save us from deceiving ourselves by pride or vanity. ...
> Incline us oh God! to think humbly of ourselves, to be severe only in the examination of our own conduct, to consider our fellow creatures with kindness, and to judge of all they say and do with that charity which we would desire from them ourselves.[7]

After Allerton, Marianne failed to examine her own conduct at all. She had none of the Christian's understanding of the sinfulness of her own heart; and she showed a notable lack of Christian charity towards Colonel Brandon, Mrs Jennings, and the Middletons. Elinor alone had exercised the self-examination prescribed for the Christian, by questioning the state of her heart in relation to Edward, and, even more, her complex and disagreeable feelings about Lucy. Elinor never had the same certainty that Edward loved her which Marianne always felt about Willoughby. 'She was far from depending on that result of his preference of her, which her mother and sister still considered as certain' (p. 22).

The most interesting feature of the character of Elinor, and a real technical achievement of *Sense and Sensibility*, is that this crucial process of Christian self-examination is realised in literary terms. Elinor is the first character in an Austen novel consistently to reveal her inner life. The narrative mode of *Sense and Sensibility* is the first sustained example of 'free indirect speech', for the entire action is refracted through Elinor's consciousness as *Northanger Abbey* could not be through the simple-minded Catherine's. Other technical changes necessarily follow. Dialogue is far less important in *Sense and Sensibility*, since the heroine is not so much in doubt about the nature of external truth, as concerned with the knowledge of herself, her passions, and her duty. Judging by the narrative mode alone, *Sense and Sensibility* is, like *Mansfield Park* after it, an introspective novel. And yet it is clearly important to recognise that both are introspective only within closely defined limits. The inner life led by Elinor, and later by Fanny, is the dominant medium of the novel, but it is entirely distinct from the irrational and emotional states which the post-Romantic reader thinks of as 'consciousness'.

Technically, as well as intellectually, Elinor's scrupulous inner life has great importance in the novel, and Jane Austen brings it out by giving similar qualities to the two male characters who approach a moral ideal. Edward Ferrars and Colonel Brandon have the same wary scepticism about themselves. Rather to the detriment of their vitality, Jane Austen's characteristic word for both of them is 'diffident'. Diffidence helps to explain Edward's unwillingness to expatiate on matters of taste; and 'the epicurism, selfishness and conceit' of Mr Palmer are contrasted with Edward's 'generous temper, simple tastes and diffident feelings (p. 305). Robert Ferrars's complacent comparison of himself with his brother Edward enforces a similar point (pp. 250–1). And diffidence, especially in relation to Marianne, is also the characteristic of Colonel Brandon as a lover (p. 338).

But it is Elinor alone who can be seen living through the moments of self-examination that are evidently typical of both men. The most interesting sequence in which she is shown doubting herself occurs after she has heard Willoughby's confession. Many modern critics interpret this passage as evidence that Jane Austen is qualifying her own case, in order to arrive at a compromise solution somewhere between 'Sense' and 'Sensibility'. According to Mr Moler, for example, Elinor feels after she has heard Willoughby that her own 'Sense' has been inadequate: 'Elinor's rationality causes her to reach a less accurate estimate of Willoughby than Marianne and Mrs Dashwood reach with their Sensibility.'[8]

Such interpretations are interesting as evidence of the difficulty the twentieth-century reader has with the notion of an objective morality. What happens in this episode is surely that Elinor is shaken by her feelings, for she finds both that she pities Willoughby and that she has a renewed sense of his 'grace', or personal attractiveness. Her judgement is assailed by involuntary sympathy: part of her wants to excuse his injuries to Marianne and Miss

Smith. Yet the fact that Willoughby was tempted – by the two young women on the one hand, and by an education in worldliness on the other – does not in fact absolve the adult man, or not, at least, if one employs the objective ethical code rather than the relativist subjective one. The progressive supposedly sees the evil in individual men as social conditioning, the operation of impersonal forces which the individual cannot help. Elinor now considers Willoughby from this point of view – which is, of course, his own – and she finds it impossible to absolve him. 'Extravagance and vanity had made him coldhearted and selfish' (p. 381). This is not Jane Austen qualifying Elinor's sense with a dash of Marianne's sensibility. On the contrary, she shows Elinor's judgement reasserting itself, with some difficulty, after a most effective and deeply felt appeal has been made to her sympathies:

> Willoughby, in spite of all his faults, excited a degree of commiseration for the sufferings produced by them, which made her think of him as now separated for ever from her family with a tenderness, a regret, rather in proportion, as she soon acknowledged within herself – to his wishes than to his merits. She felt that his influence over her mind was heightened by circumstances which ought not in reason to have weight; by that person of uncommon attraction, that open, affectionate and lively manner which it was no merit to possess; and by that still ardent love for Marianne, which it was not even innocent to indulge. But she felt that it was so long, long before she could feel his influence less.
>
> (p. 333)

It is easy to mistake Elinor's sense for coldness. She is intended to be quite as loving and quite as accessible to 'feeling' as Marianne. The difference between them is one of ideology – Marianne optimistic, intuitive, un-self-critical, and Elinor far more sceptical, always ready to study the evidence, to reopen a question, to doubt her own prior judgements. She can be ready to revise her opinion of Willoughby. She can admit her mistakes, as she does of her wrong estimate of Marianne's illness.[9] The point about both episodes is that Elinor was never intended to be infallible, but to typify an active, struggling Christian in a difficult world. Indeed, Jane Austen clearly argues that we do not find the right path through the cold, static correctness of a Lady Middleton, but through a struggle waged daily with our natural predisposition to err.

It is the role of Marianne Dashwood, who begins with the wrong ideology, to learn the right one. After her illness she applies her naturally strong feelings to objects outside herself, and her intelligence to thorough self-criticism in the Christian spirit. In what for her is the crisis of the book, her confession of her errors to Elinor (pp. 345ff.), Marianne resembles Jane Austen's other heroines Catherine, Elizabeth, and Emma, all of whom arrive at the same realisation that (in the words of Jane Austen's prayer) 'pride' and 'vanity' have blinded them in relation both to themselves and to external reality.

It is quite false to assume that merely because Marianne is treated with relative gentleness, Jane Austen has no more than a qualified belief in the evils of sensibility. She spares Marianne, the individual, in order to have her recant from sensibility, the system. Even this is possible only because Marianne, with her naturally affectionate disposition and her intelligence, is never from the start a typical adherent of the doctrine of self: youth and impetuosity for a time blinded her, so that she acted against the real grain of her nature.[10] Because Marianne is not representative, other characters are needed, especially in the second half of the novel, to show the system of self in full-blooded action. Jane Austen provides them in the group of characters who fawn upon and virtually worship that false idol compounded of materialism, status-seeking and self-interest, Mrs Ferrars.

The leading characters who take over from Marianne the role of illustrating what worship of the self really means are Lucy Steele and Fanny Dashwood. It is clear, of course, that neither Lucy nor Fanny is a 'feeling' person at all. Both are motivated by ruthless self-interest, Lucy in grimly keeping Edward to his engagement, Fanny in consistently working for her immediate family's financial advantage. But both Lucy and Fanny, though in reality as hard-headed as they could well be, clothe their mercenariness decently in the garments of sensibility. Lucy flatters Lady Middleton by pretending to love her children. She acts the lovelorn damsel to Elinor. Her letters are filled with professions of sensibility. Similarly, in the successive shocks inflicted by Lucy's insinuation of herself into the family, 'poor Fanny had suffered agonies of sensibility' (p. 371). It is no accident that at the end the marriages of the two model couples, Elinor and Marianne and their two diffident, withdrawing husbands, are contrasted with the establishments, far more glorious in worldly terms, of Lucy and Fanny and their complacent, mercenary husbands.[11] Lucy and

Fanny may quarrel, but it is suitable that they should end the novel together, the joint favourites of old Mrs Ferrars, and forever in one another's orbit. However it begins, the novel ends by comparing the moral ideal represented by Sense with a new interpretation of 'individualism'. The intellectual position, originally held in good faith by Marianne, is abandoned; what takes its place is selfishness with merely a fashionable cover of idealism – and, particularly, the pursuit of self-interest in the economic sense. Willoughby's crime proves after all not to have been rank villainy, but expensive self-indulgence so habitual that he must sacrifice everything, including domestic happiness, to it. Lucy's behaviour is equally consistent, and it, too, is crowned with worldly success:

> The whole of Lucy's behaviour in the affair, and the prosperity which crowned it, therefore, may be held forth as a most encouraging instance of what an earnest, an unceasing attention to self-interest ... will do in securing every advantage of fortune, with no other sacrifice than that of time and conscience.
>
> (p. 376)

Jane Austen's version of 'sensibility' – that is, individualism, or the worship of self, in various familiar guises – is as harshly dealt with here as anywhere in the anti-Jacobin tradition. Even without the melodramatic political subplot of many anti-Jacobin novels, Mrs Ferrars's London is recognisably a sketch of the anarchy that follows the loss of all values but self-indulgence. In the opening chapters especially, where Marianne is the target of criticism, 'sensibility' means sentimental (or revolutionary) idealism, which Elinor counters with her sceptical or pessimistic view of man's nature. Where the issue is the choice of a husband, Jane Austen's criteria prove to be much the same as Mrs West's: both advocate dispassionate assessment of a future husband's qualities, discounting both physical attractiveness, and the *rapport* that comes from shared tastes, while stressing objective evidence. Both reiterate the common conservative theme of the day, that a second attachment is likely to be more reliable than a first.[12] By all these characteristic tests, *Sense and Sensibility* is an anti-Jacobin novel just as surely as is *A Gossip's Story*.

The sole element of unorthodoxy in *Sense and Sensibility* lies in the execution, and especially in the skilful adjustment of detail which makes its story more natural. *Sense and Sensibility* is not natural compared with Jane Austen's later novels. Any reader will notice the stiffness of some of the dialogue, particularly perhaps

those speeches early in the novel where Elinor sums up the character of Edward (p. 20). And yet, especially in the second half of the
novel, it is remarkable how the harsh outlines of the ideological
scheme are softened. Often the changes are small ones, such as
turning the jilted heroine's near-obligatory decline and death into a
feverish cold caught, plausibly, from staying out to mope in the
rain. Alternatively the difference may show in the born novelist's
sense of occasion, her flair for a scene. Twice in the latter half of the
novel, for example, there are theatrical entrances, consciously
worked for: Edward's, when at last he calls on Elinor in London,
only to find her with Lucy Steele; and Willoughby's, when he comes
to Cleveland in response to the news that Marianne is dying.
Developments like this do more than rub away some of the
angularities of the old nature–nurture dichotomy. They begin to
make so many inroads on it (particularly in relation to Marianne)
that many readers have had the impression Jane Austen was trying
to break it down altogether. Certainly there is plenty of evidence in
the second half of the novel that Jane Austen was impatient with
the rigidity of her framework; and yet all the modifications she
makes are a matter of technique, not ideology. Lucy Steele resembles Isabella Thorpe and Mary Crawford, George Wickham, Henry
Crawford, Frank Churchill, and William Walter Elliott in that
she does not come, like some other authors' representations,
vociferously advocating free love, or revolution, or the reading of
German novels. She is a harbinger of anarchy for all that.

Compared with the common run of anti-Jacobin novels it is a
considerable achievement, and yet it has never been found quite
good enough. *Sense and Sensibility* is the most obviously tenden-
tious of Jane Austen's novels, and the least attractive. The trouble is
not merely that, for all the author's artistic tact, the cumbrous
framework and enforced contrasts of the inherited structure remain.
It matters far more that the most deeply disturbing aspect of all
anti-Jacobin novels, their inhumanity, affects this novel more than
Jane Austen's skilled mature work. In a way *Sense and Sensibility* is
worse affected than many clumsy works by lesser writers, because it
is written naturally, and with more insight into at least some
aspects of the inner life. The reader has far too much real sympathy
with Marianne in her sufferings to refrain from valuing her precisely
on their account. There is plenty of evidence that Jane Austen,
anticipating this reaction, tried to forestall it. As far as possible she

tries to keep us out of Marianne's consciousness: Marianne's un-
wonted secrecy, after Willoughby has left Barton, and after her
arrival in London, functions quite as effectively in restricting the
reader's sympathy as in restricting Elinor's. Merely to have
Marianne's sufferings described after she has received Willoughby's
letter is sufficient, however, to revive all the reader's will to identify
himself with her. The effort to point up Elinor's feelings instead will
not do: either we do not believe in them, and conclude her frigid, or
the felt presence of suffering in the one sister helps us to supply
imaginatively what we are not told about the inner life of the other.
It is difficult, in short, to accept the way consciousness is presented
in this novel. Marianne, and to some extent also Elinor, are drawn
with strong feelings which the reader is accustomed to sympathise
with, and actually to value for their own sake. But it is the argument of the novel that such feelings, like the individuals who
experience them, are not innately good. Unfortunately, in flat
opposition to the author's obvious intention, we tend to approach
Marianne subjectively. Right or wrong, she has our sympathy: she,
and our responses to her, are outside Jane Austen's control. The
measure of Jane Austen's failure to get us to read her story with the
necessary ethical detachment comes when she imposes her solution.
What, innumerable critics have asked, if Marianne never brought
herself to love Colonel Brandon? The fact that the question still
occurs shows that in this most conscientiously didactic of all the
novels the moral case remains unmade.

From Marilyn Butler, *Jane Austen and the War of Ideas* (Oxford,
1975), pp. 182–96.

NOTES

[In many ways paralleling Duckworth's contemporaneous argument,
Marilyn Butler reminds us that the contrast-novel was an established didactic
form in the late eighteenth and early nineteenth centuries and sees Austen as
obeying the genre by contrasting the responses of Marianne and Elinor to
almost identical situations. Elinor represents the Christian wisdom that
knows correct judgement is hard, that mankind is fallible and the world full
of pitfalls; Marianne represents the naïvely optimistic idealism of sentimentalism. The differences between the two characters are not simply moral
since both are types found in many contemporary novels which were well
understood by readers to personify political issues. The property-owning
classes in England were fearful that the example of the French Revolution

would increase support for those British radicals who were demanding political and economic equality for all of Britain's citizens. These radicals were from around 1800 termed Jacobins, a term which originated in a Parisian egalitarian political club which met first in 1789 in the old convent of the Jacobins (i.e. followers of St Jacques). *Sense and Sensibility* was seen by contemporaries as one of a genre of anti-Jacobin novels, Marianne signifying the disturbance caused by revolutionary fervour, by a commitment to passion and to the ideal that brooks no social conventions, and to the individual's selfish will rather than social conformity. Like Elizabeth in *Pride and Prejudice*, she is a threat, fascinating, but needing to be repressed.

Butler sees *Sense and Sensibility* as much more interesting than the general run of anti-Jacobin novels because Austen's artistic inclinations lead her to develop scenes and characters in a way that erodes the rigidity of the genre, and indeed tends to make Marianne far too interesting (and insufficiently transgressive of social conventions), but she also views the novel as finally a limited achievement. References to *Sense and Sensibility* are to the edition by R. W. Chapman (London, 1923). Ed.]

1. W. Austen Leigh and R. A. Austen Leigh, *Jane Austen, her Life and Letters, A Family Record* (London, 1913), p. 80.

2. Maria Edgeworth does not completely discard the contrast-novel, which recurs in one of the *Popular Tales, The Contrast (1804)* and in *Patronage* (1814). Jane Austen does not quite discard it either – for *Mansfield Park* is a contrast-novel, of the consecutive rather than the continuous type.

3. *Nature and Art* appears to borrow its format from Thomas Day's Rousseauistic *Sandford and Merton* (1783–9), with its spoilt little aristocrat Tommy Merton, and its robust, simple farmer's son, Harry Sandford.

4. The very terminology adopted by some of the titles is revealing. Mrs Inchbald sees the issue in terms of 'nature' versus 'art', art in this context having the connotation of artificiality. 'Sense' gives nurture a very different bearing. By the mid-nineties sensibility is commonly a pejorative word. See E. Erämetsä, *A Study of the Word 'Sentimental'* (Helsinki, 1951).

5. *Sense and Sensibility*, p. 42. Elinor's involuntary admiration of Willoughby is important in the light of their last interview together.

6. Tests of the heroine's virtue in, respectively, Mrs West's *Gossip's Story*, and Mrs Hamilton's *Memoirs of Modern Philosophers*.

7. 'Prayers composed by Jane Austin', in *Minor Works*, ed. R. W. Chapman (Oxford, 1963), pp. 453–4 and 456.

8. Kenneth Moler, *Jane Austen's Art of Allusion* (Lincoln, 1968), p. 70. For other expositions of the view that Austen is 'ambivalent' between

sense and sensibility, see Mary Lascelles, *Jane Austen and her Art* (Oxford, 1939), p. 120; Andrew Wright, *Jane Austen's Novels: A Study in Structure* (London, 1954), pp. 30–1 and 92; and Lionel Trilling, 'A Portrait of Western Man', *The Listener*, 11 June 1958, p. 970.

9. For Mr Moler, Elinor's complacent first opinion, that Marianne will soon recover, is further evidence that Austen meant to show the limits of sense, and to strike a balance with sensibility. *Jane Austen's Art of Allusion*, pp. 62–73.

10. Marianne's intelligence is of a kind which gives her moral stature within Jane Austen's system of belief. Although she begins the novel professing an erroneous system, it is always clear that she has the capacity for the searching self-analysis of the Christian. Simple, good characters like Mrs Jennings are valued by Jane Austen, but she never leaves any doubt that individuals with active moral intelligence are a higher breed.

11. Some critics have called Elinor's marriage 'romantic', Lucy's 'prudent', and the end another instance of Austen's compromise between sense and sensibility. (Cf. Andrew Wright, *Jane Austen's Novels*, p. 92). But this shows a continued misunderstanding of Austen's interpretation of her two terms: her 'sense' approximates to the traditional Christian personal and social ethic, her 'sensibility' to a modern individualist ethic in two different manifestations, Marianne's and Lucy's.

12. Marianne, Colonel Brandon, Edward Ferrars, the late Mr Dashwood, and even perhaps Lucy Steele are better matched in their second choice than in their first.

3

Sense and Silences

ANGELA LEIGHTON

In both Romantic and twentieth-century literature we find the need to transgress the limits of the written word, in order to explore the peculiar resonance of what cannot be written. Fragments of language are shored up against the more difficult and strange expressiveness of Silence. However, what is significant is that these Silences always touch, at some point, the limit of language. They do not float freely, but remain in some kind of relation to words, to Sense. To write about Silence, toward Silence, is not the same as to *give up* writing, but it is to *go on failing* to resolve the choice which Silence offers. This is the dilemma that afflicts those most loquacious authors of Silence: the subjects of Beckett's novels. Thus 'the Unnamable' struggles with his own story:

> I want it to go silent, it can't, it does for a second, then it starts again, that's not the real silence, it says that's not the real silence, and what can be said of the real silence, I don't know.[1]

He speaks yearningly, despairingly, relentlessly, for the Silence which, like Godot, might resolve all his words.

However, there is another literary Silence, which is not that of failed creativity, or of the Romantic sublime, or of twentieth-century shame. Instead, this is the Silence of something which the text refuses to say openly, but which it allows, as a deliberate alternative to its own words. It is tempting to equate these escaping meanings with the Freudian unconscious, as Macherey does when he writes:

> The speech of the book comes from a certain silence ... for in order
> to say anything, there are other things *which must not be said*. Freud
> relegated this *absence of certain words* to a new place ... which he
> paradoxically *named*: the unconscious.[2]

However, I would argue that the alternative Silences of what is not
said in the literary text are too much deliberated to be like the
unconscious. In *The Language of the Self* Lacan writes:

> No doubt ... we have to lend an ear to the 'not-said' which lies in the
> holes of the discourse, but this does not mean that we are to do our
> listening as if it were to someone knocking from the other side of a
> wall.[3]

However, in literature the 'not-said' makes itself heard very much
like 'someone knocking', and that 'someone' is very often a woman.
Such Silences become evident where there are gaps or inconsistencies or ironies in the main text, but they become evident *as*
voices knocking against the 'wall' of the language which hides
them. To recover the Sense of Jane Austen's Silences, then, is to
hear the voices which her notoriously conservative and limiting
language would conceal: the voice, in particular, of her younger,
Romantic heroine, Marianne.

The story of Marianne, in *Sense and Sensibility*, is of one who, at
the age of seventeen, falls romantically in love with a Byronic hero,
Willoughby, is jilted, sinks into a mental and physical decline, comes
close to death, and is finally married to a man eighteen years her
senior, Colonel Brandon, who suffers from bouts of rheumatism,
wears a 'flannel waistcoat', and, in the course of the novel, scarcely
finds one occasion to speak to her directly. As Marianne progresses
from an early self-indulgent emotionalism to very real humiliation
and despair, however, her story is heard, ever more silently, on the
other side of what Austen rationally and censoriously chooses to tell.
Her discreet, ironic, and finally dismissive style only makes more
expressive those things which she leaves out, and by the end of the
novel what she leaves out is the voice of Marianne herself. *Sense and
Sensibility*, like all Austen's novels, is a drama of language in which
her heroines *suffer* what can and cannot be said.

If the literary work is read as a palimpsest in this way, where the
surface text conceals and half reveals another, less obvious text, or
where the narrative is deliberately complicated by secrets and
enigmas, things unsaid and voices unheard, we may begin to hear in

these Silences the sounds of women 'knocking'. For good as well as ill, the association of women with Silence has become a richly commonplace formula in contemporary theory. Mary Jacobus writes, in her essay 'The Difference of View', that

> femininity itself – heterogeneity, Otherness – becomes the repressed term by which discourse is made possible. The feminine takes its place with the absence, silence, or incoherence that discourse represses.[4]

Similarly, in an essay called 'Is There Such a Thing as Women's Writing?' Xavière Gauthier writes that

> blank pages, gaps, borders, spaces and silence ... emphasise the aspect of feminine writing which is the most difficult to verbalise because it becomes compromised, rationalised, masculinised as it explains itself.[5]

Both passages imply a choice, where Silence entails a negation of speech. On the one hand, to make Sense of 'spaces and silence' is to compromise them. On the other hand, if 'spaces and silence' are not hedged about with rational and verbalised thought, they must remain unexplained and always on the outside of language. It seems that women are faced with a choice between two versions of an all too familiar defeat: they should either be Silent or come to their Senses.

However, Gauthier herself does suggest an alternative to making this choice when she writes:

> If ... 'replete' words (*mots pleins*) belong to men, how can women speak 'otherwise', unless, perhaps, we can *make audible* that which agitates within us, suffers silently in the *holes of discourse*, in the unsaid, or in the non-sense.[6]

It might be possible, in Gauthier's terms, to '*make audible*' without making 'replete' that agitation and suffering which the 'non-sense' of women bespeaks. It is necessary that the Silence which especially belongs to women be protected *by* them, even while they themselves refuse to be protected *in* it. The text which articulates this dilemma is a text which is in difficulty, a text which needs both to suppress and to protect its Silences.

Sense and Sensibility is a novel in which the Silences of two women are made powerfully '*audible*'. The narrative is punctuated by their repeated but different refusals to speak. Elinor, on the side of Sense, withholds her words from considerateness for others, from a promise to keep their secrets, from admirable self-command, or occasionally from affronted intelligence, as when she refuses to pay Robert Ferrars 'the compliment of rational opposition'. Marianne, on the side of Sensibility, refuses to speak because she is careless of social proprieties, because she will not compromise the truth for politeness' sake, or because the strength of her feeling defies representation in words. Broadly, the Silences of Elinor are those of reserve and integrity; the Silences of Marianne are those of nonconformity and emotional powerlessness. While Elinor bravely suppresses the private language of her feelings, in order to engage in the public world of sometimes trivial and common Sense, Marianne retreats from that world into the serious and desperate privacy of her Sensibility. The main difference is that Elinor's Silences result from *self*-censorship – she listens 'in silence and immovable gravity' to Robert Ferrars, for instance – but Marianne's do not. *Her* reticence is never resigned or heroic. It is either a sign of her indifference to the conversations of others, as when she refuses to give an opinion as to the respective heights of Harry Dashwood and William Middleton, because 'she had never thought about it', or else it is a sign of the inexpressibility of her feelings. Marianne, after all, stands for the cause of Romanticism in this novel.

However, although both heroines retreat into Silence at various points, it is the Silence of Marianne which remains problematic, because it is not incorporated into the narrative, like Elinor's. Elinor's Silences have Austen's approval; they signify heroic reticence and control, and are contained by the language of Sense. Marianne's Silences signify emotions which have escaped control, and which are therefore in opposition to Austen's art. Marvin Mudrick writes that 'Marianne represents an unacknowledged depth of her author's spirit'.[7] I would add that this depth takes the form of a Silence which lies on the other side of the control of Austen's language. Marianne's suppressed 'scream' on receiving Willoughby's letter of repudiation, her growing depression and mental isolation, her decline into feverish raving and near-death – all these are covered by a fine veneer of understatement and qualification. By the end of the novel the divergence between the Sense of Austen's prose and the Silence of Marianne, which it throws into relief, has become painfully acute.

> Precious as was the company of her daughter to her ... [Mrs Dashwood] ... desired nothing so much as to give up its constant

enjoyment to her valued friend; and to see Marianne settled at the Mansion-house was equally the wish of Edward and Elinor. They each felt his sorrows and their own obligations, and Marianne, by general consent, was to be the reward of all.

The importance of what remains unspoken in Austen's works does not go unnoticed among critics. Barbara Hardy remarks that

> as we think of the busy social life in her novels and of the fully-occupied social lives of her characters, we also remember silence, solitude, isolation and privacy.[8]

However, with the possible exception of Tony Tanner,[9] they tend to concentrate on Elinor's self-censored story rather than on Austen's censorship of Marianne's. Gilbert and Gubar too stress the opposition between Marianne's shrill 'indulgence in sensibility' and 'Elinor's stoical self-restraint'.[10] Somehow we are left with the impression that Sensibility makes more noise than Sense. But this is not entirely true. By a different reading, it is Marianne who retreats from social intercourse, refuses to pay polite visits, and is finally rendered speechless in misery and illness. Marianne, I want to claim, with a bias that goes contrary to the apparent sympathies of the author, is the place where the familiar dilemma of women, to speak or not to speak, is played out. The Silences of Marianne are those which her author most needs to censor and protect.

One of Austen's most interesting comments on the nature of the difference between her two heroines is given in the following passage:

> 'What a sweet woman Lady Middleton is!' said Lucy Steele. Marianne was silent; it was impossible for her to say what she did not feel, however trivial the occasion; and upon Elinor therefore the whole task of telling lies when politeness required it, always fell.

Sense and Sensibility is usually interpreted as an argument of mind against heart, judgement against feeling, policy against spontaneity, Classicism against Romanticism, and, as a corollary of these, of reticence against self-expression. By this reading, Elinor's stoical reticence triumphs over Marianne's naïve outbursts. But in this passage Austen seems to be saying something different. Here it is Elinor who has access to the language of polite 'lies', while it is Marianne who remains silent. Sense has the privileges and powers of public speech, while Sensibility is a private and therefore powerless eloquence. The palimpsestic nature of this novel continually offers a choice of readings which depend on the angle of our gaze. In one light, Marianne's is merely an inconsequential adolescent drama, likely to be embarrassing for a time, but susceptible to cure. In another light, her long, if histrionic, misery challenges the conventions of polite lying.

The sensibility of Marianne, which, in its Romantic inheritance, represents what lies beyond the power of speech, is at once her prison and her weapon. Marianne defies the conventions of social intercourse because she is victimised by them, and her Silences speak against Sense because they are refused a hearing in the main text. This is not at first obvious, but it becomes so, as Austen's technique changes. At first her portrayal of Marianne relies on comic mockery and heavy irony. But as Marianne's feelings lose their fictionality and become true, Austen censors their expression by understating them, transferring them into mere physical illness, and finally by seeming to leave them altogether out of account.

At the start of the novel Austen's verbal exaggeration and irony serve to point the falsehood of the sentiments. Here she is still using the techniques of her earlier work, *Love and Freindship*, in which Laura is writing to one Marianne of the tragic events which cause her and her friend Sophia, who is 'all Sensibility and Feeling', regularly to sigh and faint and rave and run mad. The ironic violence of this earlier work is echoed in some of the language used to describe the sensibility of Marianne in the later work. At the start, she is described as having an 'excess' of 'sensibility', and on having to leave Norland she and her mother encourage each other 'in the violence of their affliction'. Similarly, when Willoughby departs, Marianne is subject to a 'violent oppression of spirits', and a 'violence of affliction', which, the language clearly signals, are false. The idea of 'violence' is usually too large for Austen's prose to contain it, and so it is presented only as exaggerated action or emotion. Violence such as Marianne's when Willoughby goes away is to be smilingly tolerated; Austen hedges it round with forbearing mockery. However, as Marianne's histrionic grief turns to very real humiliation, Austen ceases to use irony against her; she ceases to point out the comic disparities between her feelings and her reactions, and instead forces her heroine into a long retreat from language, as if to keep her protests at a safe distance. Marianne stifles her scream and at her lowest ebb raves incoherently. Her self-expression explores the furthest reaches from Sense.

The crisis of the novel is when Marianne receives Willoughby's cruelly explicit letter of repudiation. Elinor discovers her 'stretched on the bed, almost choked by grief'. Marianne thrusts a bundle of Willoughby's letters into Elinor's hands, and then, Austen writes, 'covering her face with her handkerchief, almost screamed with agony'. The word 'almost', used twice in this short passage as a qualification of Marianne's actions, is crucial. It is as if the public language of Austen's prose can scarcely contain the violence of choking or screaming. But here, instead of mocking it with ironic exaggeration, she suppresses it. Marianne *'almost* screamed with agony'. Such passion must be suppressed; her scream must not be heard. The language here acts out the actual event. The sound of screaming is stifled and silenced by polite understatement and circumspection and qualification. The word 'almost' smothers the protest, imprisons the sound in the inarticulateness of mere Sensibility, and seems to assert the authority of rational control. The phrase magnificently enacts the whole drama of Marianne's rebellion in this novel. The more her protestations of grief must be concealed and contained by an enforced Silence of public propriety and passivity, the more eloquently violent does that Silence become.

This kind of linguistic censorship of Marianne's words and actions continues throughout the second part of the novel. When Mrs Jennings hands Marianne a letter which for a moment she desperately believes to be from Willoughby, but quickly discovers to be from her mother, Austen writes of her:

> The cruelty of Mrs Jennings no language, within her reach in her moments of happiest eloquence, could have expressed; and now she could reproach her only by the tears which streamed from her eyes with passionate violence.

The authenticity of this later 'violence' of feeling in Marianne is conveyed by the wordlessness to which it reduces her. There is no falsifying 'eloquence' in her response. Instead, she is trapped in 'Sensibility', in a prison which gives no access to the language of articulate protest, but the Silence of which is now resonant and violent. Such 'passionate violence' is no longer of the surface but of the depths, and the sign of it is a kind of speechlessness which is not only Marianne's but also Jane Austen's.

The narrative turning point of the novel is Marianne's illness, which takes her to the brink of madness and death. But characteristically this event too is a drama of language. Marianne's speech during this illness becomes almost entirely unintelligible; it takes the form of 'frequent but inarticulate sounds of complaint'. The avenging spectre of her long unhappiness is a language so alienated and private that it becomes almost entirely inaccessible to others. She shows a 'feverish wildness', her 'ideas' are 'fixed incoherently on her mother', and Elinor fears never again to see her 'rational'. Such uncharacteristic melodrama in the main plot is not easily explained in ironic or moral terms, those two Senses for which Austen is famed. For Marianne's decline into near insanity and death is prompted by the trivial event of a solitary walk. The real cause of her decline is evaded in Austen's main plot, but it is hinted at in the language she uses to describe Marianne's escapade. Once again Austen's Sense seems to slant into Silences.

Here is the passage in which she describes the cause of Marianne's illness:

> Two delightful walks on the third and fourth evenings of her being there, not merely on the dry gravel of the shrubbery, but all over the grounds, and especially in the most distant parts of them, where there was something more of wildness than in the rest, where the trees were the oldest, and the grass was the longest and wettest, had – assisted by the still greater imprudence of sitting in her wet shoes and stockings – given Marianne a cold so violent.

Austen teasingly implies that Marianne's Romantic propensity for the superlative, for the 'oldest' trees, the 'longest and wettest' grass, is rightly punished by a cold. However, as that cold develops and worsens, bringing Marianne to the brink of death, this seemingly innocuous escapade acquires connotations that are perhaps not so trivial. It foreshadows a parallel occasion in *Mansfield Park* where Maria Bertram will not wait for Mr Rushworth to bring his key, and with it 'authority and protection', but instead, with Henry Crawford's help, negotiates the iron gate into the park. 'I think it might be done', he urges, 'if you really wished to be more at large, and could allow yourself to think it not prohibited'. Here the event clearly foreshadows their more serious infringement of what is 'prohibited' toward the end of the novel. In the case of Marianne, the analogy to some more serious crime is totally suppressed in terms of plot, but still hinted at in the language. Once again it is her characteristic 'imprudence' which urges her to cross some hidden boundary and to trespass in that territory which lies beyond the social – 'where there was something more of *wildness*'. The boundary is internal and moral, of course, but it becomes evident in Austen's language as the boundary to excess. What Austen refuses to explain here, either in narrative or moral terms, is still 'audible' if we are attuned to her Sense.

I suggest that this incident is related to another seemingly unexplained element in the book: that unnecessary and stagey subplot which tells of the fates of the two Elizas, and which is narrated by Colonel Brandon. Despite the unlikely melodrama of the two stories, their facts remain curiously unmemorable to the reader. One of the reasons for this might be Colonel Brandon's embarrassment and confusion when he tells them to Elinor. Another, I suggest, is Austen's own need to distance their implications from the main narrative. The first Eliza was 'an orphan', brought up with Colonel Brandon; she is tricked on the eve of her elopement with him and forced to marry his brother, whom she subsequently leaves for another. Having been abandoned by this lover, and given birth to his child, she sinks into prostitution, debt, imprisonment, and death by consumption. The second Eliza is her child, who, in spite of Brandon's custody, is seduced and abandoned like her mother, by no other than Willoughby.

I suspect that these two stories are not interpolated just for the sake of contrast or sensation. Although Marianne is not in fact seduced and does not in fact die, her passion for Willoughby, and subsequent illness when he jilts her, are shot through with implications which Austen seems at pains to emphasise in the subplot. Marianne's own story begins with a fall, a fall which occurs on another imprudent walk, and she falls practically at Willoughby's feet – or, in Austen's own more tactful phrase, 'within a few yards' of him. In the case of the first Eliza, the 'fall' is figurative; it is a 'fall' from virtue which results in the surprisingly explicit facts of pregnancy, prostitution, debt, imprisonment, and eventual death by consumption. But there are points at which Austen seems at pains to ensure that her reader does not miss the connection:

> 'Your sister, I hope, cannot be offended', said he, 'by the resemblance I have fancied between her and my poor disgraced relation. Their fates, their fortunes cannot be the same ...'

Colonel Brandon generally protests too much, especially as he goes on to tell the tale of the younger Eliza, whose affection for

Willoughby is 'as strong, still as strong' as Marianne's own. Austen's purpose is not just to warn, or to emphasise Willoughby's unregenerate nature; it is also to suggest another writing of Marianne's story, for which her reader would have been prepared. As Marilyn Butler writes, 'Mrs West, Mrs Hamilton, or the young Maria Edgeworth – would almost certainly have had Marianne seduced and killed off, after the errors of which she has been guilty.'[11] (Austen's punishments, however, take a different form.) But an analogy between Marianne and the younger Eliza continues to link the two stories. Toward the end, the sight of Marianne laid low in sickness inevitably reminds Colonel Brandon yet again of 'that resemblance between Marianne and Eliza already acknowledged, and now strengthened by the hollow eye, the sickly skin, the posture of reclining weakness, and the warm acknowledgement of peculiar obligation'. The figure of the fallen woman seems to haunt the imagination of Colonel Brandon, and in the confusion of his mind's eye there might be written, behind the text as we have it, another story, another novel.

However, *Sense and Sensibility* purports to be a story of eventual recovery and happiness, a story which moves from innocent Sensibility to experienced Sense. Thus Austen's version of the female Awakening goes contrary to our post-Romantic expectations. Instead of coming to understand the thwarted sexual nature of her own sensibility, Marianne must grow out of her private and exclusive love for Willoughby and come to accept marriage based on 'no sentiment superior to strong esteem and lively friendship'. She awakens into a knowledge of herself which is that commanded by the society around her, and which is also that of Austen's curt and realist prose at the end. Marianne's development from love to 'lively friendship', from illness to health, from egocentric Sensibility to conforming Sense, also takes the form of a development from private inarticulateness to public speech.

There is an interesting episode after Marianne's recovery, in which she and Elinor return to the place of her first fall. She says:

> 'There, exactly there' – pointing with one hand, 'on that projecting mound, – there I fell; and there I first saw Willoughby.'

But the sign of her recovery comes a few lines later, where she admits to Elinor, 'I *can* talk of it now, I hope, as I ought to do'. While her fall has taken the form of a lapse into Silence, inarticulateness, and raving, her recovery and reintegration in society through marriage take the form of submission to the prescribed language of conventional morality: 'I *can* talk of it now ... as I ought to do.' The reaction against sentimentalism and the novel of sensibility in the late eighteenth century, of which Austen is a prime example, usually works by a reassertion of 'the ethical sense' against 'unlimited toleration'[12] and sympathy. For Austen, however, 'the ethical sense' is no more (and no less) than conformity to a certain public language. Unlike her two surrogates, Marianne *does* return to the public world of community, respectability, and Sense. She returns from Silences and learns to 'talk'. ... Or does she?

As in so many of her novels, Austen's conclusion in *Sense and Sensibility* is perfunctory and swift. However, it is precisely in these last pages, in her *envoi* to her once Romantic heroine, in her detached and public tidying of events, and in her tone of realism and worldly wisdom, that Austen's Silences become deafening. At the point where she most ruthlessly claims the victory of Sense, she undermines that victory with a host of things unsaid. Let me quote once again those passages in which the future of Marianne becomes assured:

> ... to see Marianne settled at the Mansion-house was equally the wish of Edward and Elinor. They each felt his [Colonel Brandon's] sorrows and their own obligations, and Marianne, by general consent, was to be the reward of all.
> With such confederacy against her ... what could she do?

> Colonel Brandon was now as happy as all those who best loved him believed he deserved to be; in Marianne he was consoled for every past affliction ... and that Marianne found her own happiness in forming his was equally the persuasion and delight of each observing friend.

These last passages seem to be about the need for an affectionate, respectable, appropriate marriage; about Marianne's reconciliation with family and friends; about a 'sensible' kind of happiness. But again, to read the text like a palimpsest, with an ear attuned to its Silences, is to begin to suspect that this tone of realism, like so much of the public speech of Austen's novel, only works as a polite lie. If Marianne is freed from the prison of her own sensibility at the end, it is only to be crowded out by the voices of all her well-wishing friends. We are told of *their* feelings, beliefs, persuasions, and delights. But behind this bustle of public opinion Marianne, it seems, has once more nothing to say. Having learned to 'talk', it seems that at this crucial moment in her life she is to have no voice. Marianne has learned, through long trial and suffering, to be Silent.

It is this secretiveness which characterises Austen's deceptive and ironic style. The point about irony is that it always tells either more or less than the truth, and therefore requires that the reader be constantly attuned to that meaning which slips the evidence of words. That which slips the evidence of these, Jane Austen's last words, is Marianne herself. Austen's irony forbids the reader to take any act or speech at face value, and is characteristic of an art that shows language itself to be a suspect social institution. For much of the dialogue of her novel has been a cunning exploration of how the spoken word does not quite match the speaker's intention, or else of how the commonly expressed opinion fails to match the truth. It forces us to read the text as many-levelled, rather than as linear. At the end, the truth of Marianne's feelings is totally ousted behind the convenience of happiness among friends and family. Once again Austen's language conceals and suppresses, as she linguistically impersonates their tyrannical wills and wishes. Their 'persuasion and delight' are thinly disguised weapons, by which a 'confederacy' of well-wishers enforces 'happiness' on Marianne. She is victim to their 'general consent', and her feelings are referred to Silence once more. This Silence, which in the past expressed her rebellion and defiance and uncompromising Sensibility, has now become the penalty which society exacts in order to proclaim its own common-Sense version of the happy ending. It seems, after all, that Marianne's story was only a choice of Silences.

Thus I return to the dilemma of 'the feminine', which Mary Jacobus summarises when she writes:

> The feminine takes its place with the absence, silence, or incoherence that discourse represses ... [adding that] here again there's a problem for feminist criticism. Women's access to discourse involves submission to phallocentricity, to the masculine and the Symbolic; refusal, on the other hand, risks re-inscribing the feminine as a yet more marginal madness or nonsense.[13]

The answer must be not to choose, but to play out the choice: the choice of making Sense or keeping Silences. This is the choice which Austen's ironic and deceptive language continually dramatises, and which is played out in the story of Marianne. For Marianne escapes from the marginalised language of Sensibility only to be tamed and punished by the public language of Sense. What appears to be, on the surface of the narrative, an escape from her own vulnerability, or a growth into knowledge and experience, is in fact only a more absolute affirmation of the social irrelevance of her voice. 'With such confederacy against her ... what could she do?' While for a time Marianne uses Silence as an outcry and a violation of proper speech, by the end it is used against her, to reaffirm the marginality of her place and of her speech: 'that Marianne found her own happiness in forming his was equally the persuasion and delight of each observing friend.' Silences, in this novel, represent the protest of 'the feminine', but also, in the end, her punishment. Jane Austen's greatness lies in the fact that, beneath her artistic championing of Sense, she can make us *hear* those Silences that always lie on the other side of it.

From *Jane Austen: New Perspectives*, ed. Janet Todd (New York, 1983), pp. 129–41.

NOTES

[Angela Leighton approaches Jane Austen through the sophisticated textual theory which was developed in the 1970s and is generally subsumed under the term 'poststructuralism'. Leighton's version of poststructuralism synthesises materialist, feminist and psychoanalytic elements to draw attention to the way that the not-said functions in *Sense and Sensibility*. The not-said, rather than being a mere nothing, is that which enables discourse to occur, and that which indicates the censorship which ideology imposes through language upon its users. The loudest silence in *Sense and Sensibility* is that of Marianne, a person seen always and selectively through Elinor's repressing, censoring and silencing 'objectivity', reduced to non-sense because to admit her reason would be to violate the ideological closure of the text. Elinor's world-view allows for the silence of self-repression which is necessary for self to submit to its social place. But her world-view does not allow for a silence which says 'No!', as when Marianne refuses to utter the platitudes required by polite society, nor does it allow the silence which is unspeakable because aware of experiences which cannot be conveyed in the language of patriarchal sense. Leighton's reading travels in parallel with the work of many recent feminists who have drawn attention to the traces in texts of what has been written out of history in order for it to be His-story. It eloquently indicates that whilst Austen may well have situated herself with Elinor, as Butler and Duckworth suggest, the silencing of Marianne was not accomplished without screams, ill-muffled by the suffocating hand. Ed.]

1. Samuel Beckett, *The Unnameable,* in *Molloy, Malone Dies, The Unnameable* (London, 1959), p. 412.

2. Pierre Macherey, *A Theory of Literary Production*, trans. Geoffrey Wall (London, 1978), p. 85.

3. Jacques Lacan, *The Language of the Self: The Function of Language in Psychoanalysis*, trans. Anthony Wilden (New York, 1968), p. 71.

4. Mary Jacobus, 'The Difference of View', in *Women Writing and Writing about Women* (London, 1979), p. 12.

5. Xavière Gauthier, 'Is There Such a Thing as Women's Writing?' in *New French Feminisms: An Anthology*, ed. Elaine Marks and Isabelle de Courtivron (Amherst, 1980), p. 164.

6. Ibid., p. 163.

7. Marvin Mudrick, 'Irony and Convention Versus Feeling', in B. C. Southam (ed.), *Jane Austen: Sense and Sensibility, Pride and Prejudice and Mansfield Park: A Casebook* (London, 1976), p. 114.

8. Barbara Hardy, *A Reading of Jane Austen* (London, 1979), p. 21.

9. Tony Tanner, 'Secrecy and Sickness in Sense and Sensibility', in *Casebook*, ed. Southam, pp. 131–46. I am indebted to this introduction for first analysing the importance of silence in the novel.

10. Sandra M. Gilbert and Susan Gubar, *The Madwoman in the Attic: The Woman Writer and the Nineteenth-Century Literary Imagination* (New Haven and London, 1979), p. 156.

11. Marilyn Butler, *Jane Austen and the War of Ideas* (Oxford, 1975), p. 189. [Reprinted in this volume – see p. 38. Ed.]

12. Ibid., p. 23

13. Jacobus, 'The Difference of View', p. 12.

4

Closure and Narrative Danger

D. A. MILLER

> *'Such a development of every thing most unwelcome'*
>
> Que serait le récit du bonheur? Rien, que ce qui le prépare, puis ce qui le détruit, ne se raconte.[1]

The narrative of happiness is inevitably frustrated by the fact that only insufficiencies, defaults, deferrals, can be 'told'. Even when a narrative 'prepares for' happiness, it remains in this state of lack, which can only be liquidated along with the narrative itself. Accordingly, the narrative of happiness might be thought to exemplify the unhappiness of narrative in general. Narrative proceeds toward, or regresses from, what it seeks or seems most to prize, but it is never identical to it. To designate the presence of what is sought or prized is to signal the termination of narrative – or at least, the displacement of narrative onto other concerns.

It is clear that the category of the non-narratable cannot be limited to Gide's specification of it (as 'le bonheur') in my epigraph. What leaves a novelist speechless is not always what makes him happiest, and there is a wide spectrum of ways in which a novel may characterise the function of the non-narratable. In traditional fiction, marriage is a dominant form of this *ne plus ultra*, but death is another, and these are not the only ones. Narrative closure may coincide with the end of a quest, as in a story of ambition, or with the end of an inquest, as in a detective story. The closure, moreover, may be reinforced by other, secondary determinations, such as a proper transfer of property. But whatever the chosen privatives might be, it is evident that traditional narrative cannot dispense with the function that they motivate – namely, that of both constituting and abolishing the narrative movement. We might say, generally, that traditional narrative is a quest after that which will end questing; or that it is an interruption of what will be resumed; an expansion of what will be condensed, or a distortion of what will be made straight; a holding in suspense or a putting into question of what will be resolved or answered.[2]

What I have called the non-narratable in a text should not be confused with what is merely unnarrated by it. In a broad sense, of course, every discourse is uttered against a background of all those things that it chooses, for one reason or another, not to say. Three subjects that Jane Austen's novels do not treat, for instance, are the Napoleonic wars, the sex lives of the characters, and the labour of the tenants who farm their estates. The first of these is only an unincluded subject of discourse; the second is an unincluded and also forbidden topic; the third is unincluded and perhaps (there are more than sexual taboos) forbidden as well. It is by no means a negligible fact that Jane Austen does not take up these subjects. To notice omissions of this order, however, seems to me mainly useful in establishing the level at which the novelistic representation is pitched (in Jane Austen's case, below the threshold of world history, above the threshold of primary biological functions and of work). This can help us to see the limits and lacunae of the novelistic representation, but it does not adequately account for the dynamics of the representation within the field so defined. Subjects like these have no place – not even the shadow of a place – in the novels, and the novels never invoke them to terminate their discourse. The marriage of the heroine in Jane Austen, on the other hand, does inhibit narrative productivity in this way. The 'perfect union' of Emma and Mr Knightley virtually *must* end the novel; otherwise, it would not be a 'perfect' union. It would be brought back to the state of insufficiency and lack that has characterised the novelistic movement. What I am calling the non-narratable elements of a text are precisely those that (like Emma's marriage) serve to supply the specified narrative lack, or to answer the specified narrative question. It is not the case that such elements cannot be designated by the text's language, or that they literally cannot be mentioned. The non-narratable is not the unspeakable. What defines a non-narratable element is its incapacity to generate a story.

Properly or intrinsically, it has no narrative future – unless, of course, its non-narratable status is undermined (by happiness destroyed, an incorrect solution, a choice that must be remade).

I want to begin, in the case of Jane Austen, by characterising the eminently narratable states of affairs in her novels in relation to complementary non-narratable states of affairs. Which kinds of character, or situation, or language seem inherently to lend themselves to the narrative production, and which to the narrative closure? Or, if one prefers to stress the difference between the representation and the construction, with which characters, situations, and languages does the narrative discourse motivate its productivity and its closure?

...

'That the Miss Lucases and the Miss Bennets should meet to talk over a ball was absolutely necessary; and the morning after the assembly brought the former to Longbourn to hear and to communicate' (*Pride and Prejudice*, p. 18). Even so commonplace an occurrence as a ball needs to be screened: to what hopes, dangers, did it give rise? what legitimate inferences does it allow? what hazardous extrapolations does it not quite warrant? The novelist's joke here aside, we see how 'absolutely necessary' it is 'to talk over' experience, if only to oneself, being demonstrated throughout the novel. Elizabeth catches the cool greeting exchanged between Darcy and Wickham: 'What could be the meaning of it? – It was impossible to imagine; it was impossible not to long to know' (p. 73). Later she must engage Wickham in 'a full discussion' (p. 115) of the reasons for his absence from Mr Bingley's ball. And after the first evening of her visit to Charlotte Collins ('spent chiefly in talking over Hertfordshire news, and telling again what had been already written'),

> Elizabeth in the solitude of her chamber had to meditate upon Charlotte's degree of contentment, to understand her address in guiding, and composure in bearing with her husband, and to acknowledge that it was all done very well. She had also to anticipate how her visit would pass, the quiet tenor of their usual employments, the vexatious interruptions of Mr Collins, and the gaieties of their intercourse with Rosings. A lively imagination soon settled it all.
>
> (pp. 157–8)

When experience throws up so many provocative and often provoking mysteries, the typical response is to take some step, whether ratiocinative or imaginative, to settle them. 'Till this moment, I never knew myself' (p. 208), says Elizabeth, beginning to realise her true feelings for Darcy, and she has turned even her relationship to herself into a mystery that has now been solved. What are Emma Woodhouse's fantasies, in a sense, but a less reasoned and more freely inventive version of this same need to anticipate the narrative gaps in experience, to give speech to its muteness? Because Harriet's parentage is unknown, 'Emma was obliged to fancy what she liked' (*Emma*, p. 27); because there is a perceptible incoherence, however slight, in Jane Fairfax's behaviour, Emma's fancy 'received an amusing supply' (p. 214)

Whether cautiously indulged or not, this obsessive need to settle it all arises in response to the imposition of its opposite: an uncomfortable suspension of settlement, an awkward silence of signification. With a confidence and an anxiety oddly belying one another, the heroines engage to do the work of closure, which is to make sense. Ignorance, incoherence, or ambiguity must never be enjoyed, but always submitted to as an enforced evil. (It is better, of course, to recognise this evil for what it is – like, *grosso modo*, Elinor and Fanny – than to liquidate it prematurely in the manner of Emma or Elizabeth.) To make sense is a right and proper task, but it is essential to the novelistic production that it be frustrated: undermined by the parodic endeavours of matchmakers like Mrs Bennet and Mrs Jennings; misled by the false representations of tricksters like Wickham and Frank Churchill; resisted by the confusingly various behaviour of the Crawfords and the dogmatism of Marianne Dashwood; even simply deflected by the heroines' own blindness. If the novel is to be kept going, all the senses made excepting the last must be untrue, incomplete, or merely unconfirmed. The assertiveness of these may anticipate the closural act of nomination, but their inadequacy only validates its sovereignty as the moment of full, true explanation.

Jane Austen mobilises a full range of pseudo-closures: mendacious or equivocating, suspended or only partial solutions.[3] Wickham gives Elizabeth a false account of Darcy's coolness toward him, which she mistakenly takes for true. The Dashwoods' servant unwittingly equivocates when he announces that Lucy Steele has become Mrs Ferrars, for 'Mrs Ferrars' can be construed as either Mr *Edward* Ferrars or Mrs *Robert* Ferrars. Emma suspends Frank Churchill's confession ('In short, Miss Woodhouse – I think you can hardly be quite without suspicion –'), erroneously believing that she already knows its purport (*Emma*, p. 260). And the news of Willoughby's intended marriage to Miss Grey, a partial explanation of events, accounts for his cutting Marianne at the London party, but not for his initially amiable behaviour toward her. These pseudo-closures make a nice instance of the way narratable and closural systems intersect in the text. In so far as they fail to measure up to Jane Austen's rigorous ideal of a wholly and properly intelligible world, the wrongheaded, equivocal, interrupted, or scanted attempts at closure only promote further narrative. Yet in so far as they implicitly or by contrast anticipate the form that closure will assume, they promote further narrative only in the direction of closural rectification or completion. The narratable lie postulates as its future a corresponding closural truth. A switchword is equivocal, but at least narrows the closural possibilities down to two, one of which will be chosen. And we know that a suspended solution will be resumed, much as an incomplete one will be completed.

It becomes clear, then, that Jane Austen's novels must proceed (in a rather literal sense) by trial and error, if they are to proceed at all. Only narratable errors can mark the 'progress' toward an increasingly definitive closural truth. It might be argued, of course, that other novelists proceed in the very same way; but here, what might well be a common novelistic *modus operandi* goes patently against the drift of the novelist's highly unexperimental moral ideology, which is always suggesting that the knowledge of what one 'ought to have done' is available to the conscience of characters from the start. The particular effects of this ambivalence would not occur, say, in George Eliot's fiction, where an ideology of process and becoming perfectly accounts for the narrative procedures. In Jane Austen, the ideology articulated in the representation can never fully rationalise the necessities of novelistic construction, except as lapses, that is, events that really need not have happened. From the standpoint of her moral ideology, Jane Austen's novel is always on the wrong track; according to the exigencies of her novelistic construction, however, it must be on the wrong track when it moves on a track at all. For the novelist's ideal – what she calls 'the reality of reason and truth' (*Sense and Sensibility*, p. 361) – is a great good place where movement (unless already known and reduced to an iterative mode) is impossible.

What I have been discussing as the equivocation of Jane Austen's form – its tendency to disown at an ideological level what it embraces at a constructional one – shows up in miniature in the moral casuistry of the heroines, who limit the excitement they feel to fewer dimensions than their actual response often seems to warrant

...

The moral standards of Austen's heroines *are* moral standards, and certainly can be discussed as such. They also, however, allow the heroines to savour the forbidden without having to acknowledge their affective and imaginative kinship to it. They are visibly the condition of a repression, which permits repressed material to emerge by denying such material as *its own*. Freud calls this mental sleight of hand 'negation' (*Verneinung*). 'Negation is a way of taking cognisance of what is repressed; indeed, it is already a lifting of the repression, though not, of course, an acceptance of what is repressed.'[4] Freud's suggestive concept allows us to formulate in a new way the equivocation operated by the novelist between the demands of construction and the pretensions of representational ideology. If the narratable in Jane Austen turns out consistently to coincide with a lapse from the novelist's moral vision, how can the narratable be entertained at all, without her text getting ideologically contaminated by it? By being entertained, precisely, I would argue, in a mode of negation. A moral negation exculpates the novelist from the sin of narrating, and hence permits the act of narration to go forward.

...

This strategy of negation protects the novelist from the morally deplorable structures of the narratable, and so allows them to generate her novels. Jane Austen's peremptory standards, her absolute moral vision, her definitive nominations never lend themselves to narrative – indeed, they are virtually unaffected by it. Of course, the novels often tease us with the possibility that this moral ideology will fail to be incarnated. It is just possible that Edward Ferrars will marry Lucy Steele, or that Captain Wentworth will go away again. If these possibilities were realised, however, they would have the status of sheer and utter mistakes. Our knowledge of what the proper settlement ought to have been would remain unshaken. Contingencies are allowed (if never ultimately) to threaten the incarnation of the right names and relationships in a social settlement, but never the rightness of these, which is intact no matter what happens in the novels. Revising the *mot* of Gide's immoralist, we might say, 'What would be the narrative of transparent conduct and definitive language? Nothing but their disappearance or defalcation, nothing but a weak trace of them can be told.' A morally insistent voice, installed in 'the reality of reason and truth', always qualifies what *can* be told in Jane Austen, always reminding us that it doesn't quite make the mark, always denying it a certain ideological rightness or fullness. A reader becomes aware of this even on so elementary a level as that of screening eligible candidates for the heroine's hand. No, not Mr Collins – too stupid; not Colonel Fitzwilliam – too impoverished; not Wickham – his manners are too easy; and not Darcy either (in the first half of the novel) – his manners are too rude. The proper solution cannot be these, but these define the proper solution in the only way a narrative text would seem able to define it before coming to an end – that is, by contrast, by what the proper solution is *not*.

'It was *not* my mother', says the patient, from which the analyst infers, 'So it *was* his mother.'[5] At one level, Jane Austen's narrator insinuates, 'the narratable can relate to my ideology of closure only as a lapse. They have no necessary, or mutually dependent relationship with one another, for one is all insufficiency and void, and the other is all adequacy and plenitude.' From which, at another level, we might infer that the transcendent or absolute status of this closural ideology is covertly dependent on its being voided in the moment of narratability. Much as in the child's game of *Fort!/Da!* described by Freud,[6] the reappearance of an ideally transparent world becomes meaningful only through its previous disappearance. Moreover, just as the child's game takes place in the context of an original loss of his mother, so Jane Austen's symbolic staging of the disappearance and retrieval of 'the reality of reason and truth' would seem to take place within a certain anxiety about whether the full meanings of her ideology can ever be established once for all. Negation allows the patient at least to thematise his mother in the analytical discourse. Similarly, Jane Austen's moral negation permits her to bring into language what otherwise, according to a strict construction of her ideology, could never properly be mentioned. Her novels can bring forward a fascinated delight with unsettled states of deferral and ambiguity, provided that they also, gently or firmly, repudiate them as not belonging (so to speak) to their real selves. Reading Jane Austen, we engage a blinded dialectic, knowing itself in only the partial mode of denial.

...

'The night was cold and stormy. The wind roared round the house, and the rain beat against the windows; but Elinor, all happiness within, regarded it not' (*Sense and Sensibility*, p. 316). For Marianne is now on the road to recovery from her fever, and implicitly, from her attachment to Willoughby as well. Suddenly, there is heard driving up to the house a carriage, which Elinor expects is bringing her mother.

> Never in her life had Elinor found it so difficult to be calm, as at that moment. The knowledge of what her mother must be feeling as the carriage stopt at the door – of her doubt – her dread – perhaps her despair! – and of what *she* had to tell! – with such knowledge it was impossible to be calm. All that remained to be done, was to be speedy; and therefore staying only till she could leave Mrs Jenning's maid with her sister, she hurried down stairs.
>
> The bustle in the vestibule, as she passed along an inner lobby, assured her that they were already in the house. She rushed forwards towards the drawing-room, – she entered it – and saw only Willoughby.
>
> (p. 316)

Willoughby's arrival is a surprise, of course, but it fits into a series of surprising episodes in the novel, in which one character is expected and another arrives. At Barton, for instance, Marianne thinks that 'a man on horseback riding towards them' is Willoughby returning to her; it turns out to be Edward Ferrars, in disquietingly 'low spirits' (pp. 86, 96). In London, a knock is heard at the door, and both sisters instantly assume that it is Willoughby coming to call on his mistress; in walks Colonel Brandon instead (p. 161). The same mistake is repeated, less explicitly, later in the London stay (p. 203). Once more back at Barton, Elinor imagines that 'the figure of a man on horseback' is Colonel Brandon on a visit, and her visitor proves to be Edward Ferrars, come to propose (p. 358). These recurring cases of mistaken identity serve a number of functions in the novel. Most obviously, they are comic blunders, meant to reveal the heroines' characters and the particular blind-nesses attending each. Typically, Marianne assumes that events will fulfil her wishes, Elinor that events will frustrate hers, and actuality adheres to the programme of neither. Yet if these mistaken identi-ties are clearly *mistakes*, the novelist may also be hinting that they are, in some sense, identities too. It is as though events were assert-ing an interchangeability that threatened to obtain among the three men and between the two sisters. Both sisters are erotically involved with all three men, whatever safeguards are imposed by the categories (love/esteem/disgust/mistrust/quasi-sororal affection) that differentiate this involvement. Do Elinor and Marianne cultivate their difference from one another in part to avoid the threat of a sameness of situation and choice? An interesting gloss is suggested on the novel's governing antithesis – on the need for such an antithesis, despite the novelist's apparent preference for one of its terms. Elinor, we know, is not unfeeling, nor is Marianne entirely senseless. When they play their different dominant traits off one another, this is (whatever else) their way of making a preliminary classification on the basis of which they can be distinguished, along with the eligible men who approach them.

For our purposes, however, these mistaken identities most importantly refer us to the workings out of novelistic closure. They frustrate the pseudo-closures that in different ways Elinor and Marianne are both eager to impose, and ultimately work toward the real closures of the novel. The London visitor is not Marianne's lover, but the man she will later learn to love, in a lasting way; the Barton visitor is not Colonel Brandon, come to give an accurate account of Elinor's definitive loss of Edward, but Edward himself, come to propose marriage. In this scene at Cleveland, Elinor expects her mother – a figure of comfort who will allow their situation to settle into a state of equilibrium. Willoughby comes instead, who has always been a figure of disturbance, but we have been taught to suspect that what frustrates one closure may be made to issue in another.

For in so far as Willoughby's confessional visit meets an obvious closural requirement, his appearance is no surprise at all. There must be no mysteries left over at the end of a Jane Austen novel, and although it is unlikely that Willoughby's actions can be justified, they still must be explained. Some problems of motivation have not yet been laid to rest. What was the meaning of his initial treatment of Marianne? Of his sudden departure from Barton? Is his character libertine, mercenary, or just plain weak? Willoughby's explanations to Elinor cannot clear his conduct, but they do the next best thing by clearing it up. A better knowledge of his character comes to reinforce his removal from the novel's centre stage.

Yet from another angle, Willoughby's justification of himself reintroduces into his motives and intentions the same suspense that has made him a puzzle all along. Only the ante has been raised.

What once was an apparent affection for Marianne has now become an explicitly acknowledged one, whose reality is no longer suspect; and what was a seeming dismissal of Marianne at the London party now ought to become an effective one, through his marriage to Miss Grey. The ambiguity of his desire has been preserved at a more dangerous level, and the ambivalence of a response to him must be riven by attraction and repulsion more potently than ever. Furthermore, Willoughby wants his dangerous narrative – charged as it is with the suspense of which further narrative could be made – relayed to Marianne herself. 'Will you repeat to your sister ... what I have been telling you? ... Tell her of my misery and my penitence. Tell her that my heart was never inconstant to her, and if you will, that at this moment she is dearer to me than ever' (p. 330). Is Willoughby putting an end to their affair, or hoping to renew it? One sees the possibilities that his ambiguous performance opens up. It is just possible, for instance, that Marianne might yet run off with Willoughby, if this declaration met her with all its force. This at least seems the point of including the stories of Eliza Williams and her daughter in the novel, and their motifs of marital infidelity, of prostitution, of seduction and abandonment. By a kind of melodramatic projection, these stories double for the issues potentially at stake in Marianne's own. We may of course want to trust Marianne more than this implies; at the very least, however, a direct confrontation with Willoughby's 'still ardent love' for her would impede the enforced oblivion that a decent settlement must entail. If Marianne is never capable of the behaviour of a Lydia Bennet or a Maria Rushworth, she always courts something like the fate of a Mary Crawford: the inability to put the man she has loved and lost 'sufficiently out of her head' (*Mansfield Park*, p. 469).

Willoughby's narration can move in the direction of either sense or suspense. The sense of his disclosures tranquillises the disturbing inconsistencies enigmatically propounded by his conduct; it fixes him, or ought to, outside the pale of whatever might constitute settlement for Marianne. To the extent, however, that Willoughby's meaning betrays an easily exploitable ambiguity, it is troubled by a suspense that undermines its closural fixity. Elinor recognises the dangerously ambiguous status of Willoughby's narration, and her reply to his request that she repeat it to her sister marks the beginning of a strategy of redaction: 'I will tell her all that is necessary to what may comparatively be called your justification' (*Sense and Sensibility*, p. 330). She has implicitly reserved the right to edit Willoughby's confession – to bowdlerise his text so that an impressionable young woman such as Marianne might read it without harm. Elinor is the character best fitted for this task, but even for her it is no easy labour (proof of an emotional sensitivity in her that goes unperceived under cover of the boisterous demonstrations of her sister and her mother). The most important fact about Elinor's revision of Willoughby's narration (part of which takes effect immediately, and part gradually) is that it is an *exertion*. This is a word that the novelist has frequently used to describe Elinor's mental processes, and it refers us not only to the work involved in them, but also (in its root sense of a 'thrusting out') to the purpose of the work. The forces at play in the work of Elinor's censorship need to be followed in some detail.

Elinor responds to Willoughby's appeal more intensely and fully than she ever has done, only when a protective context of 'sadness' has been invoked:

> Elinor, for some time after he left her, for some time even after the sound of his carriage had died away, remained too much oppressed by a croud of ideas, widely differing in themselves, but of which sadness was the general result, to think even of her sister.
>
> Willoughby, he, whom only half an hour ago she had abhorred as the most worthless of men, Willoughby, in spite of all his faults, excited a degree of commiseration for the sufferings produced by them, which made her think of him as now separated for ever from her family with a tenderness, a regret, rather in proportion, as she soon acknowledged within herself – to his wishes than to his merits. She felt that his influence over her mind was heightened by circumstances which ought not to have weight; by that person of uncommon attraction, that open, affectionate, and lively manner which it was no merit to possess; and by that still ardent love for Marianne, which it was not even innocent to indulge. But she felt that it was so, long, long before she could feel his influence less.
>
> (p. 333)

The sadness has been implicitly grounded in the pathos of irreversibility with which she has invested Willoughby's case. If she cannot quite say, in view of the facts, 'O! what a noble soul is here o'erthrown', she thinks something a bit like it:

> Her thoughts were silently fixed on the irreparable injury which too early an independence and its consequent habits of idleness, dissipation, and luxury, had made in the mind, the character, the happiness, of a man who, to every advantage of person and talents, united a disposition naturally open and honest, and a feeling, affectionate temper.
>
> (p. 331)

Elinor's melancholy depends upon and preserves a preliminary judgement that the 'injury' is 'irreparable'. In this sense, her sadness coincides with the relief of closure – to be sad over Willoughby implies that he is now essentially *hors jeu*, 'now separated for ever from her family'. This, however, is a proposition that Willoughby's ambiguous narration by no means entirely confirms, for as we have seen, Willoughby only half sees his actions from Elinor's perspective. The confessional nature of his explanations suggests that he may be seeking remission of his sins; and if he talks the language of irreparability and permanent loss, there is some question whether he really means it. The chief point of some of Elinor's interventions has been, precisely, to insist on an irreversibility that Willoughby, in the slight hope of fresh peripeties, never fully wants to accept.

> 'Marianne to be sure is lost to me for ever. Were I even by any blessed chance at liberty again – '
> Elinor stopped him with a reproof.
> 'Well' – he replied – 'once more good bye. I shall now go away and live in dread of one event.'
> 'What do you mean?'
> 'Your sister's marriage.'
> 'You are very wrong. She can never be more lost to you than she is now.'
>
> (p. 332)

Yet even Elinor's own insistence on the irreversibility of events can grow fainter under the intensity of that tender and regretful response that it permits and controls, and it needs to be continually reaffirmed. For a moment, she 'wished Willoughby a widower. Then, remembering Colonel Brandon, reproved herself, felt that to *his* sufferings and *his* constancy far more than to his rival's, the reward of her sister was due, and wished any thing rather than Mrs Willoughby's death' (p. 335). Like a magic wand breaking a spell, the recollection of Colonel Brandon would seem to dissolve the force of Willoughby's 'influence' – except that his influence later revives, and the wand will have to be applied repeatedly, like the unmagical rod of discipline. Soon after her arrival, Mrs Dashwood begins projecting the very match that her prudent daughter has envisioned, but Elinor is no longer so certain of its validity. Mrs Dashwood insists that 'Marianne would yet never have been so happy with [Willoughby], as she will be with Colonel Brandon', but Elinor 'could not agree with her', and she withdraws 'to think it all over in private, to wish success for her friend, and yet in wishing it, to feel a pang for Willoughby' (pp. 338, 339).

Ultimately, however, Elinor's complex response to Willoughby's narration gets simplified, as she rethinks and retells it. She has been reluctant to keep her promise to Willoughby (qualified though that was) because she feared 'she had that to communicate which might again unsettle the mind of Marianne' (p. 343). But not only is a revived Marianne now prepared to respond to the sense (rather than the suspense) of his narration, she also understands that this sense can complete her cure ('If I could but know *his* heart, everything would become easy' [p. 347]). Rather than risk a lingering response to the empirical Willoughby whom she remembers, with his apparent sincerity and apparent duplicity, she needs to know what his conduct *meant*. Reassured by Marianne's proper attitude (more proper than her own has been when she wished Willoughby a widower), Elinor hazards her narration:

> She managed the recital, as she hoped, with address; prepared her anxious listener with caution; related simply and honestly the *chief points* on which Willoughby grounded his apology; did justice to his repentance, and *softened only his protestations of present regard*. Marianne said not a word. – She trembled, her eyes were fixed on the ground, and her lips became whiter than even sickness had left them. A thousand inquiries sprang up from her heart, but she dared not urge one. She caught every syllable with panting eagerness; her hand, unknowingly to herself, closely pressed her sister, and tears covered her cheeks.
>
> Elinor, dreading her being tired, led her towards home; and till they reached the door of the cottage, easily conjecturing what her curiosity must be though no question was suffered to speak it, talked of nothing but Willoughby, and their conversations together; and was carefully minute in every particular of speech and look, *where minuteness could be safely indulged*.
>
> (pp. 347–8)

Elinor's repetition of Willoughby's narration involves censoring it as well, as those parts of the passage I have emphasised easily bear witness. Moreover, the way in which the novelist presents Elinor's recital (in summary rather than scene) strongly supports an impression that Elinor's mode of telling must differ radically from Willoughby's. In that coolly ordered parade of semi-coloned clauses, we are tempted to recognise both Elinor's rational style of discourse (versus Willoughby's melodramatic theatrics) and its efficient dispatch (versus Willoughby's insidious diffuseness). When at Marianne's request ('Tell mama'), Elinor rehearses Willoughby's narration a second time to Mrs Dashwood, the same principles of abridgment and reorganisation are at work, not only in the way she packages the material for consumption by others, but in her own increasingly constricted response.

> Had Mrs Dashwood, like her daughter, heard Willoughby's story from himself – had she witnessed his distress, and been under the influence of his countenance and his manner, it is probable that her compassion would have been greater. But it was neither in Elinor's power, nor in her wish, to rouse such feelings in another, by her retailed explanation, as had at first been called forth in herself. Reflection had given calmness to her judgement, and sobered her own opinion of Willoughby's deserts; – she wished, therefore, to declare only the simple truth, and lay open such facts as were really due to his character, without any embellishment of tenderness to lead the fancy astray.
>
> (p. 349)

('*Only* the simple truth'? There would be, then, more to tell.) By the time the two sisters are ready to discuss Willoughby's character, there is no remaining trace of his influence over Elinor, who makes her judgement with untroubled confidence: 'Your marriage must have involved you in many certain troubles and disappointments .... The whole of his behaviour, from the beginning to the end of the affair, has been grounded on selfishness .... His own enjoyment, or his own ease, was, in every particular, his ruling principle' (pp. 350, 351). Now that Willoughby's story has been completely rewritten in the interest of the knowledge that passes debate (and bypasses all further narrative possibilities), even a moral can be drawn from the tale: proof, if any were needed, that his story has become a closed book to the Dashwood family. 'One observation may, I think, be fairly drawn from the whole of the story – that all Willoughby's difficulties have arisen from the first offence against virtue, in his behaviour to Eliza Williams. That crime has been the origin of every lesser one, and of all his present discontents' (p. 352). This may seem odd morality for Elinor to conclude with, in a group of women, since the crime whose punishment is supposed to edify them could only have been committed by a man. Of course, however, the real point of this 'observation drawn from the whole of the story' is to establish that the story is a *whole*, without further ramifications worth considering. Confirming Willoughby's fallen state, Elinor's observation also confirms how thoroughly vacated is the place that he might have occupied in their lives, and in the mention of Eliza Williams, it points clearly enough to a new and permanent locum tenens in Colonel Brandon.

I have dwelt on this sequence in *Sense and Sensibility* because it offers us, in miniature and in plain, almost diagrammatic form, the mechanics of closure. Willoughby's narrative, dangerously open, gives way to Elinor's retailing, modifying it in order to close it up. Willoughby's account does not inherently resolve itself; only when reconstructed and reduced by Elinor's account does it acquire a meaning of closural force. His account has a quasi-empirical richness of detail (his 'person of uncommon attraction', his 'open, affectionate, and lively manner', the hints that more is being said and unsaid than he quite knows), troubling and complicating Elinor's cognitive and moral judgement. Her account voids what it must see as the excesses and irrelevancies of his, in order that a judgement can stand, unsubverted by any fermenting residue. The first account mainly takes place, as it were, on the level of the signifier – that is, it offers a wealth of pointers to future possible meanings, not yet fully available. There are more signifiers, ambiguous and pointing in conflicting directions, than can be comfortably integrated into a definitive meaning by either Willoughby or even Elinor. By contrast, the second account takes place on the level of the signified – unambiguous, fully present meaning. It resolves the ambiguities of the first account and removes from it whatever 'ought not to have weight'. The work of closure, then, would seem to consist in an ideologically inspired *passage* between two orders of discourse, two separable textual styles. One of them (polyvalent, flirtatious, quintessentially poetic) keeps meaning and desire in a state of suspense; the other (univocal, earnest, basically cognitive) fixes meaning and lodges desire in a safe haven; and the passage from one to the other involves a voiding, a strategic omission – so to speak, a good riddance.[7] The interest of Jane Austen, on this perspective, is that her novels, far from merely operating the passage, tellingly dramatise it, so that one has a more complicated and less comfortable awareness of what it involves.

From D. A. Miller, *Narrative and its Discontents: Problems of Closure in the Traditional Novel* (Princeton, 1981), pp. 3–5, 51–5, 63–76.

NOTES

[Taking a transverse approach to the grain of *Sense and Sensibility*, D. A. Miller's reading is part of his larger concern with the ways in which narratives tell stories about what writers find threatening and wish to foreclose. Narrative is condemned to tell the story of that which it wishes to silence.

The genesis of this perverse situation is as much ideological as aesthetic, as much psychoanalytic as ideological: that which is outlawed makes for interesting stories whilst the good is essentially an absence, a lack of vice; the ideologically or mentally repressed is a site of disruptive energy with which civilisations and citizens are constantly engaged, tapping energy from the underground in order to maintain the lines of repression. The author strives to become *authority*, to play policeman/woman and close down disruption, but each attempt at closure appears to let something get away, or create new grounds for dissent, so the process of closing is never-ending. No sooner has Jane Austen written out one illicit character than another comes in view. One outbreak follows another as one novel follows another, yet curiously the author remains immune, like a doctor in a contagion hospital, or the judge on his bench, curing the curable, burying the irredeemable, gaining in status for their ability to handle the *ordures* of society without becoming unclean. Who would guess that it is their own guilt they pleasure in, their own transgressivity which they indulge and then negate behind the mask? References and citations to Austen's work are from *The Novels of Jane Austen*, ed. R.W.Chapman, 5 vols, 3rd edn (London, 1932–4), and *Minor Works*, ed. R. W. Chapman (London, 1954). Ed.]

1. André Gide, *L'Immoraliste*, in *Oeuvres complètes*, ed. L. Martin-Chauffier, 15 vols (Paris, 1932–9), vol. 4, p. 70.

2. See Roland Barthes, 'Introduction a l'analyse structurale des récits', *Communications*, 8 (1966), 23–5; and Tzvetan Todorov, 'Le secret du récit', *Poétique de la prose* (Paris, 1971), 151–85.

3. For a full discussion of 'the structural tracks of the lie', see Barthes, *S/Z* (Paris, 1970), sections 42, 60, 62, 63, 69.

4. Sigmund Freud, 'Negation', in *The Standard Edition of the Complete Works of Sigmund Freud*, ed. James Strachey (London, 1953–74), vol. 19, p. 235.

5. Ibid.

6. Freud, *Beyond the Pleasure Principle, The Standard Edition of the Complete Works of Sigmund Freud*, vol. 18, pp. 14–16.

7. I am somewhat indebted here to Galvano della Volpe's attempt to distinguish (partly on the basis of Saussurian linguistics) between the 'univocal' language of scientific discourse and the 'polysemic' (*polisenso*) language of poetic discourse. He collapses the distinction – prematurely, I think – at the level of a 'search for truth' supposedly common to both languages. Moreover, by insisting that the *polisenso* is always reducible to what he calls a 'sociological quid', he takes away whatever force the concept might have had. See his *Critica del gusto* (Milan, 1960), especially the second chapter.

5

Ideological Contradictions and the Consolations of Form (1)

MARY POOVEY

SENSE AND SENSIBILITY

The period between 1775 and 1817, the years of Austen's life, was punctuated by challenges to the traditional hierarchy of English class society and, as a consequence, to conventional social roles and responsibilities. William Wordsworth's 1817 survey of the preceding thirty years summarises the chaotic impact of these changes:

> I see clearly that the principal ties which kept the different classes of society in a vital and harmonious dependence upon each other have, within these 30 years, either been greatly impaired or wholly dissolved. Everything has been put up to market and sold for the highest price it would buy .... All ... moral cement is dissolved, habits and prejudices are broken and rooted up, nothing being substituted in their place but a quickened self-interest.[1]

In England, the decisive agent of this change was not just the French Revolution but the more subtle, more gradual, dissemination of the values and behaviour associated with capitalism – first, agrarian capitalism in the mid- and late eighteenth century, then, in the early nineteenth century, industrial capitalism, as money made itself felt in investment and capital return. By the first decades of the nineteenth century, birth into a particular class no longer exclusively determined one's future social or economic status, the vertical relationships of patronage no longer guaranteed either privileges or obedience, and the traditional authority of the gentry, and of the values associated with their life-style, was a subject under general debate. In the midst of such changes, the assumptions that had theoretically been shared by eighteenth-century moralists and their audiences seemed increasingly problematic, requiring refinement and defence if not radical change. As the literature and political debates of this period unmistakably reveal, the crisis in imaginative and moral authority was pervasive and severe; even conservative writers generally abandoned arguments about absolute truths in favour of discussions in which one set of principles was defended against a contrary but equally coherent system of values.[2]

As the daughter of a country clergyman with numerous and strong ties to the landed upper gentry, Jane Austen was involved in this crisis of authority in an immediate and particularly complex way. As Donald J. Greene has conclusively demonstrated, Jane Austen was acutely aware of her kinship to several prominent families, among them the Brydges, who were earls and lords of Chandos, and the lords Leigh of Stoneleigh.[3] More immediately, as a clergyman Austen's father belonged to the lesser realms of the gentry, and Jane and her siblings all benefited more or less directly from the patronage that traditionally reinforced the gentry's hegemony. One of Austen's brothers, Edward, was adopted by the wealthy Knight family, of Kent, and, as heir to the valuable estate of Godmersham, he was eventually able to provide a home at Chawton Cottage for Jane, her mother, her sister, and their friend Martha Lloyd. Two of Austen's other brothers, James and Henry, became clergymen, and her two youngest brothers, Francis and Charles, entered the British navy and eventually became admirals; Francis in fact became a knight. Thus Jane Austen was raised in the heart of middle-class society; she shared its values, and she owed her own position to the bonds of patronage that cemented traditional society, even though her immediate resources never permitted her fully to emulate the gentry's life-style.

In keeping with this class affiliation, Jane Austen's fundamental ideological position was conservative; her political sympathies were generally Tory, and her religion was officially Anglican; overall, she was a 'conservative Christian moralist', supportive of Evangelical ethical rigour even before she explicitly admitted admiring the Evangelicals themselves.[4]

But neither the external evidence of Austen's social position nor the internal evidence of her novels supports so strict a delineation of her sympathies. In the first place, even the traditional practices of paternalism were influenced during this period by the rhetoric and practices of individualism. (To give but one relevant example: promotion in such prestigious professions as the navy could result from individual effort and merit [as *Persuasion* indicates]; at other times it depended on the interest of a patron [as William Price learns in *Mansfield Park*].) In the second place, the role played by Austen's class in the rise of capitalism was particularly complicated; for the agricultural improvements that preceded and paved the way for early industrial capitalism were financed and initiated in many cases by the landowning gentry, yet the legal provisions of strict settlement and entail were expressly designed to prohibit land from becoming a commodity susceptible to promiscuous transfer or easy liquidation. Despite the fact that the landowning gentry participated in the expansion of agrarian capitalism, their role was passive, not active; as a consequence, their values and life-style were not extensively altered until the more radical and rapid expansion of industrial capitalism began in the first decades of the nineteenth century. When that occurred, the gentry were suddenly awakened to the implications of the changes to which their patterns of expenditure had contributed.[5] From the more vulnerable position of the lower levels of the gentry, Jane Austen was able to see with particular clarity the marked differences between the two components of the middle class: the landed gentry and the new urban capitalist class.[6] The division of sympathies that occurs in her novels when middle-class daughters get rewarded with the sons of landed families emanates at least partly from Austen's being both involved in and detached from these two middle-class groups at a moment when they were implicitly competing with each other.

In Austen's very early works, like *Lady Susan*, this division of sympathies characteristically leads either to broad farce or to the tonal uncertainties of parody.[7] As her career progresses, however, we see Austen gradually develop aesthetic strategies capable of balancing her attraction to exuberant but potentially anarchic feeling with her investment in traditional social institutions. This balance is embodied in the thematic material she chooses and the rhetorical stance she adopts. At their most sophisticated, Austen's rhetorical strategies harness the imaginative energy of her readers to a moral design; she thus manages to satisfy both the individual reader's desire for emotional gratification and the programme of education prescribed by traditional moral aestheticians.

To understand why Austen assumed that a novel could simultaneously gratify the cravings of the imagination and provide moral instruction, it is useful to turn to Samuel Johnson, Austen's favourite eighteenth-century essayist. According to Johnson, novel-reading is an active, not passive, enterprise, for it aggressively engages the imagination of its young reader. Novels, Johnson explains,

> are the entertainment of minds unfurnished with ideas, and therefore easily susceptible of impressions; not fixed by principles, and therefore easily following the current of fancy; not informed by experience, and consequently open to every false suggestion and partial account. ... If the power of example is so great, as to take possession of the memory by a kind of violence, and produce effects almost without the intervention of the will, care ought to be taken that, when the choice is unrestrained, the best examples only should be exhibited; and that which is likely to operate so strongly, should not be mischievous or uncertain in its effects.[8]

Johnson's wariness about the power of the imagination should remind us of Mary Shelley; for, as different as these two writers were, they shared a profound anxiety about the insatiable hunger of the imagination. Johnson's answer to this anxiety was to compose not novels but moral essays that were characterised by a tremendous respect for reason's antagonist. Mary Shelley's solution was simultaneously less evasive and less effective. In fact, her novels represent the two dangers to which imaginative engagement might lead. At one extreme, as the 1818 *Frankenstein* proves, a 'romantic' novel might so thoroughly activate the imagination as to undermine all moral authority; at the other extreme, as in *Falkner*, the moral novel might so dogmatically focus the imagination that all subversive exuberance would be driven into the background of the fiction, only to return to the forefront in troubling reminders of what cannot be contained.

To a certain extent, Jane Austen shared this ambivalence with regard to the imagination. When Anne Elliot advises Captain Benwick in *Persuasion* to admit 'a larger allowance of prose in his daily study' so as to 'rouse and fortify' a mind made 'tremulous' by immersion in Romantic poetry, she is warning against the 'susceptibility' of the indulged imagination.[9] But while Austen might well agree with Johnson that novels should 'serve as lectures of conduct, and introductions into life', her major works are not as defensive as either his *Rasselas* or Shelley's *Falkner*; they do not, that is, 'initiate youth by mock encounters in the art of necessary defence'.[10] Instead, Austen attempts to convert the pleasure generated by imaginative engagement into a didactic tool. As the 'productions' that provide 'more extensive and unaffected pleasure than those of any other literary corporation in the world', novels are best suited for such education. For in the best novels, Austen continues in *Northanger Abbey*, 'the greatest powers of the mind are displayed, ... the most thorough knowledge of human nature, the happiest delineation of its varieties, the liveliest effusions of wit and humour are conveyed to the world in the best chosen language'.[11]

Such a balance was not easy and Jane Austen's first published novel, *Sense and Sensibility* (1811), suggests how persistent this problem proved to be for her early in her career.[12] *Sense and Sensibility* is a much darker novel than any of the juvenilia or the parodic *Northanger Abbey* (1818), and we might speculate that one origin of its sombre tone and the eruptions of anarchic feeling that punctuate it lies in the anxiety with which Austen viewed individualism's challenge to paternalism. For in *Sense and Sensibility*, as, in a slightly different way, in *Lady Susan* and *Northanger Abbey*, the most fundamental conflict is between Austen's own imaginative engagement with her self-assertive characters and the moral code necessary to control their anarchic desires.

In the greater part of *Sense and Sensibility*, Austen's aesthetic strategies endorse the traditional values associated with her 'sensible' heroine, Elinor Dashwood. One of these strategies consists in measuring all of the characters (including Elinor) against an implicit, but presumably authoritative, moral norm. As early as the second chapter, in that free, indirect discourse that is the hallmark of her mature style, Austen shadows the opinion of a single fallible character with this implicit moral standard.[13] Irony in *Sense and Sensibility* arises for the most part from the novel's action; the dialogue between Mr and Mrs John Dashwood points up as surely as any overt narrative commentary the parsimony behind their dwindling good will. But our response to this dialogue is initially shaped by such sentences as the following: 'To take three thousand pounds from the fortune of their dear little boy, would be impoverishing him to the most dreadful degree'; 'How could he answer it to himself to rob his child, and his only child too, of so large a sum?'[14] The hyperbole expressed in the words 'impoverishing', 'dreadful', and 'rob' conveys both the strategy of Mrs Dashwood's rhetoric and its absurdity, and the repeated use of the word 'child' suggests how effective she is in manipulating John Dashwood's generosity. Because these sentences belong to the narrative and not to direct dialogue, they mimetically convey the tone of the conversation and simultaneously judge it by reference to an implicit system of more humane values – the undeniably Christian values that one should love one's neighbour as one's self and that the man who hoards treasures in this world (or the woman who encourages him to do so) will never get into the kingdom of heaven.

But despite this ground of Christian principles, nearly everything in the plot of *Sense and Sensibility* undermines the complacent assumption that they are principles generally held or practically effective. Almost every action in the novel suggests that, more often than not, individual will triumphs over principle and individual desire proves more compelling than moral law. Even the narrator, the apparent voice of these absolute values, reveals that moral principles are qualified in practice. The narrator's prefatory evaluation of John Dashwood, for example – 'he was not an ill-disposed young man, unless to be rather cold hearted, and rather selfish, is to be ill-disposed' (p. 5) – directs our attention most specifically to the way in which what should, in theory, be moral absolutes can, and in practice do, shade off into infinite gradations and convenient exceptions. Is it always morally wrong to be 'rather' selfish, especially in a society in which such selfishness is the necessary basis for material prosperity? What efficacy will moral absolutes have in such a society? How could Elinor's patient, principled fidelity win the passive, principled Edward if it were not, finally, for Lucy Steele's avarice?

A second strategy that is apparently designed to forestall such questions by aligning the reader's sympathies with Elinor's 'sense' involves the juxtaposition of Elinor and her sister Marianne at nearly every critical juncture in the novel. Consistently, Elinor makes the prudent choice, even when doing so is painful; almost as consistently, Marianne's decisions are self-indulgent and harmful, either to herself or to someone else. But this neat design is less stable than an absolute and authoritative moral system would seem to require. Many readers have found Marianne's 'spirit' more appealing than Elinor's cautious, prim, and even repressive reserve, and they have found Marianne's passionate romance with Willoughby more attractive than the prolonged frustration to which Elinor submits. That such preferences may be in keeping with at least one countercurrent of the novel is suggested by the fact that whenever Austen herself explicitly compares the two putative heroes – Colonel Brandon and Edward Ferrars – with the less moral, more passionate Willoughby, it is Willoughby who is appealing. On two occasions when Willoughby is expected but one of the more subdued lovers appears instead, the disappointment is unmistakable; and when the reverse situation occurs, in the climactic final encounter between Elinor and Willoughby, Elinor is aroused to a pitch of complex emotion we never see Edward inspire in anyone. Moreover, Willoughby repeatedly bursts into the narrative with 'manly beauty and more than common gracefulness', but Edward and Brandon seem inert fixtures of the plot, incapable of energetic gallantry and attractive only to the most generous observer. The initial description of each of them is dominated by negative constructions and qualifying phrases, and even Elinor cannot unreservedly praise the man she wants to marry. 'At first sight', she admits, 'his address is certainly not striking; and his person can hardly be called handsome, till the expression of his eyes, which are uncommonly good, and the general sweetness of his countenance, is perceived. At present, I know him so well, that I think him really handsome; or, at least, almost so' (p. 20). Colonel Brandon, 'neither very young nor very gay', is 'silent and grave' much of the time (p. 34), and his 'oppression of spirits', like Edward's chronic depression, can scarcely compete with Willoughby's charm.

The most telling dramatisation of the contest between the potentially anarchic power of feeling and the restraint that moral principles require takes the form of a conflict within Elinor herself. This scene, in the final volume, owes much to conventional eighteenth-century didactic novels, but Austen's placing it at a moment when the generally self-disciplined Elinor is unusually susceptible to emotion gives it a particularly complicated effect. Colonel Brandon has presented a living to Edward Ferrars, and Elinor is finally, but sadly, reconciled to the fact that her lover will marry someone else. In the midst of this personal disappointment, she is also particularly sensitive to her sister's condition, for Marianne, whose own romantic disappointment had sent her into a dangerous decline, has just been declared out of danger. Elinor's 'fervent gratitude' for this news is especially great because of the joy and relief it will bring to her mother, whose arrival is expected at any moment. It is this hectic peace – as Marianne sleeps quietly upstairs and a violent storm assaults the house – that Willoughby invades when he melodramatically steps into the drawing room.

Elinor's first response is 'horror' at his audacious intrusion; but before she can leave the room, Willoughby appeals to something even more powerful than Elinor's 'honour' : her curiosity. Elinor is momentarily captivated by Willoughby's 'serious energy' and 'warmth', and she listens 'in spite of herself' to the story he unfolds – the chronicle of his passions, both honourable and base. At the end of his dramatic recital, Willoughby asks Elinor for pity, and, even though she feels it is her 'duty' to check his outburst, she cannot repress her 'compassionate emotion'. It is this emotion that governs her judgement of Willoughby – a judgement that verges disconcertingly on rationalisation:

> Elinor made no answer. Her thoughts were silently fixed on the irreparable injury which too early an independence and its consequent habits of idleness, dissipation, and luxury, had made in the mind, the character, the happiness, of a man who, to every advantage of person and talents, united a disposition naturally open and honest, and a feeling, affectionate temper. The world had made him extravagant and vain – Extravagance and vanity had made him cold-hearted and selfish.
>
> (p. 331)

When Willoughby departs, he leaves Elinor in an even greater 'agitation' of spirits, 'too much oppressed by a crowd of ideas ... to think even of her sister'.

> Willoughby, in spite of all his faults, excited a degree of commiseration for the sufferings produced by them, which made her think of him as now separated for ever from her family with a tenderness, a regret, rather in proportion, as she soon acknowledged within herself – to his wishes than to his merits. She felt that his influence over her mind was heightened by circumstances which ought not in reason to have weight; by that person of uncommon attraction, that open, affectionate, and lively manner which it was no merit to possess; and by that still ardent love for Marianne, which it was not even innocent to indulge. But she felt that it was so, long, long before she could feel his influence less.
>
> (p. 333)

One purpose of this episode is clearly to dramatise the odds against which Elinor's 'sense', or reason, ultimately triumphs and therefore to increase, not undermine, our admiration for that faculty. But a second effect of the passage is to subject the reader to the same temptation that assails Elinor. Because the presentation is dramatic and because, for a moment at least, the character whose judgement has thus far directed our own hesitates in her moral evaluation, the reader is invited to judge Willoughby not by reference to an objective standard but by his immediate appeal to our imaginative, sympathetic engagement. As Elinor temporises, the moral principle for which she otherwise speaks seems dangerously susceptible to circumstances, to the appeal of 'lively manners', and to the special pleading of aroused female emotion.

Jane Austen seems anxious to control the moral anarchy that strong appeals to feeling can unleash; yet, significantly, she does not exclude passion from the novel, nor does she so completely qualify it as to undermine its power. Instead, Austen attempts to bend the imaginative engagement it elicits in the reader to the service of moral education. To do so, she restricts the reader's access to the romantic plot by conveying its details and its emotional affect only through indirect narration. At the beginning of the novel, for example, the incident in which Willoughby rescues Marianne is summarised by the dispassionate narrative persona, who supplies sentimental clichés but *not* Marianne's response to her rescue: 'The gentleman offered his services, and perceiving that her modesty declined what her situation rendered necessary, took her up in his arms without farther delay' (p. 42). Similarly, the episode in which Willoughby cuts and kisses a lock of Marianne's hair is given to Margaret to relate (p. 60), and the emotional specifics of Willoughby's farewell at Barton Cottage can be deduced only from their aftermath (p. 82). Most of Marianne's outbursts of passion to Willoughby are confined to letters, which are concealed from the reader until after Willoughby has snubbed Marianne. In fact, the only emotionally charged encounter between the lovers that Austen presents dramatically is their final meeting at the London ball, and there Marianne's passion is transmuted by Willoughby's silence into the terrible muffled scream that both voices and symbolises her thwarted love. So careful is Austen to keep the reader on the outside of such 'dangerous' material that she embeds the most passionate episodes within other, less emotionally volatile stories. Thus the story of the two Elizas – related, as we will see, by a character whose relationship to the tale immediately activates our judgement – is contained within the story of Marianne's passion for Willoughby – a relationship whose emotional content is conveyed to the reader more by innuendo, summary, and indirection than by dramatic presentation. And this second story, in turn, is contained within the story of the relationship that opens and closes the novel – Elinor's considerably less demonstrative affection for Edward. By embedding these stories in this way, Austen seeks to defuse their imaginative affect and increase their power to educate the reader: from the fates of the two Elizas we learn to be wary of Marianne's quick feelings, and from the consequences of Marianne's self-indulgent passion we learn to value Elinor's reserve.

Instead of being allowed to identify with Marianne, then, for most of the novel we are restricted to Elinor's emotional struggles. This enables Austen to dramatise the complexities of what might otherwise seem an unattractive and unyielding obsession with propriety; it also permits her to filter the two stories of illicit passion through a character whose judgement generally masters emotion. That the passion bleeds from the narrators of these two tales into Elinor's 'sense' attests to the power of this force and to the dangerous susceptibility that, without proper control, might undermine the judgement of even the most rational reader.

Austen also attempts to control the allure of Marianne's romantic desires by refusing to consider seriously either their social origin or their philosophical implications. As Tony Tanner has pointed out, Austen really avoids the systematic examination of 'sensibility' that the novel seems to promise.[15] The novel begins like a novel of social realism. In the first paragraphs the narrator sounds like a lawyer or a banker; family alliances, the estate that is the heart of paternalistic society, even the deaths of loved ones, are all ruthlessly subordinated to the economic facts. Given this introduction, the reader has every reason to believe that the most important fact – that Mrs Dashwood will have only five hundred pounds a year with which to raise and dower her daughters – will govern the futures of Elinor, Marianne, and Margaret. And given this probable development, the reader can understand why romantic fantasies are appealing. It is no wonder that Marianne – facing a life of poverty, the spiritual banality of relatives like the John Dashwoods, and the superficial urbanities of a neighbourhood composed only of the Middletons and Mrs Jennings – turns to Cowper for imaginative compensation; nor is it surprising that she fancies (in accordance with the promises of romantic novels) that her beauty will win the heart and hand of an errant knight. Beneath Marianne's effusions on nature and her passionate yearning for a hero lies the same 'hunger of imagination' that Mary Wollstonecraft tried and failed to analyse in *Maria*. But to take Marianne's passions and longings seriously on their own terms would be to call into question the basis of Christian moral authority, the social order that ideally institutionalises that authority, and, finally, the capacity of orthodox religion or society to gratify imaginative desires.[16] Elinor's sense, despite its admirable capacity to discipline and protect the self, cannot begin to satisfy this appetite, and no other social institution in the novel does any better. Instead of taking this implicit criticism to its logical conclusion, as Wollstonecraft tried to do, Jane Austen defuses its threat by directing our judgement away from bourgeois society and toward the self-indulgent individual. Austen caricatures just enough of Marianne's responses to nature and love to make her seem intermittently ridiculous, and, when her desires finally explode all social conventions, Austen stifles her with an illness that is not only a result but also a purgation of her passion. At the end of the novel, Austen ushers Marianne into Brandon's world of diminished desires in such a way as to make Marianne herself negate everything she has previously wanted to have and to be.

> Marianne Dashwood was born to an extraordinary fate. She was born to discover the falsehood of her own opinions, and to counteract, by her conduct, her most favourite maxims. She was born to overcome an affection formed so late in life as at seventeen, and with no sentiment superior to strong esteem and lively friendship, voluntarily to give her hand to another! ... Marianne could never love by halves; and her whole heart became, in time, as much devoted to her husband, as it had once been to Willoughby.
>
> (pp. 378–9)

To further defuse the questions raised by Marianne's assertive subjectivity, Austen seconds the opinion of eighteenth-century moralists that women's appetites are particularly dangerous and more akin to inexplicable natural forces than to socialised – hence socialisable – responses. Except for Elinor, nearly all of the women in *Sense and Sensibility* are given to one kind of excess or another. Mrs John Dashwood and her mother, Mrs Ferrars, attempt to dominate the opinions, the professions, and even the emotions of the men who are closest to them; Willoughby's aunt, who is empowered by money and age, is even more tyrannical; and Sophia Grey, Willoughby's fiancée, enacts her passion and her will when she commands Willoughby to copy her cruel letter for Marianne. Austen implies that these women are exceptional only in the extent of their power, not in the force of their desires. The narrator describes a 'fond mother', for example, as 'the most rapacious of human beings' (p. 120) – a description borne out by the monomanical Lady Middleton – and she refers lightly to the 'suffering' endured by every lady who has the 'insatiable appetite of fifteen' (p. 33). Until her compassion is necessary to the plot, even Mrs Jennings seems dominated by a single uncontrollable desire, the hunger to live vicariously through the romantic attachments of her young friends.

Austen's female characters certainly do not monopolise passion, nor are their little contrivances finally more destructive than Willoughby's deceit. But the implications of her characterisations of such women can be identified by contrasting them with her presentation of male characters. Austen consistently provides men's behaviour with a realistic explanation by describing the social or psychological contexts that shaped it. Mr Palmer's general contempt, Elinor concludes (without any narrative qualification), 'was the desire of appearing superior to other people' (p. 112) – a desire that is an understandable compensation for Palmer's initial error: 'his temper might perhaps be a little soured by finding, like many others of his sex, that through some unaccountable bias in favour of beauty, he was the husband of a very silly woman' (p. 112). Austen's comparable references to Mrs Palmer's history are both cursory and curt: her mantelpiece, the narrator informs us, is adorned with 'a landscape in coloured silks of her performance, in proof of her having spent seven years at a great school in town to some effect' (p. 160). Austen also more extensively explains the differences between the Ferrars brothers than between the oldest Dashwood sisters; she makes no attempt to account for the temperamental contrast between Elinor and Marianne but carefully attributes the differences between Robert and Edward to their education. The only female character Austen appears to explain is Lucy Steele. Initially, Lucy's 'deficiency of all mental improvement' seems to be the effect of her neglected education: 'Lucy was naturally clever; her remarks were often just and amusing ... but her powers had received no aid from education, she was ignorant and illiterate, and her deficiency of mental improvement ... could not be concealed from Miss Dashwood' (p. 127). Soon we discover, however, that this 'explanation' is really only Elinor's generous and erroneous first impression. Austen explicitly ridicules the notion that Lucy's 'want of liberality' could be 'due to her want of education' by having Edward cling to this rationalisation to the end. But in jilting Edward for his brother Robert, Lucy conclusively proves herself inherently flawed. Like Shelley's 1831 characterisation of Frankenstein, and like both portrayals of the monster, female nature appears to be fated, fixed. Austen's final comments on Lucy are decisive: her behaviour exposes 'a wanton ill-nature' (p. 366), characterised by 'an earnest, an unceasing attention to self-interest' (p. 376).

The harshness with which Austen disposes of Lucy Steele exceeds the necessities of the plot, but it is perfectly in keeping with her moral design. For, like Shelley, Austen wants to convince the reader that female nature is simply inexplicable and that propriety must restrain this natural, amoral force. At least one other set of female characters also supports this argument, but, paradoxically, the episode in which they appear alludes not to an innate female nature but to the constraints imposed on women by patriarchal society. Because of this, the episode threatens to subvert the argument for propriety it theoretically should support. The characters are the two Elizas, and their story belongs to Colonel Brandon.

Colonel Brandon relates the story of the two Elizas to Elinor ostensibly to persuade her to warn Marianne about Willoughby. But both the hesitations with which he interrupts his narrative and the fact that he focuses not on the second Eliza (Willoughby's victim) but on her mother ('his' Eliza) suggest that Brandon does not fully recognise his own motives for telling the story. As the tale unfolds, it becomes clear that Brandon's deepest intention is to warn Marianne about the dangerous nature of her own passion; paradoxically, however, the overall effect of the episode is to reveal to the reader the depth – and consequences – of *Brandon's* sexual anxiety.[17] This anxiety, initially aroused by the first Eliza, is now being reactivated by Marianne. But there is one critical difference between the two situations: unlike the first Eliza, Marianne's passion is not for Brandon but for Willoughby. Thus Brandon's anxiety is doubly displaced: it is a past fear of too much emotion *and* a present fear of too little love. The first Eliza *did* love him, Brandon asserts, as if to enhance his own appeal, but she could not withstand her guardian's pressure to marry Brandon's older brother, heir to the family's encumbered estate. As he tells the story, Brandon stumbles over the details that wounded him most:

> 'My brother did not deserve her; he did not even love her. I had hoped that her regard for me would support her under any difficulty, and for some time it did; but at last the misery of her situation, for she experienced great unkindness, overcame all her resolution, and though she had promised me that nothing – but how blindly I relate! I have never told you how this was brought on. We were within a few hours of eloping together for Scotland. The treachery, or the folly, of my cousin's maid betrayed us. I was banished ... and she was allowed no liberty, no society, no amusement, till my father's point was gained. I had depended on her fortitude too far, ... – but had her marriage been happy, ... a few months must have reconciled me to it. ...

This however was not the case. My brother had no regard for her. ...
The consequence of this, upon a mind so young, so lively, so inexperi-
enced as Mrs Brandon's, was but too natural. ... Can we wonder that
with such a husband to provoke inconstancy, and without a friend to
advise or restrain her ... she should fall? Had I remained in England,
perhaps – but I meant to promote the happiness of both by removing
from her for years. ... The shock which her marriage had given me',
he continued, in a voice of great agitation, 'was of trifling weight –
was nothing – to what I felt when I heard, about two years afterwards, of her divorce. It was *that* which threw this gloom, even now
the recollection of what I suffered – '.

(pp. 205–6; ellipses added)

The story begins and ends in Eliza's infidelity to Brandon; only as
an extension of this does her infidelity to her husband matter, only
as the origin of his pain does Eliza's unhappiness figure. The weakness of this woman – and her sexual abandon – are 'natural',
according to Brandon; only the presence of a male guardian could
have protected her from herself. Once Eliza has fallen, her fate is so
predictable (and disturbing) that it warrants only summary description – except in regard to Brandon's own misery:

So altered – so faded – worn down by acute suffering of every kind!
hardly could I believe the melancholy and sickly figure before me, to
be the remains of the lovely, blooming, healthful girl, on whom I had
once doated. What I endured in so beholding her – but I have no
right to wound your feelings by attempting to describe it – I have
pained you too much already.

(p. 207)

Given the fate of the mother, Brandon is not surprised at the fall of
the second Eliza, the daughter, who has been bequeathed to his protection. At seventeen, her mother's fatal year and Marianne's current age, she too evaded her male guardian and ran away with
Willoughby. Now pregnant, abandoned, poor, and miserable, this
Eliza is a second monument to the passionate excesses of women.

The intense anxiety that Brandon betrays here is produced by his
fear of female sexual appetite. If female sexuality had caused the first
Eliza to betray him, how vulnerable might the excitable Marianne be
to Willoughby, who had seduced the second Eliza? Yet Brandon
expressly admires Marianne for the very passion that occasioned the
downfall of the two Elizas. Brandon wants Marianne to be emotionally responsive, but he wants her sexuality to answer only to his
command. When Elinor wishes that Marianne would renounce sen-

timental prejudices, Brandon's response is swift: 'No, no, do not desire it, – for when the romantic refinements of a young mind are obliged to give way, how frequently are they succeeded by such opinions as are but too common, and too dangerous! I speak from experience' (pp. 56–7). The allusion is clearly to the first Eliza; Brandon fears that beneath the 'romantic refinements' of the girl lurks a woman's sexual appetite, which is both 'common' and 'dangerous'. Better far to keep women innocent, to protect them from themselves – and to protect men from their 'natural' volatility.

The anxieties Brandon unwittingly reveals suggest that Austen at least intuits the twin imperatives that anchor patriarchal society: men want women to be passionate, but, because they fear the consequences of this appetite, they want to retain control over its expression. This anxiety explains why women in this society must experience so problematic a relation to their own desire. In order to win the husband necessary to their social position, women must gratify both of men's desires by concealing whatever genuine emotions they feel so as to allow men to believe that *they* have all the power. Women must use indirection, in other words, the allure of 'romantic refinements', and the subterfuges of manners and modesty in order to arouse male desires and assuage male anxieties.

The implications of this passage are very close to those Mary Wollstonecraft specifically addresses in both *The Rights of Woman* and *Maria*. But in *Sense and Sensibility* Jane Austen will no more pursue the criticism of patriarchy that is inherent in this insight than she will pursue the grim reality that is implicit in the narrator's account of the Dashwood's economic situation. Despite its gestures toward realism, *Sense and Sensibility* repeatedly dismisses the analysis of society that realism might imply and instead embraces the idealism of romance. But Austen's idealism never completely banishes her realistic impulse either. Instead, Austen retains both 'principles' and romance. Thus Marianne debunks her own youthful romance, and the novel as a whole endorses the 'heroism' (the word itself appears on pp. 242 and 265) of Elinor's self-denial. Nevertheless, Austen rewards both characters at the conclusion of the novel precisely in terms of romantic love and of lives lived happily ever after.

Some of the tensions that we finally feel in *Sense and Sensibility* emerge, then, from the conflict between the realism in which the action is anchored and the romantic elements that Austen harnesses to this realism. Throughout, she attempts to use realism to control the imaginative excesses that romances both encourage and depict:

not only does the point of view repress the romantic plot, but Austen also suggests that Elinor's self-denial – her refusal to reveal Lucy Steele's secret and her willingness to help Edward even to her own disadvantage – ultimately contributes to her own happiness as well as to the happiness of others. The prerogatives of society, Austen suggests, sometimes make secrecy and repression necessary; but if one submits to society, every dream will come true. The last part of this formulation reminds us, of course, that, just as Austen uses realism to control the irresponsible and morally anarchic imagination, she also enlists the power of the reader's wishes to buttress her moral design. Theoretically, if her readers will submit to a version of the frustration Elinor suffers or even the compromise to which Marianne grows accustomed, their wish for a happy ending will be legitimised and gratified. This fusion of realism and romance in the service of aesthetic closure decisively distinguishes between Wollstonecraft's *Maria* and Austen's early novels. For notwithstanding her imaginative engagement in 'romantic expectations', Wollstonecraft's persistent goal is to criticise the social institutions that seem to her to thwart female feeling. Jane Austen, on the other hand, despite her recognition of the limitations of social institutions, is more concerned with correcting the dangerous excesses of female feeling than with liberating this anarchic energy. Her turn to aesthetic closure enables her to dismiss many of the problems her own divided sympathies have introduced. That the need for such closure grows out of society's inability to grant happiness to everyone in the terms it promises is a problem that can remain unexamined because it is, ideally, irrelevant to this fiction. The most troubling aspect of *Sense and Sensibility* is Austen's inability to establish narrative authority because she is ambivalent toward both realism and romance. Her inability to establish moral authority is clearly related to this ambivalence. But its complexities and implications are more clearly apparent in her next novel, *Pride and Prejudice*.

From Mary Poovey, *The Proper Lady and the Woman Writer: Ideology as Style in the Works of Mary Wollstonecraft, Mary Shelley and Jane Austen* (Chicago, 1984), pp. 180–94.

NOTES

[Mary Poovey's *The Proper Lady and the Woman Writer* is concerned with the way in which the bourgeois concept of 'the proper lady' is re-produced in the work of Mary Wollstonecraft, Mary Shelley and Jane Austen. Poovey traces the concept through its formation in the eighteenth century as the middle class takes control of society and locates its women as commodities for exchange in a marriage market that acts as a key institution in the relations between old landed wealth, political power and new merchant and industrial capital. She sees the concept of the proper lady as liberating in that it gives women definite social roles and spheres of influence – as moral exemplars, as domestic managers, as educators – and as imprisoning in that it denies to them freedom, independence, passion, and physical, commercial and economic activity. As a member of the lower gentry, Jane Austen was in a vulnerable position between the enclosing large landowners and the new urban capitalist class. The ideology of Austen's novels is a coming to terms with this situation, as her works are literally a capitalisation of the vantage it gives her. In *Sense and Sensibility* Austen measures all characters against a normative ideology of humane values that is deeply conservative, yet the action in the novel shows that Marianne's anarchic spirit is more attractive than Elinor's moral constraint. Austen does not merely banish the moral anarchy of Marianne's passion so much as portray Elinor's struggle to transform its provocation into something valuable. The recuperation of Marianne, and the personal development of Elinor, effect a compromise between a conservative ideology of Christian submission to a hierarchical social structure and a recognition that the dynamic of history cannot be simply repressed; it must be accepted and harnessed. Succeeding in this one can have happiness after all.

References to Jane Austen's work are to *The Works of Jane Austen*, ed. R. W. Chapman, 2nd edn, 5 vols (London, 1926), and vol 6, *Minor Works*, ed. R. W. Chapman (London, 1954), cited as *Works*. References to Austen's letters are to *Jane Austen's Letters to her Sister Cassandra and Others*, ed. R. W. Chapman, 2 vols (Oxford, 1932), cited as *Letters*. Ed.]

1. William Wordsworth, letter to Daniel Stuart, 1817, quoted by Alistair M. Duckworth, *The Improvement of the Estate: A Study of Jane Austen's Novels* (Baltimore, 1971), p. 81.

2. For a discussion of the spirit of 'party' and the 'contrary systems of thought' typical of the literature of this period, see L. J. Swingle, 'The Poets, the Novelists, and the English Romantic Situation', *Wordsworth Circle*, 3 (1979), 218–28, and David Simpson, *Irony and Authority in Romantic Poetry* (Totowa, NJ, 1979).

3. Donald J. Greene, 'Jane Austen and the Peerage', *Publications of the Modern Language Association* (1953), 1017–31, reprinted in *Jane Austen: A Collection of Critical Essays*, ed. Ian Watt (Englewood Cliffs, NJ, 1963), pp. 156–7.

4. See Marilyn Butler, *Jane Austen and the War of Ideas* (Oxford, 1975), pp. 161–7, 284–5, and Duckworth, *The Improvement*, pp. 2–80. For another discussion of Jane Austen's religion, see Warren Roberts, *Jane Austen and the French Revolution* (New York, 1979) pp. 109–54.

5. See Terry Lovell, 'Jane Austen and the Gentry: A Study in Literature and Ideology', *The Sociology of Literature: Applied Studies*, ed. Diana Laurenson (Hanley, 1978), pp. 20–1.

6. See ibid.

7. For an excellent discussion of the complexities of parody, see George Levine, 'Translating the Monstrous: *Northanger Abbey*', *Nineteenth-Century Fiction*, 30 (1975), 337.

8. Samuel Johnson, *Rambler 4*, in *The Yale Edition of the Works of Samuel Johnson*, ed. W. J. Bate and Albrecht B. Strauss, 14 vols (New Haven, 1969), vol. 3, pp. 21, 22.

9. *Persuasion, Works*, vol. 5, p. 101.

10. Johnson, *Rambler 4*, pp. 23, 21.

11. *Northanger Abbey, Works*, vol. 5, pp. 37, 38. Patricia Meyer Spacks also points out that education in an Austen novel requires imaginative engagement; see her 'Muted Discord: Generational Conflict in Jane Austen', in *Jane Austen in a Social Context*, ed. David Monaghan (Totawa, NJ, 1981), pp. 170, 174, 177–8.

12. The precise order in which Austen composed her major works is unknown, but B. C. Southam, having consulted Cassandra's original memorandum and the surviving manuscripts, argues persuasively for the following chronology: *Elinor and Marianne* – completed before 1796; *First Impressions* – October 1796–August 1797; *Sense and Sensibility*, the revision of *Elinor and Marianne* – begun November 1797, revised again at Chawton 1809–10; *Northanger Abbey*, originally entitled *Susan* – circa 1798–99, never substantially revised; *Pride and Prejudice*, the revision of *First Impressions* – conducted in 1809–10 and 1812; *Mansfield Park* – February 1811–June 1813; *Emma* – 21 January 1814–29 March 1815; *Persuasion* – 8 August 1815–6 August 1816 (Southam, *Jane Austen's Literary Manuscripts*, pp. 52–8). The dates given in parentheses in my text are the publication dates.

13. For a discussion of Austen's 'free, indirect speech', see Norman Page, *The Language of Jane Austen* (New York, 1972), pp. 123 ff.

14. *Sense and Sensibility, Works*, 1, p. 8.

15. Tony Tanner, Introduction to the Penguin edition of *Sense and Sensibility* (Harmondsworth, 1969), p. 32.

16. See Tanner, ibid., p. 30.

17. I am indebted to Patricia Meyer Spacks and to her Yale College seminar on Jane Austen for many of the observations about this episode.

6

Ideological Contradictions and the Consolations of Form (2)

MARY POOVEY

PRIDE AND PREJUDICE

In *Pride and Prejudice* (1813) the challenge that feeling and imaginative energy offer to moral authority is particularly persistent and problematic, for it is posed by the heroine herself. As the outspoken champion of the prerogatives of individual desire, Elizabeth Bennet should jeopardise both the social order, which demands self-denial, and the moral order, which is based on absolute Christian principles. Yet, despite the dangers she seems to embody, Elizabeth Bennet was Jane Austen's special favourite. 'I think her as delightful a creature as ever appeared in print', she wrote to Cassandra.[1] And, as a favourite, Elizabeth is handsomely rewarded: she marries the richest man in all of Jane Austen's novels and is established as mistress of Pemberley, one of those great country estates that superintend and stabilise patriarchal society. In fact, Elizabeth's triumph signals the achievement of the balance that characterises Austen's mature novels, for it is the result, on the one hand, of the gradual transformation of social and psychological realism into romance and, on the other, of a redefinition of romance. Essentially, Austen legitimises romance by making it seem the corrective – not the origin or the product – of individualism. By such narrative magic, Austen is able to defuse the thematic conflict between sense and sensibility – or reason and feeling, or realism and romance – that troubled her earlier works. What is more, by forcing her reader to participate in creating the moral order that governs the novel's conclusion, Austen is able to make this aesthetic 'solution' seem, at least momentarily, both natural and right.

Pride and Prejudice depicts a world riven by ethical relativity, a fact that both mocks any pretence to absolute moral standards and enhances the quality of everyday life in a small country village. 'The country', Darcy remarks, 'can in general supply but few subjects for such a study. In a country neighbourhood you move in a very confined and unvarying society.' 'But people themselves alter so much', pert Elizabeth responds, 'that there is something new to be observed in them for ever.'[2] This principle of infinite variety within apparent unity extends from the object of study to the observer, of course; the fact that Elizabeth can praise Bingley for his compliance when he offers to remain at Netherfield and call that same trait weakness when he stays away (pp. 50, 135) tells us more about Elizabeth's desires than the principle of tractability. And the fact that Elizabeth can excuse Wickham for preferring a practical marriage when she will forever blame Charlotte for making the same choice reveals more about Elizabeth's personal investment in these two situations than Jane Austen's views on matrimony or money. Judgement is always inflected – modulated – by personal desire, Austen suggests, just as vision is always governed by perspective. 'Principles' are often merely prejudices, and prejudices simply project one's own interests on to the shifting scene outside so as to defend and reinforce the self.

Ideally, in such a world, conventions of propriety and morality make living together possible by compensating for the competing desires of individuals and by stabilising standards of judgement and value. But in *Pride and Prejudice*, as in Austen's other novels and, presumably, in her society as well, social conventions no longer necessarily serve this end; instead, as Wollstonecraft complained, social institutions have ossified until they threaten to crush the desire from which they theoretically grew and which they ought to accommodate. Beside the arrogant Miss Bingley, parading around the drawing-room in hopes of catching Darcy's eye, or Mr Collins, pompous embodiment of unyielding propriety itself, Elizabeth's impulsiveness, outspokenness, and generosity seem admirable and necessary correctives. When she bursts into Netherfield to see her sick sister, for example, the mud on her skirts becomes completely irrelevant beside the healthiness of her unself-conscious concern for Jane. That Miss Bingley despises Elizabeth for what she calls 'conceited independence' simply enhances our sympathy for conceit and independence, if these are the traits Elizabeth embodies. And when Elizabeth refuses to be subdued by Lady Catherine, whether on the subject of her music or her marriage, we feel nothing but admiration for her 'impertinence' – if this is what her energy really is.

Yet the juxtaposition of Elizabeth's lively wit with this pretentious and repressive society cuts both ways; for if the vacuity of her surroundings highlights her energy, it also encourages her to cultivate her natural vivacity beyond its legitimate bounds. As the novel unfolds, we begin to recognise that Elizabeth's charming wit is another incarnation of wilful desire, which, by rendering judgement unstable, contributes to moral relativity. As Elizabeth embellishes her surroundings with imaginative flourishes, we begin to see that indulging the imagination can harm others and that it in fact serves as a defence against emotional involvement. Through this juxtaposition, then, Austen is able to enlist the reader's initial imaginative engagement with Elizabeth in the service of moral education – an education for the reader, which shadows (but does not correspond precisely to) Elizabeth's own education, and which schools the imagination by means of its own irrepressible energy.

One of the first indications that Elizabeth's quick wit and powerful feelings may be unreliable moral guides emerges in her initial conversation with George Wickham. Until this moment, Elizabeth's companions and the settings in which she has appeared have enhanced her charm and appeal. But as soon as Elizabeth enters into her intimate conversation with Wickham, Austen encourages us to recognise that something is wrong. The problem here is not that a responsive young woman is attracted to a handsome young militia man; instead, the problem is that Elizabeth is unconsciously using Wickham to reinforce her prejudice against Darcy and is, as a consequence, allowing herself to be used by Wickham to reinforce his own false position. There are no disinterested or straightforward emotions in this scene; what appears to be Elizabeth's simple response to Wickham's physical and emotional charm is actually being fed by the subterranean force of her anger at Darcy. Elizabeth is flattered by Wickham's particular attention to her, but she is equally aroused by the fact that his story justifies her anger at Darcy. As a consequence of this double flattery, Elizabeth is blinded to the impropriety of this stranger's intimacy, she is seduced into judging on the grounds of Wickham's 'countenance' rather than some less arbitrary principle, and she is encouraged to credit her feelings instead of testing her perceptions against reality.

The action of *Pride and Prejudice* generally reveals that, despite what looks like a generous overflow of irrepressible energy, Elizabeth's 'liveliness' is primarily defensive.[3] More specifically, her 'impertinence' is a psychological defence against the vulnerability to which her situation as a dependent woman exposes her. Elizabeth's prejudice against Darcy is so quickly formed and so persistent because, at the first assembly, he unthinkingly confronts her with the very facts that it is most in her interest to deny. 'She is tolerable', Darcy concedes, rejecting Bingley's overtures on Elizabeth's behalf, 'but not handsome enough to tempt *me*; and I am in no humour at present to give consequence to young ladies who are slighted by other men' (p. 12).

Despite the fact that Elizabeth's 'playful disposition' enables her to turn this 'ridiculous' remark against Darcy, his cool observation continues to vex and haunt her for much of the novel and to govern not only her anger toward Darcy but also her 'mortification' at the antics of her family. It has this effect for two closely related reasons. First of all, in spite of her professed unconcern, Elizabeth, like everyone else, is immediately attracted to this handsome, eminently eligible bachelor, and, if only for a short time, he engages her natural romantic fantasies. We discover this later, when Darcy offers to make her dream come true and Elizabeth retorts by acknowledging that, though she once considered him as a possible husband, she no longer does so: 'I had not known you a month', she exults, inadvertently acknowledging the longevity of her fantasy, 'before I felt that you were the last man in the world whom I could ever be prevailed on to marry' (p. 193). But, given Elizabeth's social position and economic situation, even to dream of marrying Darcy is an act of imaginative presumption. The second reason for her lingering pain, then, is that Darcy's rejection deflates not only her romantic fantasies of marriage to a handsome aristocrat but, more important, the image of herself upon which such fantasies are based.

Darcy's casual remark suggests that the fact that Elizabeth is momentarily without a partner indicates that she will always be so 'slighted', that her 'tolerable' beauty will never attract the permanent partner she desires. And this remark strikes very close to home. For the inevitable result of an entail in a household more blessed with daughters than frugality is, at best, a limited choice of suitors; at worst, the Bennet's shortage of money for dowries and their equivocal social position foretell spinsterhood, dependence on a generous relative, or, most ominous of all, work as a governess or lady's companion. Austen never lets the reader or Elizabeth forget how very likely such a future is. Darcy lays the groundwork for this scenario when, alluding to their uncles in trade and law, he remarks that such connections 'must very materially lessen [the sisters'] chance of marrying men of any consideration in the world' (p. 37). Even closer to home, when Charlotte Lucas rejects romance, she does so for its opposite, the matter-of-fact assessment that a 'comfortable home' is more substantial than romantic fantasies. Elizabeth's mother is even more brutally frank. 'If you take it into your head', she warns Elizabeth, 'to go on refusing every offer of marriage in this way, you will never get a husband at all – and I am sure I do not know who is to maintain you when your father is dead' (p. 113). In the context of such dark realism, even Mr Collins's compensatory retaliation sounds ominously like a self-evident truth. 'Your portion is unhappily so small', he smugly informs Elizabeth, 'that it will in all likelihood undo the effects of your loveliness and amiable qualifications' (p. 108).

Elizabeth chooses to ignore all of these warnings, of course, because, with the arrogance born of youth, natural high spirits, and intellectual superiority, she believes herself too good for such a fate. But Darcy challenges her self-confidence, and, in the disappointment he indirectly inflicts on Jane, he proves himself capable of bringing the Bennet family face to face with undeniable reality. In the face of real dependence and practical powerlessness, Elizabeth grasps at any possible source of power or distinction. As she confides to Jane in a moment of telling self-awareness, wit and prejudice have been her two sources of power, two means of distinguishing herself:

> I meant to be uncommonly clever in taking so decided a dislike to him, without any reason. It is such a spur to one's genius, such an opening for wit to have a dislike of that kind. One may be continually abusive without saying any thing just; but one cannot be always laughing at a man without now and then stumbling on something witty.
>
> (pp. 225–6)

From this statement, Elizabeth's psychological economy is clear: she directs her intelligence toward defending herself against emotional vulnerability; she bases her moral judgement at least partially on her defensiveness; and she rationalises both the romantic fantasies with which she consoles herself and the forays of wit with which she protects herself as spontaneous effusions of a lively and superior mind.

Such criticism of Elizabeth's 'liveliness' is elaborated by Austen's characterisations of both Mr Bennet and Lydia. Elizabeth is her father's favourite daughter, and Mr Bennet's witty intelligence clearly reinforces and feeds off Elizabeth's superiority. But Mr Bennet is finally a failure, for he is lax when it comes to the social duties that are most important to the Bennet family as a whole and to Elizabeth in particular. Like Elizabeth's society in general, Mr Bennet's character is a moral vacuum; his 'indolence and the little attention he has [given] to what was going forward in his family' (p. 283) finally permit, if they do not encourage, Lydia's rebellion. Mr Bennet tries to make light of his moral irresponsibility by describing social relations as an amusing game. 'For what do we live', he asks rhetorically, 'but to make sport for our neighbours, and laugh at them in our turn?' (p. 364). But the pain that unthinking Lydia visits on the rest of the family proves conclusively how serious – and how selfish – his evasion really is.

Just as her father's defensive intelligence refracts and exaggerates Elizabeth's intellectual 'liveliness', so Lydia's wild, noisy laughter helps clarify Elizabeth's 'impertinence'. But perhaps the most important function of Lydia's story derives from its placement. For Austen positions the announcement of Lydia's elopement so as to precipitate the second, and most important, stage of Elizabeth's education. Through Darcy's letter, Elizabeth has already learned that she was wrong about both Wickham and Darcy, but Darcy's proposal and her angry rejection have, if anything, increased, not lessened, her pride and sense of superiority. 'Vanity, not love, has been my folly', Elizabeth exclaims at the moment of this first 'humiliation' (p. 208); but, on second thought, she is deeply flattered by the great man's attentions, and, since she does not regret her decision, she is free to bask in the triumph his proposal gives her over his 'pride', over his 'prejudices', and over Lady Catherine and Miss Bingley as well. Thus, even though she feels that her own 'past behaviour' constitutes 'a constant source of vexation and regret' (p. 212), Elizabeth visits Pemberley with her vanity very much intact: 'at that moment she felt, that to be mistress of Pemberley might be something!' (p. 245). This dream of what she might have been is jolted into the present and then into the future when Darcy suddenly appears, proves courteous to the very relatives he had previously slighted, and then invites Elizabeth back to Pemberley to meet his sister. At this moment, Elizabeth realises that her 'power' is even greater than she had dared imagine it to be.

> She respected, she esteemed, she was grateful to him, she felt a real interest in his welfare; and she only wanted to know how far she wished that welfare to depend upon herself, and how far it would be for the happiness of both that she should employ the power, which her fancy told her she still possessed, of bringing on the renewal of his addresses.
>
> (p. 266)

While this reflection is neither cool nor calculating, it does suggest that Elizabeth feels herself more superior than ever – not so much to Darcy as to love.

Jane's letter arrives when Elizabeth is basking in this self-confidence; its effect is to strip her of self-control, self-assurance, and her confident superiority over feeling. In Darcy's presence she bursts into tears and then, suddenly recognising what she now believes she has lost, she realises that true power belongs not to the imagination but to love: 'Her power was sinking, every thing *must* sink under such a proof of family weakness. ... The belief of his self-conquest ... afforded no palliation of her distress. It was, on the contrary, exactly calculated to make her understand her own wishes; and never had she so honestly felt that she could have loved him, as now, when all love must be vain' (p. 278).

Elizabeth's fantasies no longer seem as wild or romantic as they once did, but, before her wish can be fulfilled, she must be 'humbled' by her own sister – not only so that she (and the reader) will recognise the pernicious effects of Lydia's passionate self-indulgence, but so that Elizabeth herself will understand how intimately her own fate is bound up in the actions and characters of others. Individualism is not simply morally suspect, Austen suggests; it is also based on a naïve overestimation of personal autonomy and power. To pretend that one can transcend social categories or refuse a social role (as Mr Bennet does) is not only irresponsible; it also reveals a radical misunderstanding of the fact that, for an individual living in society, every action is automatically linked to the actions of others. And to believe that one can exercise free will, even when parents do not intercede, is to mistake the complex nature of desire and the way in which social situation affects psychology and self-knowledge.

Yet, despite its sobering implications, the 'mortification' of Elizabeth's vanity does not constitute a rebuke to the premises or promises of romance, as Marianne's illness does in *Sense and Sensibility*. Instead, in order to convert the power of romance into a legitimate corrective for harsh realism, Austen redeems romance by purging it of all traces of egotism. As we have already seen, to believe that one's beauty and wit will captivate a powerful lord is really a form of vanity. But Elizabeth's actual romantic fantasies about Darcy are short-lived; the only dashing young man she fantasises extensively about is Wickham. Elizabeth's response to her aunt's query about Wickham may be only half serious, but her confusion does reveal the extent of her susceptibility.

> At present I am not in love with Mr Wickham; no, I certainly am not. But he is, beyond all comparison, the most agreeable man I ever saw – and if he becomes really attached to me – I believe it will be better that he should not. I see the imprudence of it. – Oh! *that* abominable Mr Darcy – My father's opinion of me does me the greatest honour, and I should be miserable to forfeit it. My father, however, is partial to Mr Wickham. In short, my dear aunt, I should be very sorry to be the means of making any of you unhappy; but since we see every day that where there is affection, young people are seldom withheld by immediate want of fortune from entering into engagements with each other, how can I promise to be wiser than so many of my fellow creatures if I am tempted, or how am I even to know that it would be wisdom to resist? All that I can promise you, therefore, is not to be in a hurry. I will not be in a hurry to believe myself his first object. When I am in company with him, I will not be wishing. In short, I will do my best.
>
> (pp. 144–5)

Just as Elizabeth's prejudice against Darcy originally fed her admiration for Wickham, now her attraction to the young soldier focuses her resentment against Darcy: if Wickham's story is true, after all, Darcy has been directly (although inadvertently) responsible for preventing a marriage between Elizabeth and Wickham. But Austen does not allow this or any other romance to develop or capture Elizabeth's imagination; indeed, when she dismisses this particular suitor, she does not ridicule either the claims or the attractions of romance. Instead, when Wickham declares for the wealthy Miss King, Elizabeth remains undisturbed, and the entire issue of romantic love is simply pushed to the periphery of the narrative. Wickham's decision to marry for money does, after all, leave Elizabeth's vanity intact. 'His apparent partiality had subsided, his attentions were over, he was the admirer of some one else. Elizabeth was watchful enough to see it all, but she could see it and write of it without material pain. Her heart had been but slightly touched, and her vanity was satisfied with believing that *she* would have been his only choice, had fortune permitted it' (p. 149).

Elizabeth's eventual love for Darcy is legitimate because it springs not from the vanity we ordinarily associate with romantic expectations but precisely from the mortification of pride. Yet because Elizabeth only belatedly realises that she loves Darcy, her humbling does not entail a rejection of romantic love. Indeed, unaccountable, uncontrollable romantic love continues to play a role in *Pride and Prejudice* – in *Darcy's* desire for Elizabeth. This passion, which Austen notes but does not dwell on, is the subtextual force behind much of the action. In response to love, Darcy overcomes his prejudices against Elizabeth's connections, proposes to her, returns to her even after hope seems gone, and eventually brings about the marriages of three of the Bennet daughters. The narrative does not focus on the development or pressures of this passion; even when Elizabeth playfully asks Darcy for an account of his love, her mocking celebration of 'impertinence' deflects any explanation he might have given. Romantic love remains the unexamined and unaccountable source of power in a novel preoccupied with various forms of social and psychological power and powerlessness. It not only overcomes all obstacles; it brings about a perfect society at the end of the novel.

The romantic conclusion of *Pride and Prejudice* effectively dismisses the social and psychological realism with which the novel began. Elizabeth's 'impertinence' may have originated in her need to dispel the vulnerability of her dependent situation, but when marriage with Darcy cancels all the gloomy forecasts about Elizabeth's future, Austen no longer suggests a possible relationship between social causes and psychological effects. Elizabeth's 'liveliness' persists, of course, but it is purified of its defensiveness and its egotism. In essence, in awarding Elizabeth this handsome husband with ten thousand pounds a year, Austen is gratifying the reader's fantasy that such outspoken liveliness *will* be successful in material terms, but she earns the right to do so precisely because Elizabeth's first fantasy of personal power is *not* rewarded. *Pride and Prejudice*, in other words, legitimises the reader's romantic wishes by humbling the heroine's vanity. At the level of the plot, power is taken from egotism and given to love; at the level of the reading experience, power seems miraculously both to emanate from and to reward individualistic desire.

Darcy and Elizabeth, then, learn complementary lessons: he recognises that individual feelings outweigh conventional social distinctions; she realises the nature of society's power. Their marriage purports to unite individual gratification with social responsibility, to overcome the class distinctions that elevated Lady Catherine over the worthy Gardiners, and to make of society one big happy family. The last pages of *Pride and Prejudice* described family connections radiating throughout society, closing the gap between geographical locations, social classes, and temperamental differences. The union that concludes this novel re-establishes the ideal, paternalistic society that Mr Bennet's irresponsibility and Wickham's insubordination once seemed to threaten. With Darcy at its head and Elizabeth at its heart, society will apparently be able to contain the anarchic impulses of individualism and humanise the rigidities of prejudice, and everyone – even Miss Bingley – will live more or less happily in the environs of Pemberley, the vast estate whose permanence, prominence, and unique and uniquely satisfying fusion of individual taste and utility, of nature and art, symbolise Jane Austen's ideal.[4]

Austen is able to effect an aesthetic resolution of what is essentially a moral dilemma partly because the realistic elements in her portrayal of the situation are so carefully contained. As in *Sense and Sensibility*, Austen simply does not explore to the full the social or psychological implications of her realism. Darcy, Charlotte Lucas, Mr Collins, and Mrs Bennet all warn Elizabeth that her impertinence will probably result in spinsterhood, but Austen does not imperil the integrity of the romantic ending by dramatising the perils of such a future in a character like Jane Fairfax, Miss Bates, or Mrs Smith. But even beyond curtailing the extent of her realism, Austen controls the response of her readers by drawing them into a system of values that seems, by the end of the novel, both 'natural' and right. She can generate this system of common values because one of the fundamental principles of her art is to assume that the relationship between an author and an audience is ideally (if not automatically) a version of the relationship she knew best: the family.

The model of the family governs Jane Austen's art in at least three important ways. To begin with, her own personal family served as her first and most appreciative audience. Like the Brontës after her, Jane Austen wrote her first stories for the amusement of her family; most of her surviving juvenilia are dedicated to her siblings or cousins, and it is easy to imagine these stories and plays being read in the family circle, with various members contributing jokes from time to time. Austen's first longer works – *First Impressions* (later *Pride and Prejudice*) and *Elinor and Marianne* (later *Sense and Sensibility*) – were also apparently family entertainments, and, even after she became a published author, she continued to solicit and value the responses of her family as she composed and revised her novels.[5] For Austen, the entire enterprise of writing was associated with hospitality and familial bonds. Her letters reveal that she sometimes half-jokingly talked of her novels as her 'children' and of her characters as if they were family friends. She assured her sister, for instance, that she could 'no more forget' *Sense and Sensibility* 'than a mother can forget her sucking child'; she referred to *Pride and Prejudice* as her 'own child'; and she pretended to find a portrait of Jane Bingley exhibited in Spring Gardens: 'There never was a greater likeness', Austen playfully announced; 'She is dressed in a white gown, with green ornaments, which convinces me of what I had always supposed, that green was a favourite colour with her.'[6]

The fact that Austen's completed novels and the activity of writing itself were part of the fabric of her family relationships helps to explain why she was able to avoid both the aggressive polemicism that Mary Wollstonecraft employed and the enfeebling defensiveness to which Mary Shelley resorted. Austen actively wondered what her readers thought of her novels, and she regretted that her works did not receive adequate critical attention, but she never seems to have imagined an audience openly hostile to either her novels or herself, as both Wollstonecraft and Shelley did, for different reasons. But in addition to providing a hospitable transitional area between her private imagination and the public bookstall, Jane Austen's experience of a close and supportive family also provided models both for the way an individual's desires could be accommodated by social institutions and for the context of shared values that an author could ideally rely on to provide a moral basis for art.

The notion of the family that served Jane Austen as a model for the proper coexistence of the individual and society was essentially patriarchal, supportive of, and supported by, the allegiances and hierarchy that feminine propriety implied. Its smallest unit – the marriage – embodied for Austen the ideal union of individual desire and social responsibility; if a woman could legitimately express herself *only* by choosing to marry and then by sustaining her marriage,

Austen suggests, she *could*, through her marriage, not only satisfy her own needs but also influence society. For the most part, the culminating marriages in Austen's novels lack the undercurrents of ambivalence that characterise Shelley's depictions of even happy marriages. This is true in part because the energies of Austen's heroines are not so rigorously channelled by propriety into self-denial either before or after marriage. As *Sense and Sensibility* suggests, however, Austen does discipline female energies, but, increasingly, she also suggests that the psychological toll exacted by patriarchal society from women is too high. The fact that almost all of the peripheral marriages in her novels are dissatisfying in one way or another seems to indicate that Austen recognised both the social liabilities that Wollstonecraft identified and the psychological complexities that Shelley intuited. Nevertheless, and especially in *Pride and Prejudice*, the most idealistic of all of her novels, marriage remains for Austen the ideal paradigm of the most perfect fusion between the individual and society.

As the actual basis and ideal model of the contract between an author and an audience, the family also promised a context of shared experiences, assumptions, and values against which the writer could play and to which he or she could eventually return. And it is in this sense – and for this reason – that the moral relativism theoretically unleashed by individualism does not necessarily undermine Austen's conservative moral pattern or her didactic purpose. For if an author can assume a set of basic assumptions and values, such as family members share, then he or she can depend on the reader's returning with the narrator to that common ground, in spite of liberties to stray that have been permitted in the course of the fiction. In fact, given the common ground, these liberties often contribute to the didactic design of the novel, for they foster the illusion that challenges to ethical and aesthetic authority are actually being engaged and defeated in their own terms.

In *Pride and Prejudice* Austen tries to ensure that her readers will share a common ground by making them participate in constructing the value system that governs the novel. This participation is a necessary part of reading *Pride and Prejudice* because Austen combines a predominantly dramatic presentation of the action with an irony so persistent that it almost destroys narrative authority.[7] Even what looks like omniscient commentary often turns out, on closer inspection, to carry the accents of a single character. The famous first sentence of the novel, for example – 'It is a truth universally acknowledged, that a single man in possession of a good fortune, must be in want of a wife' – points to the radical limitations of both 'truth' and 'universally'. Masquerading as a statement of fact – if not about all unmarried men, then certainly about a community that collectively assumes it to be true – this sentence actually tells us more about Mrs Bennet than anyone else. In such local instances, irony allows us a certain freedom of interpretation even when it teases us to test our 'first impressions' against our developing under-standing of individual characters and the priorities of the novel as a whole.

As Wayne Booth has noted, irony forces the reader not only to participate in interpretation and evaluation but to choose one *system* of values over another.[8] And it is through the value system developed in the overall action of the novel that Austen hopes to counter the relativism that the localised ironies might permit.[9] We can see this principle at work in Charlotte Lucas's argument about marriage. The narrator, conveying Charlotte's thoughts indirectly, takes no explicit stand on her position: 'Without thinking highly either of men or of matrimony, marriage had always been her object; it was the only honourable provision for well-educated young women of small fortune, and however uncertain of giving happiness, must be their pleasantest preservative from want' (pp. 122–3). Certainly this statement illuminates the limitations of Charlotte's romantic expectations, but is it meant to be an author-itative assessment of reality? Or is Elizabeth's indignant rejoinder more authoritative? 'You must feel, as well as I do', she exclaims to Jane, 'that the woman who marries him, cannot have a proper way of thinking' (p. 135). Elsewhere Elizabeth's 'proper way of think-ing' has proved self-interested. Is this case any different? And how are we, finally, to decide?

In such passages, Austen is both permitting momentary freedom of choice and demonstrating the vertigo that accompanies it. But through the unfolding action of the novel she seems to qualify this freedom by endorsing one option over the other: Mr Bingley and Mr Darcy *do* both want and need wives; the love matches Elizabeth believed in *do* come about, despite all the odds against them. And, most important, the paternal order established at the end of the novel both embodies an authoritative system of values and abolishes the apparent discrepancy between individual desire and social responsi-bility. Jane Austen's irony, then, enables her to reproduce – without exposing in any systematic way – some of the contradictions inherent in bourgeois ideology; for by simultaneously dramatising and rewarding individual desire *and* establishing a critical distance from individualism, she endorses both the individualistic perspective inherent in the bourgeois value system *and* the authoritarian hierarchy retained from traditional, paternalistic society. Moreover, by allowing her reader to exercise freedom of judgement in individual instances while controlling the final value system through the action as a whole, Austen replicates, at the level of the reading experience, the marriage of romantic desire and realistic necessity that she believed was capable of containing individualism's challenge to traditional authority.

In *Pride and Prejudice* this strategy effectively focuses what had remained two distinct narrative parts in *Lady Susan* and two competing centres of authority in *Northanger Abbey* and *Sense and Sensibility*. The closure of *Pride and Prejudice* is thus aesthetically successful, but whether it ensures a comparable ideological resolution is doubtful. For at the level of the plot Austen can grant moral authority to feeling by stripping desire of egotism, but she cannot guarantee that every reader will be as educable as Elizabeth or that all expressions of feeling will be as socially constructive as Elizabeth's desire for Darcy. This problem is raised specifically in *Pride and Prejudice* by Lydia, and Austen never really dismisses this character or the unruly energy she embodies:

> Lydia was Lydia still; untamed, unabashed, wild, noisy, and fearless. She turned from sister to sister, demanding their congratulations, and when at length they all sat down, looked eagerly round the room, took notice of some little alteration in it, and observed, with a laugh, that it was a great while since she had been there.
>
> (p. 315)

Even Austen's concluding comment on Lydia acknowledges that she finally finds a place within the same society that Elizabeth superintends. 'In spite of her youth and her manners', the narrator informs us, Lydia 'retained all the claims to reputation which her marriage had given her' (p. 387).

Austen's tacit assumption that her readers will renounce the moral anarchy epitomised in Lydia and generated by the pattern of localised ironies would be accurate only if her audience already shared her own experiences and values. For the purposes of her art, Austen makes this assumption because it allows her to contain not only individual interpretations but also the social criticisms implicitly raised in the course of *Pride and Prejudice*. In fact, this assumption enables her to bring the real experiences of her readers to bear on her narrative in such a way as to underscore the necessity of the aesthetic solution, which pushes aside social realism and criticism. Austen's contemporary readers would no doubt have been all too familiar with the facts and pressures that made Charlotte Lucas's cool assessment of marriage reasonable, and, merely by alluding to this shared experience, Austen enhances the gratification that Elizabeth's improbable success provides. Thus she introduces the spectres of spinsterhood, dependence, and compromise less to explore the social strictures of Elizabeth's situation than to invoke the reality that makes her own consoling art necessary. The inadequacy of the aesthetic solution to the social problems it supposedly answers remains implicit but unproblematic; for it is precisely the gap between imaginative desire and social reality – a gap that still exists – that makes the escape into romance attractive to all readers and probably made Austen's contemporaries, in particular, anxious to believe that Elizabeth's happiness was available to every daughter of the middle class.

The special resonance and impact that her contemporaries sensed in the statements and situations of Austen's novels are dim or absent altogether for twentieth-century readers. But even the experiences Austen's contemporaries shared with her, merely by virtue of their historical, geographical, and class proximity, would not have guaranteed a common set of values. For in this period of social turmoil even the dominant system of values was characterised by internal tensions and contradictions – stresses that reflected the competition between bourgeois individualism and old patterns of patronage and also the inevitable gap between the promises of individualism and the general inequalities and personal repressions that bourgeois society requires. Given the structure of bourgeois society, the system of absolute Christian principles that is the foundation of Austen's novels necessarily had to have its everyday, functional version, which allowed one to be 'rather' selfish in pursuit of material prosperity as long as one practised charity and thought good thoughts. It is precisely the latitude of interpretations permitted by this compromise of ethical and moral absolutes that finally imperils the didactic design of *Pride and Prejudice*. For the family of readers that Austen posited did not necessarily exist; even in her own day, the consensus of values she needed to assume was as wishful a fiction as Elizabeth Bennet's marriage to Darcy.

Because of the sophistication of her narrative skills, the romance Austen dramatises at the end of *Pride and Prejudice* seems not only right but plausible. But it is plausible only because, in this novel, Austen separates the power to gratify and discipline desire from the conditions that generate and frustrate that desire. The power moves from society to the realm of art; in *Pride and Prejudice* Austen substitutes aesthetic gratification – the pleasures of the 'light and bright and sparkling' plays of wit – for the practical solutions that neither her society nor her art could provide. That we do not more often feel shortchanged by this sleight-of-hand attests to the power of her artistry and to the magnitude of our own desire to deny the disturbing ideological contradictions that have made such imaginative compensation necessary.

From Mary Poovey, *The Proper Lady and the Woman Writer: Ideology as Style in the Works of Mary Wollstonecraft, Mary Shelley and Jane Austen* (Chicago, 1984), pp. 194–207.

NOTES

[As indicated in the previous context note, Mary Poovey's reading of Jane Austen is in essence that Austen intends to warn her readers about the dangers of uninhibited desire and emphasise the need for the institutions of patriarchal society to control individual conduct, especially the amorous conduct of young women. She recognises that the institutions are not perfect but sees the way toward their reform by the softening influence of those with principled feelings. In this reading Elizabeth Bennet is the champion of outspoken desire. Her recognition of her own prejudicial misreading of the world allows her vital intelligence and wit to vivify Darcy and find appropriate place in the social structure. Romance in this novel becomes not a subversive threat but a corrective tonic. At the same time, Elizabeth's charming vitality is revealed as a defensive consequence of her financially vulnerable situation: she is in historical and material terms the unportioned (therefore unpriced and valueless) gentry woman in the marriage market (as was Austen herself); in symbolic terms she is the upstart whose vulgar parents should deny her the chance of marrying the aristocratic hero. The parallels with Cinderella and Richardson's *Pamela* are evident: the narrative is a common middle-class fantasy in which the contradiction between the desire to rise in social status and the recognition of the unbreakable barriers of social class (money and manners) is magically resolved.

From Austen's point of view, Elizabeth, like Marianne, overestimates her personal autonomy and power and radically misunderstands the power of social institutions, but rather than educate Elizabeth by way of a humiliating rejection and near-fatal illness, Austen invents the more subtle narrative strategy of having Elizabeth fall for an unsuitable male, discover her mistake without harm, then be saved from a deserved penury by the romantic passion she has evoked in Darcy. Perhaps because this passion develops in a male breast, it escapes both analysis and censure and remains an unaccountable source of power in a novel which appears to want to account for everything. Austen's characteristic realism and repression are thus conveniently broached by desire and Elizabeth has to pay only the price of a little humility to succeed in having her prince. The narrative thus works a splendid aesthetic and ideological compromise: individual desires and social responsibility can be reconciled; female passion and intelligence does not have always to be repressed; rigid and insensitive patriarchy can admit to female softening; new energies can find their place in proud and prejudicial institutions; progress is possible, at least in the pages of the book if not in the real world.

References to Jane Austen's work are to *The Works of Jane Austen*, ed. R. W. Chapman, 2nd edn, 5 vols (London, 1926), and vol. 6, *Minor Works*, ed. R. W. Chapman (London, 1954), cited as *Works*. References to Austen's letters are to *Jane Austen's Letters to her Sister Cassandra and Others*, ed. R. W. Chapman, 2 vols (Oxford, 1932), cited as *Letters*. Ed.]

1. *Letters*, vol. 2, p. 297 (29 January 1813).

2. *Pride and Prejudice*, *Works*, vol. 2, pp. 42–3.

3. Bernard J. Paris makes this point in *Character and Conflict in Jane Austen's Novels: A Psychological Approach* (Detroit, 1978), pp. 118–39. While many of my observations are consistent with Paris's reading, I disagree with his central thesis that Elizabeth can be treated as a 'real' person throughout the novel. It is precisely Austen's aborting of psychological realism that interests me.

4. See Duckworth, *The Improvement of the Estate: A Study of Jane Austen's Novels* (Baltimore, 1971), pp. 123–6.

5. In 1799, for instance, Austen remarked to her sister Cassandra, 'I do not wonder at your wanting to read "First Impressions" again' (*Letters*, vol. 2, p. 52; 8 January 1799); her letters also show her sharing *Mansfield Park* with her brother Henry before its publication, and she kept a list of the responses her family and friends made to that novel and *Emma*. See 'Opinions of *Mansfield Park* and *Emma*', in *Works*, 6, pp. 431–9. For another discussion of the relationship between Austen's composition and her family, see Mary Lascelles, *Jane Austen and Her Art* (Oxford, 1939), pp. 4, 146.

6. *Letters*, vol. 2, p. 272 (25 April 1811); p. 297 (29 January 1813); p. 230 (24 May 1813). Austen's niece Catherine Hubback commented that her aunt 'always said her books were her children' (quoted by R. W. Chapman, *Jane Austen: Facts and Problems* [Oxford, 1948], p. 67), and from her nephews we learn that Austen supplied her family with information about her characters' 'after-life': 'In this tradition any way we learned that Miss Steele never succeeded in catching the Doctor; that

Kitty Bennet was satisfactorily married to a clergyman near Pemberley, while Mary obtained nothing higher than one of her uncle Phillips' clerks, and was content to be considered a star in the society of Meriton; that the "considerable sum" given by Mrs Norris to William Price was one pound; that Mr Woodhouse survived his daughter's marriage, and kept her and Mr Knightley from settling at Donwell, about two years; and that the letters placed by Frank Churchill before Jane Fairfax, which she swept away unread, contained the word "pardon" (J. E. Austen-Leigh, *A Memoir of Jane Austen* [London, 1906], pp. 148–9). Julia Prewitt Brown also discusses the importance of the family for Austen; see her *Jane Austen's Novels: Social Change and Literary Form* (Cambridge, Mass., 1979), p. 9.

7. One of the best discussions of this function of irony is in Jane Nardin's *Those Elegant Decorums: The Concept of Propriety in Jane Austen's Novels* (Albany, 1973), pp. 4–11.

8. See Wayne C. Booth, *A Rhetoric of Irony* (Chicago, 1974), p. 44 and passim.

9. See A. Walton Litz, *Jane Austen: A Study of Her Artistic Development* (New York, 1965), p. 108.

7

Women, Power and Subversion

JUDITH LOWDER NEWTON

I

One feels at once in *Pride and Prejudice* an edge, a critical emphasis given to the economic contradiction of men's and women's lives. Elizabeth Bennet has no decent fortune whatsoever. She *must* marry; she must marry with an eye to money; and the reason she must marry is that the family inheritance has been settled on a male. It would be hard to make a more central point of the fact that the conditions of economic life favoured men and restricted women.

The entailed fortune which so obviously benefits Mr Collins and so obviously restricts Jane Austen's heroine is merely the epitome of an economic privilege that is granted men in general and of an economic restriction that is imposed on women, and the details of that privilege and restriction are explicitly recorded throughout the novel. It is the right of Austen's men to have work that pays and to rise through preference and education, and we are directly told who has had access to what. We are told that Mr Gardiner and Mr Philips are established in business and in law, that Sir William Lucas has retired from trade, that Collins has been sent to the university and granted a living, and that Wickham has been set up first as clergyman, then as lawyer, and finally as officer – prospects which he persistently rejects or squanders. But men, no matter how hapless and undeserving, must be provided for, must be given every opportunity to earn their way.

Women, in contrast, are prepared for nothing but display. Their goal is not to accomplish but to be 'accomplished' or, as Miss Bingley puts it, to be 'esteemed accomplished' (p. 36). And Austen does not fail to tell us what 'accomplished' means – being able to paint tables, net purses, and cover screens. Women have no access at all to work that pays, for in this novel, in contrast, say, to *Emma*, even the life of a governess is not an option. (The governesses of *Pride and Prejudice* are not a promising lot. Mrs Annesley may be 'well-bred', but Mrs Jenkinson has been extinguished as a personality, and the immoral Mrs Younge has been reduced to letting rooms and taking bribes.) Finally, although women and men both inherit money, women inherit a lump sum, a kind of dowry, while men inherit livings, and Austen tells us precisely who has inherited what. The Miss Bingleys are worth £20,000 while their brother has an annual four or five. Miss Darcy's fortune is £30,000, her brother's £10,000 per annum. And Mrs Bennet has a total of £4,000 while her husband nets £2,000 a year.

The first two sentences of the novel make subtle and ironic point of this disparity, and they evoke the way in which economic inequity shapes male and female power:

> It is a truth universally acknowledged, that a single man in possession of a good fortune must be in want of a wife.
> However little known the feelings or views of such a man may be on his first entering a neighbourhood, this truth is so well fixed in the minds of the surrounding families that he is considered as the rightful property of some one or other of their daughters.
>
> (p. 1)

Some single men, it would appear, have independent access to good fortunes, but all single women or 'daughters' must marry for them. 'Daughters' and their families, therefore, must think a good deal about marriage while single men with fortunes do not. Families with 'daughters' may try to control men too, to seize them as 'property', but it is really 'daughters', the sentence implies, who are controlled, who are 'fixed' by their economic situation. Single men appear at liberty; they can enter a neighbourhood and presumably leave it at will. Single men, in short, have an autonomy that 'daughters' do not, and at the base of this difference in autonomy is the fact that men have access to money.

That Austen sustains a lively interest in what women and men are worth, that she suggests a causal relation between money and power, sets *Pride and Prejudice* at some distance from [Fanny Burney's]

Evelina [1778], and this distance must be explained in part by historical context. Austen, for example, experienced the effects of industrial
capitalism as Burney did not, and one effect of industrial takeoff
(which belonged to the late eighteenth and early nineteenth centuries)
was to make consciousness of money in general more universal and
more respectable as well. One could hardly ignore money, after all,
for money was being made and made rapidly in industry and
exchange, and money was lending status and power to men who had
not had either before, men in trade, for example, men with no pretence at all to the courtly patina of title, family, and long inheritance.
This difference in historical context is certainly evoked by the fact
that the only tradesmen to appear in *Evelina* are small-time, vulgar,
and low, while in *Pride and Prejudice* Mr and Mrs Gardiner, living in
sight of the Gardiner warehouses, are neither small-time nor vulgar
but the most admirable, the most decent, the most well-bred adults in
the novel, a fact which the aristocrats must be made to face.

The acquisition of industrial and trading fortunes must also have
sharpened money consciousness – and consciousness of the relation
between money, status, and power – by increasing the number of
men who could actually acquire country estates and merge with the
gentry, another change which is expressed in contrasts between
Evelina and *Pride and Prejudice*. Burney never alludes to the merging of gentry with persons of the middle stations – although this
was certainly taking place – and she even mitigates the significance
of Evelina's marriage to a lord by revealing, in the nick of time,
that Evelina herself is the daughter of a baronet. In *Pride and
Prejudice*, however, the merging of gentry and trade is endorsed
and even common. Bingley, whose fortune comes from trade and
from northern trade at that, is on the verge of finally consolidating
his genteel status by purchasing a country estate. Sir William, who
has actually retired from trade, has established his family in a country 'lodge', and Elizabeth herself, who *is* the daughter of a gentleman but who *does* have connections in business and in the lower
regions of the law, marries a man of the upper gentry.

Pride and Prejudice, therefore, evokes the fact that money was
being made, that it lent new status and power to men of the middle
stations, and that it accelerated the merging of the gentry with the
middle classes, and, in its focus on money and money matters, it
suggests the concurrence of these phenomena with a sharpened and
newly dignified money consciousness. Given this context, it is not
surprising that Austen's vision of the power and status of women is
persistently linked to their economic situation, as Burney's vision is

not. For a general consciousness of the relation between money, status, and power must have had its effect on the way in which the lot of middle-class women was perceived. Of course the lot of middle-class women was also becoming more contradictory, for genteel women continued to lose recognised economic value while genteel men were finding new access to work and new opportunities for rising.[1] The growing contradiction must have been felt as it could not have been felt in the age of Burney.

Austen's personal relation to this larger context certainly increased her consciousness of money in general and of the contradiction between the economic lots of genteel men and women. Although the Austen family was better connected than the Burneys, was distantly related to the aristocracy, and was more immediately related to the clergy, to men in professions (a surgeon and a solicitor), to a lord mayor of London, and to the smaller gentry, Austen felt the pinch of economic stringency when writing *Pride and Prejudice* as Burney did not when writing *Evelina*. Austen's father had died in 1805, and in 1813, the year *Pride and Prejudice* was published, Jane, her mother, and her sister Cassandra were dependent for their living on three sources: a small income of Mrs Austen's, a small legacy of Cassandra's, and the £250 provided annually by four of the Austen brothers. The sum was enhanced to some degree by the money Jane earned through writing, for in July of that year she reports that 'I have now ... written myself into £250 – which only makes me long for more'.[2] But the £140 brought by *Sense and Sensibility* and the £110 from *Pride and Prejudice* did not go far, and Austen's letters for that year, as for every year, are full of references to small economies.

In fact, to read Jane Austen's letters – with their steady consciousness of bargains, pence, and shillings – is to be aware of the constancy with which money and money matters impinged upon her own experience as an unmarried woman of the middle stations. In May of 1813, for example, she writes that she is 'very lucky' in her gloves, having paid 'four shillings', that sarcenet and dimity (at 2/6) are not bargains 'but good of their sort', and that a locket at eighteen shillings cost more than Cassandra intended but is 'neat and plain, set in gold'. In September she is tempted by some edging which is 'very cheap' and regretful at having spent six shillings for a white silk handkerchief. She wavers too over some 'very pretty English Poplins' (4s/3d), does not buy them, and then decides to treat herself after all with the four pounds which 'kind, beautiful' brother Edward has given her. October finds her planning to dye her blue gown, scheming to save Cassandra postage, and inquiring after the price of butcher's meat. In November she notes a fall in the price of bread and hopes that 'my Mother's Bill next week will show it'.[3]

Austen's family situation, moreover, imposed upon her a heightened awareness of the economic contradiction between the lots of genteel women and genteel men, for Austen had five brothers and they had what she did not: access to work that paid, access to inheritance and privilege, and access to the status that belonged to being prosperous and male. In 1813 all but one brother was rising in a career. James was earning £1,100 a year as a curate, Henry was a partner in a successful banking firm, Frank was the captain of a ship in the Baltic, Charles was the flag captain of another, and Edward, the only brother without a profession, was living as a country gentleman on one of the two estates he had inherited from his adopted family.

The difference which money made in the relative autonomy of Austen women and Austen men was also striking, yet there is little emphatic indication in the letters that unequal economic privilege or unequal power was a source of oppression or discomfort to Jane. Her letters, for the most part, form a casual patchwork of details about her own economies and her brothers' expenditures, about her desire for money and their attainment of it, about her dependence in travelling and their liberties with horseback, carriage, and barouche, about the pressure she felt to marry and the freedom they assumed to marry or not to marry as they chose. Here and there, of course, we find some humorous consciousness of inequity, and there is more than one joke about the economic pressure to marry: 'Single Women have a dreadful propensity for being poor – which is one very strong argument in favour of Matrimony.'[4] But, for the most part, Jane Austen's attitude toward the economic restrictions of being a woman and toward the resulting absence of autonomy – the dependence, the confinement, the pressure to marry – is, in the letters, amused and uncomplaining.

II

It is in Austen's fiction that we begin to feel an edge, a telling emphasis, being given to the difference between the economic restriction of women and the economic privilege of men. Austen's fiction, like Burney's, was obviously a means of coming to terms with a discomforting experience, was an outlet for critical energies which she could not otherwise express, and those energies are evident in the first sentences of the novel, where Austen implies a relation between money and autonomy which her letters reflect but do not articulate. The outcome of those energies, however, is not what one might expect, for while the rest of the novel does sustain an awareness of the economic inequality of women and men, it does not sustain a felt awareness of the causal connection between money and power. Indeed, for all its reference to money and money matters, for all its consciousness of economic fact and economic influence, *Pride and Prejudice* is devoted not to establishing but to denying the force of economics in human life. In the reading of the novel the real *force* of economics simply melts away.

Despite the first two sentences, despite the implication that access to money in some way determines autonomy, the difference between men's economic privilege and that of women is *not* something we are invited to *experience* as a cause of power and powerlessness in the novel. Men, for all their money and privilege, are not permitted to seem powerful but are rather bungling and absurd; and women, for all their impotence, are not seen as victims of economic restriction. What the novel finally defines as power has little to do with money, and the most authentically powerful figure in the novel is an unmarried middle-class woman without a fortune – a woman, we may note, who bears a striking resemblance to Jane Austen.

While *Evelina* ultimately justifies the control of ruling-class men, *Pride and Prejudice* sustains a fantasy of female autonomy. As in Burney, however, there is no overt indication that Austen protested the economic contradiction on which the inequities of power between men and women were based. Indeed, where the economic inequity of women's lot seems most unfair, Austen is deflecting criticism. Mrs Bennet and Lady Catherine, for example, are the only persons in the novel allowed to object to the entail, and neither is permitted to engage our sympathies. Mrs Bennet, in fact, is made to confound potential and plausible criticism by giving it an implausible direction. The entail 'was a subject on which Mrs Bennet was beyond the reach of reason; and she continued to rail bitterly against the cruelty of settling an estate away from a family of five daughters, in favour of a man whom nobody cared anything about' (p. 58). Any reasonable objection to the automatic selection of male inheritors is obscured here by Mrs Bennet's unreasoning protests.

But if, by deflecting criticism, Austen appears to accept, indeed to apologise for, the unequal division of money and privilege – a division which it would have been futile to protest in 1813 – she also appears to limit, subtly and from the outset, what that inequity can mean. Although the Austen of the letters seems well aware of the status and sense of achievement involved in earning or preserving money, she omits from the novel almost any reference to and all observation of activity which has an economic reward. The effect is to mystify one major area in which upper- and middle-class men had access to a sense of power that upper- and middle-class women did not. We do hear that Mr Bennet oversees the farm, and we know that business prompts Mr Gardiner to postpone a vacation and to meet with Mr Stone. We are aware that Darcy writes letters of business and that he cares for his tenants and his library. We understand that Collins reads, writes sermons, and tends to parish duties, and we are left to imagine that Wickham does something more than gamble in his capacity as officer. But we never see them at work. Both sexes appear only at leisure – eating, reading, attending balls, paying visits, writing personal letters, and playing backgammon, piquet, quadrille, casino and loo. If the enforced idleness of genteel women seems oppressive in this novel, it is not out of contrast with the more productive activities of males.

It is principally in their personal rather than in their working lives that men appear at first to have more autonomy than women, more power to make decisions, to go and to do as they please. Throughout *Pride and Prejudice* men have a mobility that women, even women with money, do not, and that mobility suggests a greater general self-rule. From the first sentence on, men are linked with entry and removal, women with being 'fixed'. Bingley, for example, first enters the scene in a chaise and four and then leaves almost immediately for London, prompting Mrs Bennet to worry – in woman's traditional fashion – that he will 'be always flying about from one place to another' (p. 7). Bingley, in fact, prides himself on his alacrity in leaving – '… if I should resolve to quit Netherfield, I should probably be off in five minutes' – and he does leave Jane abruptly and painfully, only to saunter up again some ten months later (p. 39). Bingley's mobility is typical of that of the other single men in the novel, for the militia too enter and then leave, as do Wickham, Collins, and Darcy.

Women, in contrast, do not usually enter or leave at all except in the wake of men. The Miss Bingleys move with their brother; Lydia pursues the regiment; and Charlotte Lucas, Lydia, Elizabeth, and Jane all follow the men they marry. Lady Catherine's rude excursion to Meryton, Jane's visit to London, and Elizabeth's to

Hunsford and Derbyshire are seen as deviations from the more usual pattern of women's self-initiated activity, the movements back and forth within a small radius, 'the walks to Meryton, sometimes dirty and sometimes cold' (p. 143). So limited is women's usual movement – the walk to Meryton is only a mile – that a walk of three miles, at a rapid pace and without a companion, is an event. Indeed, women's usual state is not to move at all but to hear news or to read letters about the arrivals and departures of males. At most, perhaps, women look out of a window or throw up a sash, but they are essentially 'fixed', and it is not surprising that it is women in the novel who are dull or bored, who feel that the country is 'bare of news', who suffer when it rains, who repine at 'the dullness of everything', who feel 'forlorn' (pp. 25, 223, 311).

The patterns of movement in the novel do suggest a dramatic difference between the autonomy of women and men as the patterns of movement in *Evelina* do not. But they are finally background, like the fact that men work, and they are neither emphasised nor overthrown. It is in relation to the marriage choice that men's potential autonomy is brought most into conscious focus, and it is in relation to the marriage choice that their autonomy is also most emphatically subverted. As the first two sentences of the novel suggest, men do not need to marry. They may 'want' or desire wives, as it turns out, but they do not *need* to want them as women must want husbands. Men in *Pride and Prejudice*, therefore, are conscious of having the power to choose and they are fond of dwelling on it, of impressing it upon women. Mr Collins, for example, assumes that there is nothing so central to his proposal as a rehearsal of his 'reasons' for marrying – and for choosing a Bennet in particular – nothing quite so central as the information that there were 'many amiable young women' from whom he might have made his selection (pp. 101, 102).

Darcy is scarcely less agreeably aware of his power to choose, and from his first appearance he acts the role of high-class connoisseur, finding Elizabeth 'tolerable; but not handsome enough to tempt *me*' (p. 9). Like Mr Collins, moreover, Darcy remains preoccupied with the privilege of choice in the very act of proposing, for his first words are not 'I love you' but 'in vain have I struggled' (p. 178). Bingley, Colonel Fitzwilliam, and Wickham, the other single men in the novel, betray a similar consciousness. Bingley chooses his male friend over Jane. Fitzwilliam maintains that 'younger sons cannot marry where they like', but Elizabeth protests that they often choose to like and to propose to 'women of fortune' (p. 173). And Wickham, ever confident in his power to choose, first chooses Georgiana Darcy and then, in succession, Elizabeth Bennet, Mary King, and Lydia Bennet.

Male privilege, then, and access to money in particular, makes men feel autonomous. It also makes them feel empowered to control others, especially the women to whom they make advances. For, as givers of economic benefits, men expect their advances to be received and even sought after. Mr Collins dwells warmly upon the 'advantages that are in [his] power to offer' and tactfully reminds Elizabeth that she is bound to accept him, for '... it is by no means certain that another offer of marriage may ever be made you. Your portion is unhappily so small that it will in all likelihood undo the effects of your loveliness and amiable qualifications' (pp. 102, 104).

Darcy is also pleasantly aware of his power to bestow value, whether it is his desirable attention or his desirable fortune and station. At the first ball, for example, he will not dance with Elizabeth because he says he is in 'no humour at present to give consequence to young ladies who are slighted by other men' (p. 9). His first proposal – like Mr Collins' – is 'not more eloquent on the subject of tenderness than of pride', and it betrays his confidence in having his way: '[Elizabeth] could easily see that he had no doubt of a favourable answer. He *spoke* of apprehension and anxiety, but his countenance expressed real security' (p. 179).

Mr Bennet, too, seems to relish the power he has over women and to seek opportunities for its display. Aware of having wasted his power of choice by choosing Mrs Bennet, he is fond of reminding his wife and his daughters that he has control over their economic wellbeing: '[The letter] is from my cousin, Mr Collins, who, when I am dead, may turn you all out of this house as soon as he pleases' (p. 58). Indeed, with the possible exceptions of Bingley, who is seen as an anomaly, and of Mr Gardiner, who scarcely exists, virtually every man in the novel reacts in the same fashion to his economic privilege and social status as a male. All enjoy a mobility which women do not have. All relish an autonomy which women do not feel. All aspire to a mastery which women cannot grasp. And yet, in spite of their mobility, their sense of autonomy, and their desire to master and control, we do not feel that men are powerful in this novel. Their sense of power and their real pomposity are at base a setup, a preparation for poetic justice, a licence to enjoy the spectacle of men witlessly betraying their legacy of power, of men demonstrating impressive capacities for turning potential control into ineffective action and submission to the control of others.

It is significant, I think, that the only proposals of marriage recorded in the novel are unsuccessful and that both suitors are so immersed in their sense of control that they blindly offend the woman whose affections they mean to attach and, in the process, provoke what must be two of the most vigorous rejections in all literature. Here is Elizabeth to Mr Collins: 'You could not make *me* happy, and I am convinced that I am the last woman in the world who would make you so' (p. 103). And here is Elizabeth to Mr Darcy: 'I had not known you a month before I felt that you were the last man in the world whom I could ever be prevailed on to marry' (p. 182).[5] It is also significant that two of the men in the novel who have risen through preference – another benefit of male privilege – enjoy little more than an inflated *sense* of control and succeed mainly in annoying those whom they propose to act upon. Sir William, who has 'risen to the honour of knighthood' and retired to Meryton, 'where he could think with pleasure of his own importance', does no more than provoke Darcy when he attempts to claim his society (p. 15); Mr Collins may enjoy 'the consequential feelings of early and unexpected prosperity', and he may persuade Charlotte Lucas to marry him, but he is thwarted in his attempts to act upon Elizabeth, Darcy, Mr Bennet, and even Lydia and Kitty (p. 66).

Our sense of male control is also undercut by the comic readiness with which some men submit to the control of others. Mr Collins and Sir William both manifest such slavish admiration of those who have raised them or of those who stand above them in rank that their own imagined power is constantly and ironically juxtaposed with images of self-abasement: picture Sir William 'stationed in the doorway, in earnest contemplation of the greatness before him', or Collins carving, eating, and praising 'as if he felt that life could furnish nothing greater' (pp. 151, 154). Collins, moreover, qualifies his potential autonomy by submitting virtually every decision to the 'particular advice and recommendation' of Lady Catherine, and Bingley surrenders Jane because he depends on Darcy's opinion more strongly than on his own (p. 101). Men are also prone to misusing their autonomy by making bad investments. Mr Bennet's own imprudence must account for his unhappy domestic life, and Wickham's failure of resolution yokes him to Lydia, a giddy woman without a fortune. Thus access to money and male privilege in general do grant men the potential for control of their lives and for control over women, but, against the background of their real physical mobility, the men in

Pride and Prejudice are essentially set up – to surrender, to misuse, to fail to realise the power that is their cultural legacy.[6]

In obvious contrast to men, women, in their economic dependence, have far less potential to do as they like. Most women in the novel *must* marry, and, since access to money both shapes and is shaped by traditional attitudes toward women and their proper destiny, even women with money feel pressured to get a man (the rich Miss Bingley pursues Darcy, as does Lady Catherine on behalf of the wealthy Anne). Women, for the most part, do not dwell on their power to choose, do not debate over getting a husband, and seldom give thought to the value of one husband over another. Some young women, like Lydia and Kitty, are so engrossed with male regard in general that they lose sight of their reason for securing it, which is to marry, and make the attention of men – any men – an end in itself.

Indeed, the action in almost the entire first volume of the novel consists of very little but women talking or thinking or scheming about men. There is the initial plot to meet Bingley, then the first ball with its triumphs and failures. This is followed by a review of who was admired most, by a conversation between Elizabeth and Charlotte about how Jane had best pursue Bingley, by another scheme to keep Jane in Bingley's range at Netherfield, and by Miss Bingley's pursuit of Darcy at Netherfield itself. In the meantime we also hear that the militia have arrived and that Kitty and Lydia are well supplied with 'news and happiness' (p. 25). Wickham appears; Wickham is schemed over; and the whole first movement of the novel is brought to a close with another ball and another flourish of female display.[7]

The degree of female obsession with men, the degree to which they lack autonomy or self-control, may also be measured by the degree to which they helplessly and unthinkingly discount their ties to one another when a man's attention is at stake. Caroline Bingley, of course, is the most extreme example. Her abuse of Elizabeth is unrelenting, and her friendliness and her sister's friendliness to Jane wax and wane with the absence or restoration of male regard: '… when the gentlemen entered, Jane was no longer the first object' (p. 50). Even sisterly affection is tenuous where men are concerned. Kitty and Lydia set off to inquire about Captain Carter but not to visit the ailing Jane. Kitty can only weep 'from vexation and envy' when Lydia goes to Brighton, and Lydia herself is fond of twitting her sisters about having married before them (p. 298). So languid is one sister's interest in another that, when Bingley and Darcy dine away from Netherfield,

Caroline summons Jane on the grounds that 'a whole day's tête-à-tête between two women can never end without a quarrel' (p. 27).

Women in *Pride and Prejudice*, then, do not generally act like choosers, and, since they devote a good deal of energy to compulsive scheming and plotting, they obviously do not entertain illusions of easy control. What power women do aspire to is manipulative and indirect and is further diminished by the fact that obsession makes them ineffective and unreflecting. Mrs Bennet, for example, frustrates her own ends time and time again while entertaining 'the delightful persuasion' that she is promoting Jane's marriage (p. 99). Miss Bingley's pathetic snares entangle not Darcy but herself. Mary's eagerness for display blinds her to the embarrassment of her 'pedantic air', and Lydia's passion for the attentions of a charming male wins her a husband who must be bribed to marry her and whose affection for her 'soon sunk into indifference' (pp. 22, 366).

It is important to note, however, that we are not just speaking of the Mrs Bennets, the Carolines, the Lydias, and the Marys, for all young women in the novel are caught to some degree in the same currents, and this enforces our sense of a universal female condition. All the Bennet women spend a good part of one evening conjecturing about Bingley and 'determining when they should ask him to dinner' (p. 6). All are pleased with their own or with each other's triumphs. All are bored by the 'interval of waiting' for the gentlemen, and the prospect of the Netherfield ball is 'extremely agreeable to every female of the family' (pp. 72, 92). Our first introduction to Elizabeth, in fact, finds her trimming a hat.

Women, like men, therefore appear to be determined almost uniformly by a shared economic and social condition, but, just as we are not permitted to feel that men's economic privilege necessitates power, so are we not permitted to feel that women's lack of privilege necessitates powerlessness. The first two sentences of the novel may emphasise the idea that women's compulsive husband hunting has an economic base, but we are never allowed to *feel* that base as a determining force in their experience. As I have suggested, almost every reference in the novel to economic necessity is relegated to Mrs Bennet, a woman whose worries we are not allowed to take seriously because they are continually undermined by their link with the comic and the absurd: '... Miss Lizzy, if you take it into your head to go on refusing every offer of marriage in this way, you will never get a husband at all – and I am sure I do not know who is to maintain you when your father is dead' (pp. 108–9). This is the kind of financial

threat which would be taken seriously in a novel by Charlotte
Brontë, but in *Pride and Prejudice* this threat, this sting of potential
poverty, is undercut. There is consciousness of economics, to be sure,
but that consciousness is raised and then subverted.[8] This is an odd
manoeuvre on the part of an author sometimes praised for her
awareness of social and economic forces, but it serves a purpose as
preparation for Elizabeth by defining the nature of Elizabeth's world.

The Charlotte Lucas episode is especially significant in this light,
for at a distance it might suggest that economic forces do indeed
have tragic domination over 'sensible, intelligent' young women
(p. 15). But once again this is not what we are actually invited to
feel. We are not allowed to dwell on the economic realities of
Charlotte's situation, because the shifting ironies almost continually direct us elsewhere: we look with irony at Mr Collins, for
example, or at Charlotte's family, or at Charlotte herself. When her
economic considerations *are* introduced, they are introduced ironically and at her expense: 'Miss Lucas ... accepted him solely from
the pure and disinterested desire of an establishment' (p. 117).

If we feel sympathy for Charlotte at any point, we first do so
when her family dwells on the economic and social advantages of
the match and gives no thought at all to her personal happiness. To
Sir William and Lady Lucas the fulsome Mr Collins is 'a most eligible match for their daughter, to whom they could give little fortune' (p. 117). Charlotte's brothers are relieved of their fear that
she will become a financial burden, 'an old maid', and her younger
sisters 'formed hopes of *coming out* a year or two sooner', in order
we presume to strike their own marital bargains (p. 118). But these
ironies still do not put us in contact with her economic necessities.
They may expose the selfishness and money-mindedness of
Charlotte's relations, but if anything the suggestion that Charlotte's
family is overly concerned with money puts us at a greater distance
from any real sense of Charlotte's economic needs.

It is in the paragraph on Charlotte's own reflections that we come
closest to seeing her as the victim of those economic and social
forces which tend to reduce genteel unmarried women to the status
of merchandise:

> Without thinking highly either of men or of matrimony, marriage
> had always been her object; it was the only honourable provision
> for well-educated young women of small fortune, and however
> uncertain of giving happiness, must be their pleasantest preservation

from want. This preservative she had now obtained; and at the age of twenty-seven, without having ever been handsome, she felt all the good luck of it.

(p. 118)

The reference here to marriage as the 'only honourable provision' evokes a strong pull of sympathy for Charlotte but, coming as it does in the midst of her other reflections, it is not entirely clear to what extent the narrator joins her in this point of view. The extent to which we *can* feel the authority of this reference is the extent to which we will feel the force of economic necessity in Charlotte's decision, but the authority of the reference is never clear.

Elizabeth's own judgement lays the blame for Charlotte's decision on Charlotte's perversity: 'She had always felt that Charlotte's opinion of matrimony was not exactly like her own, but she could not have supposed it possible that when called into action she would have sacrificed every better feeling to worldly advantage' (p. 121). Yet the extent to which Elizabeth's judgement has narrative authority is also cloudy. Certainly, Elizabeth can be accused of speaking from fear, fear that Charlotte's example is a portent of her own fate as a single woman of small fortune. And certainly Elizabeth is inconsistent, for she defends Wickham for the same behaviour with Mary King. If we see Charlotte with irony, we see Elizabeth with irony too, and ultimately the narrator abandons us to ambivalence. The Charlotte Lucas episode, on the whole, is left to suggest, on the one hand, the perverting force of women's economic lot and to prevent us, on the other, from feeling that force as a reality in the universe of Elizabeth Bennet.[9]

One effect of undermining the force of economic realities is to make most women, in their helpless fixation on men and marriage, look perverse or merely silly and to lay the blame on women themselves, not on their economic and social lot. Another effect, however, is to suggest, rather wishfully, that there is some way out. Men may go about acting more powerful than women – indeed, their lot in life may give them the potential for having power – but because a sense of power seems to befuddle critical vision they are not really powerful at all. Conversely, women may seem powerless as men are not, but because we are finally not to *feel* that they are victims of social and economic forces they do not have to be powerless after all. What we have in *Pride and Prejudice*, it seems, is a novel that recognises the shaping influence of economics but that denies its force. The novel, in fact, all but levels what in life we know to have been the material base of power and powerlessness and defines real power as something separate from the economic.

III

Real power in *Pride and Prejudice*, as is often observed, involves having the intelligence, the wit, and the critical attitudes of Jane Austen; and Elizabeth Bennet, as it is also sometimes observed, is essentially an Austen fantasy, a fantasy of power.[10] As a fantasy, of course, Austen's Elizabeth is to some extent like Burney's Evelina; the nature of her power is traditional and womanly; it is the power of autonomy and, specifically, the power of private opinion and self-defence. Elizabeth's opinions, however, are not so private as Evelina's. They are not confined to letters, nor, as a matter of fact, are they confined to novels. For Elizabeth's world, as created by Jane Austen, affords her a freedom which Austen's world evidently did not. It affords her scope not only to entertain critical attitudes but to express them with energy and to put them into effective action. Elizabeth can do more than quietly scorn Miss Bingley's eagerness to please Darcy – she can laugh out loud at Jane's gratitude for being admired, and she can reject outright Charlotte's schemes for securing a husband. She can put herself at some distance from gratefulness, scheming, and overeagerness to please men, and in the process she can also be rather direct and effective in challenging Darcy's traditional assumption of control as a ruling-class man.

Elizabeth's world, in contrast to Austen's, permits her something more than spiritual victories, permits her more than that *sense* of autonomy which comes with wittily observing the confinements of one's situation, with standing apart from them in spirit while having to bend to them in daily behaviour. It permits her not only the energetic expression of but also the forceful use of those critical energies which Austen herself diverted into novels and which Evelina confines, more or less, to correspondence. Austen's fantasy of female autonomy is far more rebellious, then, than Fanny Burney's, for Elizabeth's autonomy, although a version of those 'private opinions' which even 'yoked creatures' entertain, is still a version which allows them rather free expression and, most important, which allows them to modify the power relations in Elizabeth's world.

If in *Evelina* the most central expression of power is that of landed male control, in *Pride and Prejudice* the most prominent form of power is that of female autonomy, and it is not implausible to see in this distance between Burney and Austen an expression of the changing social context. Austen, for example, in allowing female autonomy to work effectively against a ruling-class male – a use of power entirely foreign to *Evelina* – evokes a more general sense that the authority of landed males had been challenged if not actually mitigated. In her endorsement of an autonomy not tied to class or fortune, Austen also reveals some affinity with an individualism that had ties to the French and the Industrial revolutions. This individualism is usually identified as middle-class and, by implication too, as male, and it is usually discussed in its economic application. Eric Hobsbawm, for example, sees 'individualist competition, the "career open to talent", and the triumph of merit over birth and connexion' as a significant result of the dual revolutions, but the 'career open to talent' is a concept which applies only to men and for the most part to men of the middle class.[11] John Owen also refers to the early nineteenth century as a 'new era of individualism and *laissez-faire*', another definition of 'individualism' which emphasises the growing economic privileges of middle-class men.[12] And Ian Watt, in his discussion of 'individualism and the novel', focuses upon 'economic individualism' as represented in the 'economic man' – although in this case 'economic man' includes Moll Flanders, a low-life female.[13]

The individualism or autonomy of Austen's heroine, however, is adapted to the purposes of a genteel unmarried woman. It is not expressed, therefore, through economic achievement, as it might be in a male, nor is it expressed through grand actions upon the world. It is an individualism, moreover, that cannot really be defined as middle-class or anti-gentry, for it is tied less to Austen's class sympathies than to her partially articulated feelings as a woman – the energy of Elizabeth's critical opinions, for example, is directed against men of middle stations, like Collins and Wickham, not just against the upper-class Darcy. Elizabeth's individualism, that is, is often directed against those very men of the middle stations, those men rising in careers, who conventionally define for us what individualism means. Austen's adaptation of individualism is thus more feminist than middle-class, for it is a disguised expression of discontent with the growing division in money, status, and power between middle-class men and middle-class women.

Elizabeth's autonomy, then, expresses an individualism adapted to female use, but because it is so adapted it is also heavily qualified and disguised, much as Evelina's far less developed powers are qualified and disguised by Fanny Burney. And the most potent qualification of Elizabeth's autonomy lies in the nature of the fictional world that Austen has created on her behalf. That we enjoy Elizabeth's critical energies as we do, that we feel safe with them, and that generations of conventional readers have found her charming rather than reckless owe much to the fact that Austen's version of Elizabeth's universe is one which mitigates the punishing potential of her critical views and challenging behaviour. If money, for example, were really a force in the novel, we might find Elizabeth heedless, radical, or at best naïve for insulting and rejecting a man with £10,000 a year, for condemning her best friend, a plain and portionless twenty-seven-year-old, because she married a man who could support her in comfort. In similar fashion, if wealthy young men were less given to bungling and dissipating the autonomy and control that are their legacy, we might feel uncomfortable or incredulous when Elizabeth takes on Darcy. It is Austen's subversion of economic realities and of male power that permits us to enjoy Elizabeth's rebellious exuberance, because it is principally this subversion which limits, from the outset, the extent to which we feel Elizabeth is in conflict with the forces of her world.

But to allow a nineteenth-century heroine to get away with being critical and challenging – especially about male control and feminine submission – is still to rebel against ideology and dominant social relations, no matter how charmingly that heroine may be represented, no matter how safe her rebellion is made to appear. When Austen allows Elizabeth to express critical attitudes and to act upon them without penalty, she is moving against early nineteenth-century ideologies about feminine behaviour and feminine fate, for by any traditional standards Elizabeth's departures from convention ought to earn her a life of spinsterhood, not a man, a carriage, and £10,000 a year. Elizabeth's universe, moreover, is real enough – its economic and social forces are kept close enough to the surface – that we believe in it and do not dismiss it as fantasy. And Elizabeth herself is so convincing that we can't dismiss her either. For all its charm and relative safety, Elizabeth's rebellion invites us to take it seriously, and it is for this reason, I assume, that the rebelliousness of *Pride and Prejudice*, like the rebelliousness of most women's writing, is even further qualified.

One major qualification of Elizabeth's resistance to male control, to men's assumption of control, and to women's submissive behaviour is that, like Austen, she accepts the basic division in men's and women's economic lots. Men have a right to money that women do not. Thus Wickham is prudent for pursuing Mary King, but Charlotte is mercenary for marrying Collins. Men also have a right to greater autonomy, to greater power of choice, for Elizabeth never does challenge Darcy's ideologically justified right to criticise women or to act the connoisseur. Nor is it entirely clear that she objects to men's general assumption of control over women. Her real aim is self-defence; she wants to resist intimidation and to deny Darcy's particular assumption of control over her, a control which he exercises through the expression of critical judgements: 'He has a very satirical eye, and if I do not begin by being impertinent myself, I shall soon grow afraid of him' (p. 21).

Elizabeth's habitual tactic with Darcy is to anticipate and to deflate him in the role of critic and chooser but never to challenge the privilege by which he is either one. One of her manoeuvres is to insinuate her own judgement before Darcy can deliver his: 'Did not you think, Mr Darcy, that I expressed myself uncommonly well just now ...' (p. 21). Another is to deprive him of the opportunity to judge at all: '... he means to be severe on us, and our surest way of disappointing him, will be to ask nothing about it' (p. 52). And still another is to defy him outright: '... despise me if you dare' (p. 48). Elizabeth's witty portraits of Darcy are also designed to cast doubt upon his reliability as critic but not upon his right to criticise. Darcy's pride and his alleged indifference to friendship, for example, must make him overly harsh and therefore untrustworthy in his judgements: 'And *your* defect is a propensity to hate every body' (p. 54).

Elizabeth, of course, in defending herself against the controlling power of Darcy's negative judgements, suggests that she is also defending herself against a desire to please Darcy and to enjoy the benefit of his positive attentions. Her defence, that is, continually implies an underlying vulnerability to his good opinion, and this is another qualification of her autonomy. Elizabeth never challenges the privilege by which Darcy bestows benefit through his regard, never entirely denies the benefit he does bestow, and is never wholly immune to enjoying it. She merely tries to avoid responding to his attentions with that show of gratefulness and pleasure which he egoistically expects and which her own feelings indeed prompt in her. At Netherfield, when Darcy asks her to dance, she is at first 'amazed at the dignity to which she [had] arrived', but her overriding defensive purpose is to deny both to herself and to him that the occasion affords her any sense of status or pleasure (p. 86). It is evident, then, that Elizabeth's resistance to Darcy is undermined by a lingering susceptibility to his attentions and by a lingering desire to please. In fact, the very energy with which she defends herself against both pleasing and being pleased argues that she is not only vulnerable to Darcy's power over her feelings but ironically and defensively controlled by it.

Elizabeth's qualified opposition to being controlled by one attractive male is juxtaposed, moreover, with her complete vulnerability to the emotional control of another, for she succumbs to pleasing Wickham and being flattered by him even before he reveals himself as an ally. Indeed, Elizabeth's readiness to believe Wickham is partially explained by the fact that, like all the young women in the novel, she is ready to approve any attractive and charming man who pays her attention, to decide absurdly that his 'very countenance may vouch for [his] being amiable' (p. 77). Elizabeth's head is full not only of what Wickham tells her about Darcy but of Wickham himself, and in dressing for the Netherfield ball she thinks both of 'seeing a confirmation of every thing in Mr Darcy's looks and behaviour' and of conquering 'all that remained unsubdued of [Wickham's] heart' (pp. 80, 85). Even after Wickham has thrown her over for Mary King, or Mary King's fortune, she continues to be flattered by 'a solicitude, an interest which she felt must ever attach her to him with a most sincere regard' (p. 144).

As it turns out, of course, Elizabeth is not only not autonomous with Darcy and Wickham, she is mistaken and wrong. She is wrong about Darcy's intentions, and she is wrong about Wickham's, and she is wrong for the same reason that she is not self-directing. Despite her intelligence, wit, and critical energies, she cares too much about male regard.[14] As she herself is aware, after reading Darcy's letter, it is her 'vanity', her vulnerability to the good opinion of men, that has blinded her both to Darcy's character and to Wickham's:

> But vanity, not love, has been my folly. Pleased with the preference of one, and offended by the neglect of the other, on the very beginning of our acquaintance, I have courted prepossession and ignorance, and driven reason away, where either were concerned.
>
> (p. 196)

If there is any punch left in Elizabeth's resistance to Darcy's traditional assumptions of control, it is certainly diminished by our continuing awareness that the rebellion itself works in the interests of tradition. That is, Elizabeth's assertion of autonomy attracts Darcy rather than putting him off. Elizabeth, we are assured, has a 'mixture of sweetness and archness in her manner which made it difficult for her to affront anybody; and Darcy had never been so bewitched by any woman as he was by her' (p. 48). Heightened aggression on Elizabeth's part is met by heightened feeling on Darcy's, by greater fears of 'the danger of paying Elizabeth too much attention' (p. 54). Thus we may enjoy Elizabeth's self-assertions, but we are never invited to value them in themselves, as we are invited by later novelists to value Jane Eyre's or Lucy Snowe's or Maggie Tulliver's. Elizabeth's qualified resistance to Darcy, attractive as relief from the extreme male centring of most women in the novel, is valued in great measure, nevertheless, because it attracts the attention of a desirable man.

Elizabeth's autonomy, then, is quiet, is not intended to alarm. It invites the conventional female reader to identify with unconventional energies but commits her to nothing more, and it permits the conventional male reader to admire Elizabeth's spirit while finding comfort in the fact that she is wrong, that she is not autonomous after all, and that her whole resistance to male control only secures and gives value to the love of a good man. It is as if Austen could not be indirect or qualified enough in presenting this self-assertive heroine, for we almost never focus on Elizabeth's rebellious energies without feeling the undermining force of one irony or another. It is, in fact, Austen's qualification of Elizabeth's power that accounts for most of the complexities and ironies in the first two-thirds of the novel, and it is these ironies, I suspect, that have permitted the most conventional readers to find Elizabeth charming – and most charming of all when she asserts her independence of Darcy's traditional control as a male.

As a power fantasy, Elizabeth is in some ways astoundingly modest. The remarkable thing, perhaps, is that her rebelliousness, undercut and qualified as it is, still maintains a quality of force, still strikes us as power. It does so in part because of its juxtaposition with Miss Bingley's ineffective machinations and Jane's well-intentioned passivity, both reminders of what it means to be traditionally feminine. And in part, too, Elizabeth's rebellious energies retain a quality of force because they really act upon her world; they change Darcy, change the way he responds to his economic and social privileges, change something basic to the power relation between him and Elizabeth. Without intending to, Elizabeth exercises influence over Darcy, renders him more courtly, less liable to impress upon her the power he has to choose and to give her benefits, and less liable to assume control of her feelings. Evelina, in contrast, must depend upon the purely voluntary goodness of Lord Orville.

Still, neither Elizabeth's much qualified self-defence nor even her unintended influence over Darcy establishes her as the powerful character she is. The most profound source of what we feel as Elizabeth's power is her ability – in the last third of the novel – to turn her critical vision upon herself, upon her own unthinking vulnerability to male approval. It is at this point in the novel that Elizabeth establishes what we could call real autonomy. It is at this point, moreover – the point at which Elizabeth redirects her critical energies from Darcy to herself – that the multiple ironies which have characterised the first two-thirds of the novel are suddenly dropped. It is a less anxiety-provoking business for a woman to assert autonomy against an aspect of herself, against the enemy within, than against the traditional power relations of her culture. And though it is necessary and vital to assess one's own blindness, in a patriarchal society, this is also a much surer and more lasting form of power than pitting one's self against the traditional privileges of men.

Elizabeth's recognition of her vulnerability to male attention does force her, however, into painful and even humiliating recognitions. It is a hard thing for a woman who has felt herself defended against the control of a ruling-class man to discover, after all, that she has been led astray by her extreme vulnerability to his good opinion. It is humiliating to feel apologetic toward an oppressor – for Darcy has greater control than Elizabeth and has made her feel it. Why has Austen put her through this? One answer, perhaps, is that Elizabeth's recognition of her 'vanity' further undercuts her rebellion against male control. But her confessions may also be seen as a hard lesson in the difficulties of confronting the enemy within, a hard lesson in the fact that the most apparently autonomous women may be creatures of their culture too.

This lesson is especially painful and realistic because, despite Austen's ironic underminings, the force of Elizabeth's community is strongly felt. But in this novel, in contrast say to Charlotte Brontë's *Villette*, the shaping force of community is evoked only to be dramatically overthrown. The degree to which Elizabeth has been immersed in the values and mystifications of her community is the degree to which we feel that she is powerful when she separates herself from both.

IV

Pride and Prejudice brings to a culmination the kind of quest plot which is only initiated and then dropped in *Evelina*, for by the end of this novel the heroine has achieved real autonomy and self-direction; indeed, no other character in the novel achieves her measure of self-knowledge or potential self-rule. The self-knowledge which comes to Darcy comes to him offstage and at the instigation of Elizabeth. Elizabeth alone is her own analyst and, in a novel where Austen brilliantly arranges for intelligence to mitigate the forces of economics and social position, Elizabeth emerges for the readers as the most powerful because the most intelligent and self-directing character in the novel. But if, in reading Darcy's letter, Elizabeth gains a measure of real autonomy, in that she gains a measure of freedom from the unthinking desire for male regard, what Elizabeth's freedom finally purchases is an ability to consider, to weigh, to choose which male's regard she really values. Elizabeth's autonomy, that is, frees her to choose Darcy, and her untraditional power is rewarded not with some different life but with woman's traditional life, with love and marriage. Quest in this novel is partly justified by and then rewarded with love.

The economic contradiction of men's and women's lives, the paucity of options for genteel women at the time, the weight of ideology as expressed in life and fiction permit Austen no other happy ending, but there is of course a major difficulty in Elizabeth's reward. For marriage in this novel, as in life, involves a power relation between unequals, and that is hardly a fitting end for a fantasy of power. What we find at the end of *Pride and Prejudice*, therefore, is a complicated and not entirely successful juggling act in which all the economic privilege and social authority of the traditional husband-hero must be demonstrated at last but demonstrated without diminishing the autonomy of the heroine.

It is not until late in the novel, for example, not until Elizabeth rejects Darcy's proposal, reads his letter, and establishes herself as the most powerful character in the book, that we are permitted firsthand exposure to Darcy's economic and social significance. Only at Pemberley, for example, are we made to *feel* the reality of his authority to act upon the world: 'As a brother, a landlord, a master, she considered ... How much of pleasure or pain it was in his power to bestow' (p. 234). Darcy's authority, moreover, is juxtaposed on this visit with the first signs that he has been influenced by Elizabeth's self-assertion: 'Never in her life had she seen his manners so little dignified, never had he spoken with such gentleness as on this unexpected meeting' (p. 235).

Darcy's rescue of Lydia is another demonstration of the hero's traditional authority, the authority belonging to money, class, and male privilege, but it is also to be construed as further demonstration that Elizabeth has influenced him, that he is more courtly not only to her but to her family, whom he is now not above serving. Darcy's second proposal, moreover, is brought on by still another spirited assertion of Elizabeth's autonomy, her refusal to conciliate Lady Catherine, and even the timing of this proposal scene is set by Elizabeth. The proposal itself, finally, is followed by Darcy's lengthy reminder that it is Elizabeth who has changed him: 'You taught me a lesson, hard indeed at first but most advantageous. By you I was properly humbled' (p. 349).

But it 'will never do' for Elizabeth to seem more powerful than Darcy (p. 361). That is not what traditional marriages, what 'good' marriages, are all about. According to Mr Bennet, in fact, Elizabeth 'could be neither happy nor respectable unless [she] truly esteemed [her] husband, unless [she] looked up to him as a superior' (p. 356). Darcy must protest, then, that he would have proposed whether Elizabeth opened the way or not: 'I was not in a humour to wait for any opening of yours' (p. 361). And Elizabeth, for her part, must betray some consciousness of and gratefulness for the traditional economic and social benefits. She must appreciate Pemberley not just for the good taste that it exhibits but for its economic grandeur,[15] for the 'very large' park and for the 'lofty and handsome' rooms (pp. 228, 229). She must acknowledge that to be mistress of Pemberley might be 'something', and she must experience 'gratitude' to Darcy for loving her (pp. 228, 248). Yet Elizabeth's own autonomy must not be diminished. She is allowed, therefore, to see more than Darcy does to the last:[16] 'She remembered that he had yet to learn to be laughed at, and it was rather too early to begin' (p. 351). We leave her, in fact, in the last paragraph of the novel, surrounded by Pemberley's splendour but seeming to hold her own, astonishing Georgiana with her 'lively, sportive manner' and her 'open pleasantry' and persuading Darcy, against his will, to make peace with Lady Catherine (p. 367).

Austen's difficulties with Elizabeth's reward, her attempt to give her marriage but to alter what marriage means, her attempt to balance love and quest, her tinkering with heroine and hero must account for the fact that most readers of *Pride and Prejudice* find the end less satisfactory than the beginning. On the one hand, the charge that Elizabeth, as witty heroine, is now too inclined to moralise and be grateful owes much to the fact that marriage requires her to dwindle by degrees into a wife. On the other hand, the observation that Darcy as hero is less convincing than as villain owes much to the requirements of Austen's fantasy, which are that Elizabeth not dwindle too far, that she maintain her equality with if not her ascendancy over her husband.[17] Darcy, therefore, though he must demonstrate all the economic privilege and social authority of the traditional hero – which are plenty – may not have everything; he may not have Pemberley, £10,000 a year, rank, looks, intelligence, flexibility, wit, and a convincing reality as well. There is some point, though an unconscious point, to his stiffness and unreality, for both function at some level to preserve the fantasy of Elizabeth's power.

The end of *Pride and Prejudice*, nevertheless, witnesses a decline in Elizabeth Bennet, for in *Pride and Prejudice* as in much of women's fiction the end, the reward, of woman's apprenticeship to life is marriage, and marriage demands resignation even as it prompts rejoicing, initiates new life while it confirms a flickering suspicion that the best is over. Given the ambivalent blessing of marriage as a happy ending, it is a tribute to Austen's genius that what we take from *Pride and Prejudice* is not a sense of Elizabeth's untimely decline but a tonic impression of her intelligence, her wit, and her power, and it is an even greater tribute that we believe in her power, that we do not perceive it as fantasy. For Austen's brilliant construction of her heroine's world, her recognition and subtle subversion of economic forces, the mobile intelligence of the heroine herself, the ironies directed at that intelligence, the complexities of Elizabeth's failure in vision and of her recovery complicate what is at base a wish fulfilment, give it an air of credibility which lends force to the spell of the fantasy upon us.

As one of my students put it, we need more fantasies like Elizabeth.

From Judith Lowder Newton, *Women, Power and Subversion: Social Strategies in British Fiction, 1778–1860* (Athens, Ga., 1981), pp. 55–85.

NOTES

[Judith Newton's *Women, Power and Subversion* shares with Mary Poovey's essays above a concern with the way in which fictions by women deal with patriarchal ideology. She recognises that Jane Austen's novels can be read as supporting the conservative view of women's role as ideally that of wife and moral guardian, and that the romance of *Pride and Prejudice* works as a compensatory fantasy for women's impotence. However, she observes that because the fantasy represents women as important, competent, intelligent, and well aware of their situation, the fantasy subverts patriarchal ideas of women as passive, emotional and incompetent. The triumph of Elizabeth Bennet redefines power in terms of intellectual ability – precisely the area where Austen and other women could compete as equals. This redefinition depends upon the fiction not representing the full extent of economic, legal and political subjugation, but the productive value of the fantasy cannot be denied and Jane Austen's fictions do represent women's lives as dominated by the marriage market. Her women characters spend their time scheming and competing to obtain control over men who are represented as absurd and bungling. Elizabeth Bennet's marriage to Darcy is, for Newton, a sad necessity of the genre, but whilst her dwindling to the role of submissive wife is politically retrograde, the image that readers carry away from the text is of the light, bright and sparkling heroine who was more than a match for any man around, and who compelled a man with money and power to set aside his prejudices and offer her all. Such a fantasy may be compensatory to women readers whose life experience is probably in total contradiction, but the fantasy invites women to be like Elizabeth and not feel abashed before patriarchal oppression. References to *Pride and Prejudice* which appear in the text are to the Rhinehart edition (New York, 1949). Ed.]

1. See Eric J. Hobsbawm's chapter, 'The Career Open to Talent', *Age of Revolution, 1789–1848* (New York, 1962), p. 226 and see Ivy Pinchbeck, *Women Workers and the Industrial Revolution, 1750–1850* (New York, 1969), p. 315.

2. Jane Austen, letter to Frank Austen, 3 July 1813, letter 8.1, in *Jane Austen's Letters to Her Sister Cassandra and Others*, ed. R. W. Chapman (London, 1959), p. 317.

3. Ibid., pp. 306–10, 328, 326, 321, 352, 361, 367.

4. Ibid., p. 141.

5. Douglas Bush suggests that rejected proposals 'have more dramatic possibilities than happy acceptances', but the 'dramatic possibilities', I feel, tend to one end – the deflation of male power. See *Jane Austen* (New York, 1975), p. 95.

6. Critics such as Frank W. Bradbrook and Kenneth Moler have observed that Darcy is set up to be deflated, that he is in fact a caricature of the Burney–Richardson hero, but the character of Darcy also reflects a larger tendency in the novel to set up and subvert male power in general. See Bradbrook, *Jane Austen and Her Predecessors* (Cambridge, 1966), p. 97; Moler, *Jane Austen's Art of Allusion* (Lincoln, 1968), p. 89.

7. See Nina Auerbach's fine chapter on *Pride and Prejudice*: 'The unexpressed intensity of this collective waiting for the door to open and a Pygmalion to bring life into limbo defines the female world of *Pride*

and Prejudice.' Communities of Women: An Idea in Fiction (Cambridge, Mass., 1978), p. 39.

8. Though see Auerbach on the way in which the Bennet women's economic invisibility is subtly expressed in the 'near invisibility of Longbourn and the collective life of the Bennets within'. Ibid., p. 42.

9. It is hardly surprising that readers of *Pride and Prejudice* are widely divergent in their assessment of the Charlotte Lucas episode. A few, for example, sympathise with Charlotte and see her, more or less, as a victim of economic and social necessity. See David Daiches, 'Jane Austen, Karl Marx and the Aristocratic Dance', *American Scholar*, 17 (1947–8), 289; and see Mark Schorer, 'Pride Unprejudiced', *Kenyon Review*, 18 (1956), 83, 85. On the other end of the spectrum, many critics are inclined to see Charlotte as a rather simple example of moral or intellectual perversity. See W. A. Craik, *Jane Austen: the Six Novels* (London, 1965), p. 65, and Jane Nardin, *Those Elegant Decorums: The Concept of Propriety in Jane Austen's Novels* (Albany, 1973), p. 51.

10. Several critics observe elements, at least, of wish fulfilment or self-projection in Austen's heroines. See, for example, Yasmine Gooneratne, *Jane Austen* (Cambridge, 1970), p. 95.

11. Hobsbawn, *Age of Revolution*, p. 218.

12. John B. Owen, *The Eighteenth Century, 1714–1815* (Totowa, NJ, 1962), p. 314.

13. Ian Watt, *Rise of the Novel* (Berkeley, 1962), p. 61.

14. See Auerbach on the safety of being 'partial, prejudiced, and ignorant. Objectivity, impartiality and knowledge might endanger the cloak of invisibility which is so intrinsic a part of Austen's perception of a woman's life'. *Communities of Women*, p. 54.

15. See Auerbach's description of Pemberley's 'architectural and natural power'. Ibid., p. 44.

16. While it is true, as Gilbert and Gubar maintain, that Austen's stories dramatise 'the necessity of female submission for female survival', the end of *Pride and Prejudice* is managed so as to mitigate the degree to which the heroine must submit. Sandra Gilbert and Susan Gubar, *The Madwoman in the Attic: the Woman Writer and the Nineteenth Century Literary Imagination* (New Haven, 1979), p. 154.

17. Several critics note that Darcy is more convincing as villain than as hero. See, for example, Henrietta Ten Harmsel, *Jane Austen: A Study in Fictional Conventions* (The Hague, 1964), p. 81. And Kenneth Moler, for one, finds Elizabeth becoming more and more like the conventional Evelina; see *Austen's Art of Allusion*, p. 107. See also Nina Auerbach's treatment of Darcy's 'shadowy reality', in *Communities of Women*, p. 53.

8

Necessary Conjunctions

JULIA PREWITT BROWN

Certain moments in literature always surprise us, no matter how many times we encounter them. One such moment is Cordelia's response to Lear, 'Nothing', in the first act of the tragedy. Another is the opening sentence of *Pride and Prejudice*: 'It is a truth universally acknowledged, that a single man in possession of a good fortune must be in want of a wife' (p. 3). Like Cordelia's unexpected reply, Austen's claim is surprising because we do not know how to interpret it. Is Cordelia's answer faint or firm, resigned or defiant? In the atmosphere of Lear's complex vanities, its stark simplicity makes it ambiguous. Similarly, the opening claim of *Pride and Prejudice* is either an instance of unalloyed irony or comic hyperbole. Read ironically, it means a great deal more than it says; read comically, it means a great deal less. Because its targets are unknown, its assurance is baffling. No matter how we read it, its finality is its irony (or comedy); it holds its 'truth' and the resistance to its truth in one – the quintessential stance of the ironic comedies.

Such instances are very few and brief in Jane Austen. They constitute a direct address from the author to the reader. They dazzle us partly because they are infrequent, and they provide in their flashing ambiguity a highly concentrated version of the novelist's perspective. The discourse of the rest of *Pride and Prejudice* issues from this initial stance and falls into two broad categories, narrative and dialogue. Perceived together, as they are meant to be perceived, the narrative and the dialogue achieve the same brilliant ambiguity of the authorial voice. Consider the first appearance of narrative comment in the novel, at the close of chapter 1:

> Mr Bennet was so odd a mixture of quick parts, sarcastic humour, reserve, and caprice, that the experience of three and twenty years had been insufficient to make his wife understand his character. *Her* mind was less difficult to develop. She was a woman of mean understanding, little information, and uncertain temper. When she was discontented she fancied herself nervous. The business of her life was to get her daughters married; its solace was visiting and news.
>
> (p. 5)

Considered in isolation, the passage seems objective, informative, and unambiguous. Yet when read as the conclusion of the following dialogue, the passage achieves a different resonance:

> 'My dear Mr Bennet', said his lady to him one day, 'have you heard that Netherfield is let at last?' Mr Bennet replied that he had not.
> 'But it is', returned she; 'for Mrs Long has just been here, and she told me all about it.'
> Mr Bennet made no answer.
> 'Do not you want to know who has taken it?' cried his wife impatiently.
> '*You* want to tell me, and I have no objection to hearing it.'
> This was invitation enough.
>
> (p. 3)

Here we have a world of opinion and report, and one in which the effect of an event takes the place of the event itself. Neither time nor place is specified except as 'day' and 'neighbourhood'. We have only the disembodied voices of wife and husband clashing in an empty space, and ricocheting back in the form of countless amplifying ironies to the novel's opening statement. The sensibility of the dialogue is ephemeral, irrational, opinionated; it is a precarious world indeed to be followed by such stable, definitive evaluations as 'She was a woman of mean understanding' or such simplistic understatements as 'Her mind was less difficult to develop'. This ostensibly objective narrative voice is true as far as it goes. It is true because its evaluations are, as evaluations, correct and useful. They are the necessary simplifications we live by, and the Bennets live by, for the paragraph reveals each as seen by the other.

Yet these evaluations cannot be mistaken for life itself, and Jane Austen knows they cannot. When Elizabeth returns from visiting Mr and Mrs Collins and her mother asks whether they 'do not often talk of having Longbourn when your father is dead', we are surprised. We are required once again to acknowledge the audacity and variety and complexity of this woman's 'mean understanding'.

The cadence of moral rationalism, the abstract, judgemental sensibility revealed in such statements as 'mean understanding, little information, and uncertain temper' are always checked by action and dialogue. Through the careful juxtaposition of narrative and dialogue, Austen prevents us from investing everything in such statements.

Elizabeth too must learn that simplifications are dangerous; both she and Darcy insist on what is only provisional and half-true as final. Of her complacent division of humanity into intricate and simple characters, for example, Elizabeth comes to say, 'The more I see of the world, the more am I dissatisfied with it; and every day confirms my belief of the inconsistency of all human characters, and of the little dependence that can be placed on the appearance of either merit or sense' (p. 135). The irony of the novel's opening sentence lies in its assurance in simplification and generalisation, its insistence that the local perception is universal, absolute, permanent. We simplify our world in order to live in it; and Austen (like Sterne) keeps telling us we do. *Pride and Prejudice* is an exhilarating work because it turns us back continually on life by showing us the failure of language and the individual mind to capture life's unexpectedness. And beneath the exhilaration lies an affection for the bizarre actuality of things. The opening hyperbole, for example, contains an element of eccentric delight in human exaggeration.

The narrative voice, then, provides some limit, some barrier, which the action strives ceaselessly (and successfully) to overcome. The narrator's provision of certitude, despite its accuracy, is temporary. Nevertheless, its role in the novel is of vital importance. Indeed, without the narrative voice, the moral structure of the novel would crumble. The terms of order in the novel are defined by the narrative voice, just as the terms of anarchy are defined by dialogue and action. In this respect, Austen works in a way similar to that of George Eliot. Eliot's compassionate narrative voice is used both to reprimand and to redeem the failing world of Middlemarch. Austen's rational narrative voice is used both to abuse and applaud the evasions of humankind – abuse the cruelties and applaud the abundance. Only through the careful and complex juxtaposition of action and narrative does each author maintain her ambiguity. The depth of both *Pride and Prejudice* and *Middlemarch* depends on the reader's sensitivity to the relationship between the action of the characters and the voice that enfolds it. As James wrote, we cannot speak of incident and narration as though they were mutually exclusive:

> I cannot ... conceive in any novel worth discussing, of a passage of
> description that is not in its intention narrative, a passage of dialogue
> that is not in its intention descriptive, a touch of truth of any sort
> that does not partake of the nature of incident, or an incident that
> derives its interest from any other source than the general and only
> source of the success of a work of art – that of being illustrative ... I
> cannot see what is meant by talking as if there were a part of the
> novel which is the story and a part which for mystical reasons is
> not.[1]

In Austen, the 'story' is made meaningful by narrative intrusion: and 'description' or reflection is made meaningful by story.

Jane Austen's narrative voice establishes a stability in a world of fluctuating opinions and exaggerations. The opening page of chapter 2, for example, dwells on the various 'reports' of Bingley and of the party he will bring with him. Bingley is 'wonderfully handsome' and 'extremely agreeable', and he is bringing 'twelve ladies and seven gentlemen' to the next assembly with him. In conclusion (and not wholly in defiance) of these reports, the narrator comments: '[The party] consisted of only five altogether; Mr Bingley, his two sisters, the husband of the eldest, and another young man ... Mr Bingley was good looking and gentlemanlike; he had a pleasant countenance, and easy, unaffected manners' (p. 10). This pattern is characteristic in Jane Austen: the responses to an event are catalogued, beginning with the most exaggerated and concluding with the true fact of the case, or the truest response.

The Bennet family's response to Mr Collins's engagement to Charlotte Lucas is another example of this progress toward truth. Sir William Lucas comes to Longbourn bearing the news, and the first reactions are attributed to the least rational of the group: 'Mrs Bennet, with more perseverance than politeness, protested he must be entirely mistaken, and Lydia, always unguarded and often uncivil, boisterously exclaimed, "Good Lord! Sir William, how can you tell such a story? – Do you not know that Mr Collins wants to marry Lizzy?"' (p. 126). After Sir William's departure, the responses flow with enthusiasm, beginning once again with Mrs Bennet and Lydia, to Mr Bennet, Jane, and finally Elizabeth, whose simple statement truly evaluates the event with regard to her friendship with Charlotte, 'Elizabeth felt persuaded that no real confidence could ever subsist between them again' (p. 128). This pattern, with its suggestion of the endless variations and subterfuge surrounding an event, implies a belief in the difficult accessibility, perhaps the inaccessibility, of truth. The reliable interpretation of a chapter or incident is usually founded on the response or evaluation stated last.

The conclusions to the ironic comedies are especially ambiguous in this respect. Each has its own ironic touch, each calls to mind the memory of some incident of absurdity or insensibility and in so doing, gently undermines the conspicuous gaiety of the marriage union. The allusion to an imperfection is often injected in the penultimate lines of the last chapter (Lady Catherine's visit to Pemberley, Mrs Elton's opinion of Emma's wedding clothes) just before the perfect happiness of the union is proclaimed. It is as if the modes of resistance to the truth become part of the truth itself.

The paradox of truth and truth's compromise accounts for the paradoxical mood of uncomfortable harmony with which most of the novels close. Emma's 'perfect happiness' and Anne Elliot's 'perfect felicity' have the slightly unsettling effect of flattery. Emma is still not above making fun of Robert Martin, as she does in a closing dialogue with Mr Knightley, and Anne Elliot assures herself that she was right to reject Wentworth in the first place. In a world that the novels themselves have so insistently pronounced to be relative, how can we accept the absolute assertions of the endings? Their ambiguity is intended and is a way of pointing out life's compromise of felicity without derogating what felicity remains. By the time we reach the conclusion of *Pride and Prejudice* we understand the limitations of such words as 'perfect' and know how to interpret them; when we close the pages of *Emma* we have learned enough about Emma and Mr Knightley and Highbury and life in general there to know exactly how much perfection and how much happiness are included in the narrator's 'perfect happiness'.

The narrative voice, then, possesses the essential perspective of the novel. Although Austen's style has been compared to that of Henry James, her use of a vigorous and daunting narrative voice distinguishes them. This voice has more in common with that of the George Eliot narrator, whose all-inclusive compassion envelops the divisions and decay of the story, or that of the Fielding narrator, whose humour is equally tolerant. Austen's authorial consciousness is also binding, for it accepts in its embrace the evasions and irrationalities of direct dialogue and the cool, clear cadence of reason of the objective narrative. It brings them together in its brief flashes of genius, such as in the opening sentence of *Pride and Prejudice*. In such moments, the two streams of discourse in Jane Austen, narration and dialogue, rush together completely. They represent the *effect* of the novel, the total perspective we are to gain, one that rises spontaneously out of the interaction between narration and dialogue.

It may seem to belie Austen's morality to insist that the evasions and even cruelties that arise from the insensibility or partial insight of the characters of *Pride and Prejudice* are somehow sanctioned by the author. Yet the acceptance of such things is securely encompassed in her wisdom, just as Lady Catherine is finally received at Pemberley. And often, particularly in the ironic comedies, the modes of resistance to what is right or true are fairly innocent. The desire to make Bingley more handsome than he really is, to make his party larger than it really is, reveals a need to make ordinary life more glamorous and drastic than it really is. Emma's requirement that life in Highbury be more vivid, elegant, and mysterious than it is reveals a similar need. It is one of the paradoxes of Austen's perspective that such requirements are both ferocious and innocent.

Pride and Prejudice, however, deals less with the problem of accepting an inelegant and unpoetic world than with accepting an irrational and absurd one. If Emma's aspirations are for more witty and more alive surroundings, Elizabeth's efforts are to restrain the anarchic energies of cynicism and insensibility in her parents. The unrelenting invasion of sense by nonsense, of sensibility by moral nullity, of humour by nihilism is a dominant theme in the novel. And determining the proper moral posture to adopt in such a world is the dilemma of individuality.

Space in *Pride and Prejudice*, as Van Ghent suggests, is 'a place for an argument'.[2] The psychic and moral distances in the novel are enormous, while the physical distances are a matter of a coach ride. The internal distance between Elizabeth and her mother, for example, we intuitively recognise to be a central structural element in the novel. Distances such as these establish the terms of sensibility and anarchy in the action. Yet what are the terms? Mrs Bennet moves in an atmosphere of repugnance that is scarcely explained. Studies of Austen's language have insisted that the moral scale of the novels is located in speech – yet is this enough? The variations in diction and sentence structure provide clues to the moral scheme, but they should of course be connected to incident.

Mrs Bennet and two other reprehensible characters, Lydia and Mr Collins, as independent personalities, are each characterised by a failure to distinguish the important from the trivial, the valid from the invalid. In language and action, they have no true discriminating sense. Their failure is both intellectual and moral; part of the underlying philosophy of *Pride and Prejudice* is a belief in the intimate bond between intelligence and morality, articulated so well in Richard Simpson's term 'intelligent love' or James's 'emotional intelligence'.[3] Consider Mrs Bennet's behaviour upon learning that Lydia will be married, perhaps her most offensive display in the whole novel.

> It was a fortnight since Mrs Bennet had been downstairs, but on this happy day, she again took her seat at the head of her table, and in spirits oppressively high. No sentiment of shame gave damp to her triumph. The marriage of a daughter, which had been the first object of her wishes, since Jane was sixteen, was now on the point of accomplishment, and her thoughts and her words ran wholly on those attendants of elegant nuptials, fine muslins, new carriages, and servants. She was busily searching through the neighbourhood for a proper situation for her daughter, and, without knowing or considering what their income might be, rejected many as deficient in size and importance.
>
> (p. 310)

When, however, Mr Bennet reveals to her 'amazement and horror' that he will not advance a guinea to buy clothes for his daughter, Mrs Bennet's astonishment knows no bounds. In a manner characteristic of Austen's narrative technique, the final sentence of the paragraph identifies the moral problem that the paragraph has been examining: 'That his anger could be carried to such a point of inconceivable resentment, as to refuse his daughter a privilege, without which her marriage would scarcely seem valid, exceeded all that she could believe possible. She was more alive to the disgrace, which the want of new clothes must reflect on her daughter's nuptials, than to any sense of shame at her eloping and living with Wickham, a fortnight before that took place' (pp. 310–11). Unable to distinguish significant from insignificant experience, Mrs Bennet can never see below the surface and views, for example, Mr Gardiner's sacrifices on behalf of her daughter as an early Christmas present.

The shamelessness of Mrs Bennet's response is both an intellectual and a moral failing. Lydia, educated and admired by her mother, is the best example of Austen's understanding of ingratitude. Lydia is not ungrateful in the way of Goneril and Regan; she is without shame, unconscious of the suffering and inconvenience she exacts from others. Lydia's behaviour at the Gardiners' house in London at the time of her wedding exemplifies her shamelessness. While she is dressing for the ceremony, Mrs Gardiner is trying to impress upon her some consciousness of her actions. Lydia says, 'However I did not hear above one word in ten, for I was thinking, you may suppose, of my dear Wickham. I longed to know whether he was wearing his blue coat' (p. 319). In another situation the pre-occupation with the blue coat would be humorous; here, because it brings to mind Mrs Gardiner's painful version of the story, it only signifies the waste of suffering and effort behind the event about to take place. Lydia's blindness is a matter of both the mind and the heart. In her letter of elopement to Mrs Forster – 'My Dear Harriet, You will laugh when you know where I am gone' (p. 291) – she reveals a numbness of perception as well as of feeling.

An important technique of moral comment, and certainly of comedy, is the suggestion or juxtaposition of antithetical experiences. When Mrs Bennet equates Jane's face with the fat haunch of venison as two things that must impress Bingley about her table, an almost metaphorical effect results, an effect that Austen's novels are frequently said to lack. Mr Collins's equations are even more astonishing; when he learns that the eldest Bennet daughter is engaged, he accommodates himself: 'Mr Collins had only to change from Jane to Elizabeth – and it was soon done – done while Mrs Bennet was stirring the fire' (p. 71). As Collins himself admits, the choice of wife is the selection of another player at the quadrille table at Rosings. Yet the humour of this mentality is often qualified by a recognition of its danger. Upon Lydia's elopement Mr Collins makes an extraordinary comparison: 'The death of your daughter would have been a blessing in comparison of this' (pp. 296–7). Here Mr Collins's insensibility is instructive, for it reminds us that the event is not tragic, and it forces us to re-adopt the perspective we may have lost through sympathising with Elizabeth.

The many outlandish equations in the speech of Mrs Bennet, Mr Collins, and Lydia create a powerful force of irrationality in the novel. Such bizarre juxtapositions have a way of neutralising the whole experience of life. It is their impoverishing, indiscriminate strength that Darcy resists through his intellectual fastidiousness and temperamental rigidity. He does not know, he says, more than six accomplished women in his acquaintance; and he will not participate in company that he considers inferior. But while his intelligence makes discriminations to excess, his moral sense, as he says, is lost in the realm of 'theory'. Bingley and Jane are at the opposite pole; to Bingley, all women are accomplished, and Jane (as Elizabeth complains) has liked too many stupid men. Because their moral optimism is untempered by any real intellectual penetration, they are rendered powerless. Bingley can be persuaded that Jane never cared for him, and Jane lacks the wit to guess what has happened. They are the opposite of Darcy; their good will overcomes their intelligence. Wickham and Charlotte form perhaps that most harmful variation on the moral-intellectual scale in that both have totally inactive moral lives yet highly effective perceptual intelligence. Although Charlotte is a far more sympathetic character than Wickham, both are seducers, always a serious sin in Jane Austen, or to be more precise, both engage in a polite form of prostitution. Mr Collins's angered insensibility to Elizabeth when she rejects him seems amateur when compared to the calm and knowing insensibility of Charlotte's inviting behaviour. Even Lydia seems vulnerable compared to the man who in his careless greed decides to let her seduce him.

All the men and women of Elizabeth's generation are actively involved in adopting their permanent, adult posture toward the world. The decisions and choices of the insensitive or unintelligent characters – Charlotte, Mr Collins, Wickham, Lydia – are revealed in the way they view the selection of spouse: as a relatively uncomplicated decision, a matter of ambition or necessity. To the intelligent and sensitive person, like Elizabeth or Darcy, the choice of adult posture, like the choice of spouse, is most complex. To a person gifted with 'emotional intelligence' in Jane Austen's world, the choice of moral stance in a world that is continually fluctuating under the active energies of sense and nonsense is as problematic as the individual's consciousness will allow. In *Pride and Prejudice* we view a variety of responses: Darcy, who is totally rigid in his refusal to give way to the exigencies of absurdity; Mr Bennet, who capitulates entirely; Lady Catherine, who exemplifies what her nephew is in danger of becoming; and Elizabeth, who is susceptible to her father's chosen stance. Darcy must learn to laugh at himself and to develop a more generous attitude toward the absurdity of others. Elizabeth is the agent of this change, who has learned the value of laughter from her father, but who, under Darcy's influence, will not give in to it entirely.

Mr Bennet is one of the most interesting characters in Jane Austen, for through him the author exposes the pieties of cynicism. Mr Bennet goes beyond seeing the absurdity of life; he *wants* life to be absurd. This attitude is his major failing; his inadequacy as a father is directly related to it. There is a kind of sin, the sin of despair, in wanting life to be absurd, a spiritual lassitude, and in the end a means of self-justification. His well-known statement about the purpose of life, at times mistaken for the author's view, is one of the more chilling comments in all of Jane Austen: 'For what do we live, but to make sport of our neighbours, and laugh at them in our turn?' (p. 364). This statement recalls Lydia's view that life is a joke. Of her elopement she writes: 'What a good joke it will be! I can hardly write for laughing' (p. 291).

On the other hand, a numbness to the absurdities of self and others is also associated with moral deficiency. If Mr Bennet represents the pieties of cynicism, Mary Bennet represents the pieties of sense and signals us to be cautious in assuming an unequivocal Johnsonian value system in the novel. Mary's inflated utterances parody Dr Johnson:

> Pride ... is a very common failing I believe. By all that I have ever read, I am convinced that it is very common indeed, that human nature is particularly prone to it, and that there are very few of us who do not cherish a feeling of self-complacency on the score of some quality or other, real or imaginary. Vanity and pride are different things, though the words are often used synonimously. A person may be proud without being vain. Pride relates more to our opinion of ourselves, vanity to what we would have others think of us.
>
> (p. 20)

Strictly speaking, her words are true, yet she is patently absurd. Like those of Darcy, Mary Bennet's good principles exist in the realm of theory only; when it comes to active goodness, to helping her family during the crisis, she is as selfish as Kitty or Lydia. Austen's belief that sense must be tempered by an appreciation of absurdity is a lasting one. It becomes an issue in *Emma*, particularly with regard to Mr Knightley, whose only failing is his blindness to the power and pleasure of absurdity. If, like Darcy, we separate ourselves from the anarchic elements of life, we must separate ourselves from the pleasures of expression altogether. It is as though every Elizabeth comes with a Mrs Bennet, and you cannot have one without the other: in the words of T. S. Eliot, they are a 'necessary conjunction'. Darcy resists his attraction to Elizabeth in the beginning in part because he cannot tolerate her mother's anarchic vulgarity. Their marriage represents his capitulation to the force of irrationality as it does her surrender to the need for rationality. Similarly, when Darcy will not dance because, as he says, 'every savage can dance', he is denying the right of the chaos in himself and others to find form in civilised life; and this is a serious denial in Jane Austen, because only through civilised forms does the chaos of human nature find meaning, and only through the inclusion of chaotic energies does civilisation find meaning. Those characters who disavow the importance of emotional and sexual urges in social existence lead surface lives, without resonance and without hope. The world of Rosings is one of meaningless formality, of material luxury and spiritual vacancy, even of ill health. And Charlotte Lucas's life with Mr Collins is not only a 'preservative from want' but a preservative from intelligence, gaiety, and love, an embalmed safety from possibility and the requirement of morality and hope.

The moral activity I have identified – the arbitration of the energies of absurdity by the discriminations of sense and the modification of the egotism of sense by the exigencies of absurdity – is directly connected to the eugenic concerns of the plot. In selecting one another, Elizabeth and Darcy counteract the influences of their parents (in Darcy's case, his surrogate parent) and set forth on an improved project for the present, which is to say, the future. Like the perception of space, the perception of time in *Pride and Prejudice* is defined internally. Literal time is a few months, just long enough for the marriageable persons to court and marry. Internal time covers the psychic distance of three generations through exposing the actions of the central generation. The past and future do not exist as mysterious abysses; Austen's time is an eternal present, which encloses in its immediate alterations both the past and future.[4] The individual is determined by his past, yet the very existence of this influence ensures the power of his will to affect the next generation. For this reason the choice of mate is the crucial act of life in *Pride and Prejudice*, the one most capable of effecting change and justifying hope.

Pride and Prejudice is far more preoccupied than Austen's other novels with the rituals and taboos concerning mating. In the course of the novel four marriages are decided: those of Charlotte Lucas,

Lydia, Jane and Elizabeth; five, if we include Colonel and Mrs Forster. Every social event is important in affecting the attachments that will result and in forwarding the heroine's education in proper selection. There is neither cynicism nor triviality in thinking these events important; selecting a mate was the arena in which women's whole future was decided. The heroine is the last to be engaged, for part of her knowledge in selection comes through observing her friend and her sisters choose.

As suggested in my discussion of the opening scene, *Pride and Prejudice* is from the beginning a world of unexplained attitudes and restrictions. Characters are judged according to their behaviour with regard to these taboos, and the taboos are clarified by the acts that break them. Wickham breaks a powerful taboo in trying to seduce Georgiana and in finally eloping with Lydia; and we know that very careful restrictions surround courtship behaviour, such as a limit on the number of times an unengaged couple can dance together at a ball. As Freud specifies, taboos are distinct from moral and religious prohibitions in that they are not based upon any divine ordinance, but may be said to impose themselves on their own account. Almost all the restrictions in Jane Austen's novels appear to the modern reader as taboos rather than moral edicts, because they are unexplained and our own age is no longer familiar with the moral rationale behind them. Like the taboos Freud describes, the moral edicts in Jane Austen's novels seem to have no ground and to be of unknown origin.[5] Jane Austen does not give explicit reasons for their necessity: those who are dominated by them take them as a matter of course. A modern critic, for example, who sees Lydia's behaviour as a positive rebellion of the will reveals that the taboos of seduction and elopement are unintelligible to him. Yet a careful reading of the novel makes these taboos meaningful.

The object of the taboos in *Pride and Prejudice* (like the object of many primitive taboos) is to protect the acts of marriage and sexual function from interference. The marriages of one generation provide the moral ethos for the next; for this reason, it is of absolute importance that marriages be responsible and secure in both the moral and the material spheres. Marriage confers a new moral status on both sexes. A married couple, for example, is allowed to take responsibility for younger, unmarried persons. Shortly after the Forsters are married, they invite Lydia to Brighton; even though Mrs Forster is as irresponsible as Lydia herself, her new status allows her this authority. Irresponsible and responsible marriages form the basis of the novel's action. Like George Eliot, Jane Austen believed in the power of moral influence. As in primitive custom, those who break a taboo must be shunned, for their example is contaminating; Kitty cannot visit Lydia, Maria Bertram is exiled to a foreign country. On the other hand, the main hope for raising the moral intelligence of the society lies in this belief in the malleability of individual beings.

Marriage of course spawns other chief acts of life: birth, initiation, and, once again, mating and marriage. The first responsibility of parents is to educate and prepare their offspring for participation in this most central process so that they will harm neither themselves or others. Mr and Mrs Bennet are guilty of not preparing Lydia for mature initiation into this rite. As a result, her marriage is emotionally vacant and economically irresponsible; the narrative review of the three marriages at the close of the novel informs us that the Wickhams are freeloaders. In a sense, one must raise one's children well so that they will raise their children well. In Jane Austen, one generation is an eternity. What we do now is affected by what our parents did and will affect what our children do. This is the sum of what Elizabeth learns in her passage into adulthood. Only when she understands the extent of her own conditioning is she capable of transcending it: '[Elizabeth] had never felt so strongly as now, the disadvantages which must attend the children of so unsuitable a marriage' (p. 236). Her self-knowledge is solidly linked to a knowledge of her past and her family; not until she sees the past borne out in Lydia's fate does she become fully conscious of herself and capable of love.

From Julia Prewitt Brown, *Jane Austen's Novels* (Harvard, 1979), pp. 65–79.

NOTES

[Judith Prewitt Brown reaches similar conclusions about *Pride and Prejudice* to those reached about *Sense and Sensibility* by D. A. Miller, although her analysis relies upon an untheoretical discrimination of Austen's narration and her dialogues. Brown observes that the ambiguity of Austen's texts derives in part from the undecidable nature of her narration, but also in large measure from the difficulty of locating decisive values when the very decided values of the narrative voice are thwarted or contradicted by the interest and vivacity of a character's actions and discourse. Where Miller saw a process of repression and escape, Brown sees a process of limitations being set and constantly transgressed, and this is fortunate since were Austen's compulsive orderliness to succeed, her works would lack all the energy and excitement that makes them interesting. The stability that is constantly sought for in Austen's world, and often achieved in a manner than looks profound, is really only provisional because Austen's work grants resoundingly moral conclusions where in reality there is only flux. Although expressed in a language free of modern critical references, Brown's account would in many ways concur with a poststructuralist, or indeed deconstructionist, reading. The certainties of Austen's work are seen as erected in negation of what has authentic life and value, and as thereby escaping the kind of scrutiny that would show they were in themselves as ill-founded and fragile as those to which they pretend superiority. References to Jane Austen's work are to *The Works of Jane Austen,* ed. R. W. Chapman, 3rd edn, 5 vols (London, 1932). Ed.]

1. Henry James, *Partial Portraits* (New York, 1888), pp. 391–2.

2. [Dorothy Van Ghent, 'On *Pride and Prejudice*', *The English Novel; Form and Function* (New York, 1951), pp. 99–111. Ed.]

3. [Richard Simpson was the first critic after Sir Walter Scott to give extended consideration to Austen's work. See his unsigned review of J. E. Austen-Leigh's *Memoir* published in the *North British Review*, 52 (April 1870), 129–52, reprinted in *Jane Austen; The Critical Heritage*, ed. B. C. Southam (London, 1968), pp. 241–65. Ed.]

4. Time in *Pride and Prejudice* calls to mind Wittgenstein's definition of eternity: 'If we take eternity to mean not infinite temporal duration but timelessness, then eternal life belongs to those who live in the present.' *Tractatus-Logico-Philosophicus.*

5. [See Sigmund Freud, *Totem and Taboo: Some Points of Agreement between the Mental Lives of Savages and Neurotics* (1913), translated by James Strachey (London, 1950). Ed.]

9

Politics, Pride, Prejudice and the Picturesque

ISOBEL ARMSTRONG

The ebullience and confident assurance of its comedy, combined with its fairy-tale gratifications, has made *Pride and Prejudice* the best known, and possibly the best liked, of all Jane Austen's novels. Two sisters without fortune marry men with money and high social standing. Despite the embarrassment of a marriage-obsessed mother and another sister's descent to the *demi-monde* of elopement and London lodging-houses, they are rewarded with marriage in a text almost as keen on the grand match as their mother, Mrs Bennet. The second daughter, Elizabeth, a girl who can rush on foot over the fields to nurse a sick sister, careless of a muddy petticoat and the sneers of her involuntary hostesses; who can stand up to the insult and invective of Lady Catherine de Bourgh and assert her right to marry Darcy, Lady Catherine's nephew, if she so chooses, eventually marries into one of the foremost aristocratic landowning families in England. Arguably the most important scene in the novel suggests that social boundaries can be crossed. When Elizabeth visits Darcy's property in Derbyshire, at a time when she is estranged from him, she meets him unexpectedly by his house: then, as she and her companions are shown his grounds, they cross a bridge on to a narrow pathway and see him for a second time, hurrying towards them. It is as if the text is asserting, through the delicate drama of this spacial moment, that it is possible to bridge temperamental and social spaces, that gaps can be closed.

The ease with which Elizabeth Bennet can be assimilated into high rank, accommodating herself to its demands, has enabled some critics to read this as an essentially conservative and 'anti-Jacobin' novel. In her *Jane Austen and the War of Ideas* Marilyn Butler sees the novel as an exemplary parable in which Elizabeth gives up her tendencies to radical protest and prejudice against the powerful.[1] In *The Way of the World: The Bildungsroman in European Culture* Franco Moretti sees *Pride and Prejudice* as a novel of settlement, a work embodying the innate tendency of the *Bildungsroman* (the novel of growth and development) to stabilise its closed world by opting for socialisation rather than free individual exploration.[2] The marriage contract between Elizabeth and Darcy is effectively a political agreement between the aristocracy and the bourgeoisie, embodying a mutual adjustment in which power on the one hand and critique on the other are softened and aestheticised into a harmonious relationship. Jane Bennet, marrying Bingley, a *nouveau riche* (his family fortune has been made by trade) who becomes a landowner, might be said to exemplify another version of this 'aesthetic' resolution. The novel, remarkable for its movement from place to place, from environment to environment, begins and ends with Bingley's tenancy of Netherfield Park, as if asserting a newly negotiated stability. Perhaps this endorses Moretti's interpretation of *Pride and Prejudice* as the classic *Bildungsroman*, which, like another Enlightenment work, Goethe's *Wilhelm Meister*, implicitly tells an admonitory story derived from conservative optimism, the story of how the French Revolution can be, and could have been, prevented.

The ending of the novel in particular creates a sense of graceful ease and lightness which tempts one, as comedy so often does, to believe that all is unproblematically resolved. But *Pride and Prejudice* is not an unproblematical novel: if it is implicitly about averting revolution, it is just as strongly concerned with challenging repression, and the double programme creates complexities which glance off its superficially glittering surface. Jane Austen herself wondered warily and self-critically whether the novel was not 'rather too light and bright and sparkling', and whether its 'playfulness and epigrammatism' required the contrast of 'anything', such as an interpolated 'history of Buonaparté', to relieve its uniform lightness.[3] Yet, encountering the text's playfulness with her own, she had realised, perhaps, that such a 'history' was already covertly present in her novel. On its last pages she remarks that the indigent couple, Wickham and Lydia, continue to be rootless with 'the restoration of peace'. Whether this is the peace settled by the Treaty of Amiens (1802), or one of the much later pauses in the Peninsular War (possibly after the relief of Portugal, 1812), or a hypothetical peace, is unclear. But what is important is the amazing insouciance with which the only overt reference to the major European events of the period, the Napoleonic Wars, occurs when the novel is almost at an end. Contemporary readers would have understood from the presence of the army that this was a novel of the post-revolutionary period set during the Napoleonic Wars, but the uncanny refusal to name these formative events is remarkable. And perhaps this arises less from a willingness to de-historicise her love-story than from a perception that the novel *is* only too strongly marked by history, however indirectly. The novel's scintillating wit reminds us that the strategy of the joke has come to be seen as a way of displacing aggression, anxiety, or pain. The text knows this: what does Elizabeth do after Darcy's humiliating public rejection of her as a dancing partner – and just as surely as a sexual partner – at the Netherfield ball but joke about it afterwards? In a similar way the displaced anxieties of the post-revolutionary period are at work in this novel. The aesthetic resolution of the 'conservative' plot is continually questioned by the narrative process and subverted by complexities of language.

To see how the text is marked, even scarred, by history it has to be remembered that the novel was composed and revised over a period of sixteen or seventeen years. An early version, *First Impressions*, seems to have been composed over 1796–7, and revised as the novel now known as *Pride and Prejudice*, published in 1813.[4] In this it resembles another anxious post-revolutionary work, Wordsworth's *Prelude*, also composed over a long period. Significantly, a title which points towards subjective, individual experience is replaced with one which emphasises abstract, moral, public, and social qualities. The change of title perhaps registers a new historical situation. The novel was begun after what was essentially a bourgeois, individualistic, middle-class radicalism had collapsed after the Terrors and when a new aggression and territorial acquisitiveness had manifested itself on the part of France during the French wars. It was completed after more than a decade of war in which Napoleon had proved himself a dictator, and when, in England, libertarian belief and public criticism of government were severely repressed. So the composition of the novel covers a long and *changing* cycle of revolutionary history in France, just as it covers a changing sequence of events in England. When the novel is thought of as a response to the French Revolution, it is salutary to ask which phase of that Revolution it responds to and with which phase of British response to revolutionary activity it is in dialogue. The question cannot in fact be answered with precision. What can be said is that the complexities of the text register a situation when bourgeois individualism and its nature required examination and critique, and a later situation when the very reverse was the case – when despotism and repression were a substantial threat. Hence the novel discloses a play of conflicting energies and positions. Hence it is a deeply questioning work.

The two titles take us some way into the questions asked in the novel. As has been noticed by Tony Tanner in his essay on *Pride and Prejudice*, the term 'impression' from the title *First Impressions* has philosophical implications.[5] It was terminology used by David Hume in his *A Treatise of Human Nature* with very specific meaning. But Hume also has a good deal to say about pride. In Book 2 of his *Treatise*, 'Of the Passions', Hume makes Pride the predominant passion and begins his discussion with an account of the social and moral significance of Pride. His demythologising of Pride (he gives it no theological significance) suggests why it became central to Jane Austen's novel and why it is dialectically linked to Prejudice, which is sometimes an attribute of Pride and sometimes the antipathetic response Pride engenders in others. For, though we know that this alliterative title seems to have been taken from the closing pages of Fanny Burney's *Cecilia*, it is by no means a simple title.[6] Earlier novels, such as *Northanger Abbey* or *Sense and Sensibility* – one a burlesque of the Gothic novel and the other partly a satire of the novel of sensibility – signal Jane Austen's dependence on literary forms and conventions. The titles are clear. Unlike *Sense and Sensibility*, however, *Pride and Prejudice* does not fall into the easy antithesis the alliteration appears to guarantee: the relationship between the two qualities is not stable and is far from clear.

What interests Hume about Pride is that, though it may be a universal passion, it is not a 'natural' one. For, unlike greed, hunger, and lust, it does not arise from specific bodily organs and internal needs. Its object is self and self alone, but Pride is pleasurable to self by virtue of demonstrable *external* attributes which are seen as *possessions*, whether they are mental or physical possessions. They are almost infinite in number and depend on the value attributed to them by custom and association; almost anything can be converted into

Pride: 'A man may be proud of his beauty, strength, agility, good mien, address in dancing, riding ... But this is not all. The passion, looking further, comprehends ... Our country, family, children, relations, riches, houses, gardens, horses, dogs, clothes; any of these may become a cause either of pride or humility.'[7] Just such arbitrary pride of family possession echoes in Lady Catherine de Bourgh's boast to Elizabeth, adapting Burke's conservative belief in an aristocratic tradition, that her daughter and Darcy are meant for one another: 'They are descended on the maternal side, from the same noble line; and, on the father's, from respectable, honourable, and ancient, though untitled families' (p. 316). Hence her ludicrous rhetorical hyperbole when she considers a marriage between Elizabeth and Darcy: 'Are the shades of Pemberley to be thus polluted?' (p. 317).

Perhaps her consciousness that the male line is *not* titled makes her arrogance defensive, for her pride rests much more vulgarly on wealth and possession than she implies. Certainly her language here points up a truth about the objects of pride which Hume had noticed: possessions are not only the contrivances of art but befall us at the caprice of fortune.[8] Carried away by 'poetic' diction, Lady Catherine forgets that it is not logically possible to pollute by physical contamination a 'shade' or ancestral ghost or phantom. Nor is it possible to defile the shadows cast on our grounds by the trees surrounding our property, because they are immaterial. But her ancestral ghosts have all the solidity of possessions for her: the very shadows of Pemberley seem to belong to her lineage; yet the good fortune of her descent is essentially the caprice of chance, as is made clear by the lucky chance, which she has remarked upon much earlier to Elizabeth, that her own estate was not entailed to the male line. The products of art and chance come to seem natural to us, Jane Austen's language suggests, just as Lady Catherine almost believes she has power over the weather and nature itself: 'The party then gathered round the fire to hear Lady Catherine determine what weather they were to have on the morrow' (p. 149). 'Determine', with its ambiguous sense of both 'considering' and 'arranging', is a significant word. As so often in Jane Austen's texts, the precision of the authorial language is far more meticulous than the language of its characters.

Dr Johnson's *Dictionary*, which would have been authoritative in Jane Austen's time, foregrounds meanings of 'Pride' which are subordinated in modern dictionaries.[9] Johnson's first meaning, for instance, is 'Inordinate and unreasonable self-esteem', whereas a modern dictionary gives the primary meaning of the noun as 'a feeling of honour and self-respect'. Johnson's second definition is 'Insolence; rude treatment of others; insolent exultation', and secondary meanings are 'Dignity of manner, loftiness of air' (3), 'Ornament' (6), and 'Splendour; ostentation' (7). The negative meanings predominate over positive signification – 'Generous elation of heart' (4). As will be seen, the signification of both 'Pride' and 'Prejudice' works in contradictory ways, but it is immediately evident from these definitions and Hume's discussion that *prejudice*, that which pre-judges, must be an inherent attribute of Pride, for in these definitions it is founded on a *pre*-judgement of one's own and one's possessions' worth. For Hume Pride is an object lesson in the way that the human passions work; as ideas and impressions reinforce one another in a self-perpetuating cycle, Pride is confirmed by the Pride it has itself generated.[10] Moral and ideological blindness are virtually inevitable. Just as the medieval sin of pride subsumed all other sins, so pride in this novel subsumes prejudice.

Late in the narrative, when Darcy has become a more acceptable figure, we learn that he had indeed intended his sister to marry Bingley, and it is left open as to whether that intention prejudiced him or not when he persuaded Bingley to leave Netherfield to avoid, as his cousin Colonel Fitzwilliam describes it, much to Elizabeth's humiliation, 'a most imprudent marriage' (p. 165). We learn from Miss Bingley, late in the novel, that on their first acquaintance Darcy had said cruelly of Elizabeth: '*She* a beauty! – I should as soon call her mother a wit' (p. 239). Darcy believes that his high social standing justifies a peremptory control of his friend's actions and deception (he is party to the concealment from Bingley of Jane's presence in London); he believes, even in a declaration of love for her, that he is justified in pointing to the low connections and indecorum of Elizabeth's family. Elizabeth, mortified by her blindness and prejudice, poignantly exclaiming that she could not have been more blind 'Had I been in love', forgets, in the revelation of Wickham's immorality, that Darcy *has* behaved badly. His friends and connections can behave, indeed, as brashly and indecorously, as stupidly, as her own. Miss Bingley's sexual signals to Darcy are as vulgar as any by Lydia: just as Lydia 'exposes' herself, as her father puts it, to the public eye in Brighton, so Caroline walks flauntingly round the Netherfield drawing room to attract Darcy. Even Darcy is 'a little ashamed of his aunt's ill breeding' when she asserts that, if Elizabeth plays on the piano in the room belonging to her daughter's companion, she 'would be in nobody's way, you know, in that part of the house' (p. 154): she would occupy the social space of a servant. Bingley's sisters laugh more cruelly than anyone else in the novel at the follies and low social standing of others. Class and money protect such people from their prejudices. Responding to Elizabeth's amazed realisation of misprision, an unwary reader can fall into another misprision, forget or repress what is glaringly obvious, and collude with a 'prejudiced' sympathy with the upper-class characters in the novel without knowing it.

Another trap in the title is that it too easily persuades a distribution of pride and prejudice between characters. If Darcy has all the pride, Elizabeth possesses the prejudice, it seems. Johnson offers a second 'accidental' meaning of prejudice as pre-judging which he describes as 'Mischief; detriment; hurt; injury'. Because prejudice is a bad thing, it *creates*, by association, bad and harmful things. Wickham's mischievous and false rumours about Darcy are such prejudicial injuries. Elizabeth accepts them too readily, but she does not perpetrate them. She accuses herself, nevertheless, of prejudice, as the narrative voice does, and her strong reactions and excess of confidence in her judgement have suggested to some people that Elizabeth is a subversive figure, rashly in conflict with authority and the accepted hierarchy of power. 'You give your opinion very decidedly for so young a person' (p. 148), says Lady Catherine. 'We are not rich enough, or grand enough for them' (p. 161), Elizabeth bursts out, when she understands Jane's grief at the sudden departure of Bingley to London. She rebels against privilege and the exploitation of privilege to manipulate advantageous marriages. Her prejudice, if it can be called prejudice at all, comes from a different source from that of Darcy. To return to Hume for a moment, it is the fierce, other-directed passion which he associates with love and hate, passions which he sees as the antithesis of Pride because they are both directed to what is external to the self. Hume aligns Pride and Humility as interdependent passions because both turn inward. We need not map Hume slavishly on to the novel to see the irony of the essential similarity of Darcy and the obsequious, possessively snobbish 'Humility' of Mr Collins at the start of the novel. Collins and Wickham are introduced into the narrative almost at the same time, perhaps because Wickham is another example of 'Humility': that is, someone whose sense of undeserved social inferiority humiliates him and stings his egotism. Desire and aggression are related, on the other hand, because they move beyond the self.[11]

Hume's scepticism allows that each set of passions can be just as dangerous – or beneficial – socially and politically as the other.

It seems as if the novel was written at a time when the very meanings of the words 'pride' and 'prejudice' were in contention and when their signification was unstable. An essay 'On Prejudice' by Anna Laetitia Barbauld, a radical poet and thinker a generation senior to Jane Austen, suggests this. We would not normally associate this radical writer with Jane Austen, perhaps, but both authors were certainly concerned with the same problems. Mrs Barbauld argues that, though we are told not to implant prejudice in our children, it is impossible to present them with a pure cultural and intellectual situation which enables them to judge on 'evidence'.[12] All cultures and societies inevitably form and prejudice children. Truly *philosophical* belief can be reached later, perhaps, and those who 'aspire to lead public opinion' cannot indulge in prejudice, but for many it is 'prejudice' which creates our first deeply held beliefs, whether these are ideological in character (and for her they are) or not.[13] Mrs Barbauld's essay is part of a debate in which Jane Austen's novel, with its investigation of prejudice, participates. Her discussion throws light on one aspect of prejudice: it arises when you either cannot see or do not know something, and no two people can ever know or see the same thing. The essay uses the imagery of sight and perspective to illustrate this and suggests why Jane Austen's novel is so dominated by the nature of vision, why it is supremely the novel of eye contact, of optics. Everyone occupies a particular spot:

> and his views of things are contracted or extended according to his position in society: as no two individuals can have the same horizon, so neither can any two have the same associations; and different associations will produce different opinions, as necessarily as by the laws of perspective, different distances will produce different appearances of visible objects.[14]

For Mrs Barbauld the opposite of what might be called the committed and passionate relativism of prejudice is deeply negative scepticism. Mr Bennet, standing aloof from affairs, enjoying the fiasco of the Bennet family's ill-judged behaviour after the Netherfield ball as if it were a 'scene' detached from him, assuming a stance of objectivity which actually allows him to express contempt for his wife and daughters, has the characteristics of scepticism. His two elder daughters, on the other hand, believe in more than he does. They both believe in the possibility of reaching a committed understanding of those close to them, and this includes the possibility of mutual sexual love. But, the novel asks, can an understanding of people ever be reached without bias or prejudice? This is an especially urgent question where sexual feeling is concerned. In a context where, 'according to his position in society', each person's 'view' of things is 'contracted or extended', the search for 'evidence', for an understanding of the psychological and moral horizon of another person, is difficult indeed. Among the upper classes horizons were limited and perspectives narrowed by the minute restrictions governing propriety. Social relations were ordered by hierarchical customs, by rules, and above all, by unspoken codes. Thus the act of *looking* becomes paramount in the novel.

The rhythm of the novel is a series of public events followed by an often anxious analytical retrospect shared by two people in private – Charlotte and Elizabeth, Elizabeth and Jane, Elizabeth and Mrs Gardiner. One of the commonest verbs in the novel is 'observe'. It means both 'to gaze attentively' and 'to make a verbal pronouncement'. The verb 'observe' thus has a paradoxical reference to the unspoken and the spoken, to the private and the public domains. To look attentively must be an individual's private act. But to speak is a public action – we observe *to* someone. The women *look* in public, but *speak* in private. Tony Tanner is right to remark on the importance for the novel of the volatile and deceptive nature of sense 'impressions', which, Hume reminds us, 'mix' with the passions and prevent the formation of precise 'ideas'.[15] But it is not easy to see why in this novel the interpretative process should be connected so insistently with the physical immediacy of vision, with the almost endless hermeneutics of the eye. The text is hypersensitive to the gaze or the averting of the gaze, to the inadvertent movement of the eyes or the deliberate stare. It abounds with these wordless moments of visual perception. On her enforced visit to Netherfield to nurse Jane 'Elizabeth could not help observing as she turned over some music books that lay on the instrument, how frequently Mr Darcy's eyes were fixed on her' (p. 44). The moment of greatest tension in the novel is the occasion of the accidental meeting at Pemberley when 'They were within twenty yards of each other ... Their eyes instantly met ... She had instinctively turned away' (p. 221).

It is the anxiety of the eye rather than its gratification which is most often registered. If the eye exposes, it also conceals. Elizabeth's 'fine eyes', of course, which gradually come to delight

Darcy and exasperate Miss Bingley, make it frankly apparent (as frankly as any post-Freudian) that the eye is the focus of erotic energy. This is why the eye is both faintly scandalous and deeply mystifying. It is the only public expression of libido available both to the perceiver and the perceived in a social order where sexual feeling is displaced into the movement of a chair (as when Darcy is disappointed by Elizabeth's answer to his question at Rosings about her readiness to move from her family), where arousal is expressed by a few steps towards a group of card players, or where a remark about the height of a man's sister discloses interest in the woman with whom she is compared. At Netherfield Darcy prefers to compare his sister with Elizabeth rather than with Miss Bingley, who pesters him to think of his sister's height in relation to herself. Interestingly, he is hesitant in saying that his sister is 'about' Elizabeth's height, 'or rather taller' (p. 33). It is as if he is uncertain whether his eye, like his heart at this stage in the novel, is playing tricks on him. Only when Miss Darcy appears much later in the novel do we discover that she *is* 'tall and on a larger scale than Elizabeth' (p. 229). It is out of such a minute detail that Jane Austen emphasises the anxiety of vision. The anxiety of the eye in the novel comes from a sense that the eye's discourse betrays, both by signifying too much and too little, and by exposing too much or concealing too much. The eye is the source of misprisions, making necessary the exhaustive process of interpretation. And because, as Mrs Barbauld reminds us, and Darcy's hesitation about his sister's height confirms, 'different distances will produce different appearances of visible objects' by the 'laws of perspective' themselves, the hermeneutic problem is endless and unresolvable.

Not knowing, not to be able to see, to be kept in ignorance, is one of the haunting concerns of the text, as the suspense over Lydia's elopement most dramatically indicates. But the novel's preoccupation with vision is richer and deeper than the fear of misprision and the fear of relativism and its uncertainty, powerful though this is. What *vision* as an act means and signifies in its culture is as important for this text as the signifying eye in a closed social order. Seeing as signification, as much as the signification of seeing, is its concern. This problem is explored through Elizabeth, the 'laws of perspective', and the aesthetic category of the picturesque when she visits Darcy's estate, Pemberley. Its complexity suggests both why she is a subversive and possibly destructive figure in her independence and intrepid individualism – a 'danger', as Darcy thinks instinctively at the beginning of his acquaintance with her – and why she is at the same time, and in contradiction to her destructive role, a source of change, a challenge to the tyranny of fixed forms.

Enlightenment fascination with the control and ordering of vision through laws such as those of perspective and colour seems to have been both cause and effect of the experiments with vision which demonstrated its complexity. To turn nature into a category of the aesthetic, which is what terminology such as the picturesque and the beautiful achieves with visual experience, is to guarantee a mastery of seeing which is effectively a mastery of the phenomenal world. Newton's ceaseless experiments with light, with reflection and refraction and colour, may have endorsed aesthetic 'laws' because he frequently used pictorial terminology: 'the light which comes from the several Points of the Object is so refracted ... as to converge and meet again at so many Points in the bottom of the Eye, and there to paint the Picture of the Object'.[16] After dissection anatomists actually see 'Pictures of Objects lively painted thereon', which are 'propagated by Motion along the Fibres of the Optick nerves into the Brain'.[17] Elizabeth, impressed and fascinated by Pemberley, literally revalues her experience with Darcy by re-vision. Moving from room to room and window to window, she sees the external landscape change as her perspective changes, new pictures as it were 'propagated by Motion'. 'As they passed into other rooms, these objects were taking different positions' (p. 216). She contrasts all this with the ostentation and fixity of things at Rosings. It is a landscape in movement, but movement governed by her relationship to it, by the 'laws of perspective'. Before she and her companions actually enter the picturesque landscape of Darcy's estate, she seeks out his portrait, and through a representation, through aesthetic experience, she assuages that sense of unequal power and shamed and irritable inferiority which had dominated her relationship with him formerly by participating in an equal gaze with the painted face. Portraits, we know from Miss Bingley's sneers earlier in the book, when she imagines paintings of Elizabeth's inferior relations hanging alongside Darcy's, are intended to aggrandise the great and confirm their power. They establish the power and mastery of the gaze unequivocally because the eyes are allowed to control the space into which they look. In an amazing moment of syntactic ambiguity which recalls and subtly alters the earlier account of Darcy's gaze, the portrait, momentarily living man and painting simultaneously, 'fixed his eyes upon herself'

(p. 220). The mutuality of this moment, when each confers power on the other, comes about because the indeterminate syntax, rare in an Austen text, allows Elizabeth to be the agent who 'fixed' the portrait's eyes upon herself.

Some people feel the book ends here: Elizabeth has changed; the horizons of each partner have altered; a new harmony has been 'fixed' according to new laws. Elizabeth is ready to modify her independence and to be absorbed into Darcy's world. But the portrait *is* a portrait, and Reynolds reminds us in his *Discourses* that portraits are 'undetermined' and provide enough of a reminder of the original in order that 'the imagination supplies the rest'.[18] Elizabeth has yet to meet the 'real' Darcy and to go out in to his grounds, and when she does the settlement through art almost immediately destabilises.

Elizabeth and the Gardiners are taken through landscape which is virtually a paradigm of the picturesque. The river winds, the irregular openings among the wooded high ground 'gave the eye power to wander' (p. 223). It is a landscape of sudden turns, defiles, and abrupt descents. 'Irregularity', 'sudden and abrupt deviation', wrote Uvedale Price, one of the principal theorists of the picturesque, are 'one of the principal causes of the picturesque'.[19] He associated the picturesque with 'curiosity' and arousal, and actually connected it with political independence and the capacity for change.[20]

It is fascinating that Elizabeth is associated not simply with a disruptive and transgressive category, but with an aesthetic classification which disrupted *other* categories in the eighteenth century. It was the most disputed aesthetic category of the time. Richard Payne Knight, in dispute with Uvedale Price, claimed that the picturesque did not and could not exist as a separate category, because it disrupted the symmetrical distinction between the beautiful (which represented smoothness, evenness, symmetry, and balance) and its opposite, the fearful grandeur of the sublime.[21] Humphrey Repton, attacked by Price for the rigid grouping of his landscaping, conceived the picturesque as a gentle and taming mean (like the English Constitution!) between extremes of savagery and despotism, whereas Price thought of it as the epitome of challenge to conformity.[22] But perhaps it is less important to discover what the picturesque represents as to see that it is a troublesome and problematical category which is hard to legitimate. Price, its most adamant defender in the late eighteenth century, claimed that the picturesque was, as it were, a movable category, appearing with the beautiful and the sublime, itself and not itself. It was above all an *experiment* with vision. Because it is concerned with the temporal process, with the effects of change and decay, and because it includes mean and even ugly objects within itself, it has broader cultural meaning and social reference than other aesthetic categories. It disrupts visual reference and association by defamiliarising objects – an aged, tanned gypsy by a hovel, for instance – in order to regroup them as picturesque. Such defamiliarisation depends simultaneously on our reconfiguring and our *knowing* the cultural and social meaning of objects.[23] Interestingly, Price genders the picturesque, including women in it, for it is not only conventionally beautiful women who inspire passionate sexual love.[24]

It is clear that the picturesque disrupts rather than bridges categories – it is fascinating, indeed, that the legitimacy of a rustic bridge in a landscape was a point of dispute between Knight and Repton, as if embodying the problem.[25] Elizabeth, associated so powerfully with the intrinsically unaccountable picturesque, 'tanned' like Price's gypsy, crossing Darcy's stream by a bridge which spans a defile and conducts her to a path only wide enough for one person, bringing with her that 'liveliness of mind' for which Darcy loves her, is the representative of nonconformity and the harbinger of change. Her very presence, her intervention in Pemberley, produces radical alteration. The objects seen through the Pemberley windows (and Elizabeth is particularly associated with views outward from windows there – her first formal visit is to a room with windows 'opening to the ground' [p. 235]) took 'different positions' (p. 216) according to the laws of perspective; but that change is reciprocally governed by the changing position of the person who relates to these objects, and, moreover, it takes a particular *awareness* to notice this change. At Netherfield Elizabeth had been the interloper. She had recognised this when she refused to join the 'charmingly group'd' and 'picturesque' figures of its inmates, who literally had no room on their path for her (p. 46); the novel implies that she remains an interloper at Pemberley.

It seems that the feminine is an intrinsically disruptive category in this novel, as it is for Price's picturesque. It signals excess: the awkwardly Malthusian Mrs Bennet who can produce only five daughters and not a single son is one form of excess. The entail against the female line is mentioned insistently in the novel.[26] Too many women are in pursuit of too few men: Miss Bingley, Miss de Bourgh, and Elizabeth of Darcy; Jane and Georgiana Darcy of Bingley; Lydia, Miss King (and even Elizabeth for a while) of Wickham. The first sentence of the novel actually implies its inverse: 'It is a truth universally acknowledged, that a single woman without possession of a good fortune, must be in want of a husband', as Charlotte, making sure of marrying Mr Collins, is only too aware.

The particular 'perspectives' and 'horizons' of women, to continue to use Mrs Barbauld's terms, must make them ask radical questions. The text asks these questions not only through Charlotte's cool deconstruction of marriage as a financial settlement but more transgressively through Lydia's cheerful subversion of sexual convention. Indeed, it is through Lydia, who jokes about the excitement of dressing an officer in drag, that the novel unsettles rigid gender distinctions. Mr Bennet complains, with sceptical irony, that his son-in-law Wickham 'simpers' (p. 292) effeminately. To say this of an army officer, normally associated with masculinity, radically questions the artificial construction of gender by society. Interestingly, Mary Wollstonecraft had challenged conventional gender distinctions by pointing to the effeminacy of pampered army officers in her *Vindication of the Rights of Woman*.[27] This is an unexpected convergence of very different texts.

Because women can so easily transgress the limits of decorum by doing or saying what will bring public censure, Jane, Elizabeth, and Charlotte are uneasily preoccupied with how much or how little it is possible to convey, especially in matters of sexual attraction. It is as if they are conscious of a meaning of 'Pride' as feminine sexuality on display, which Johnson gives as rare and contemporary dictionaries as archaic. The plot turns on the inadequacy of Jane's signals to Bingley, the 'evidence' and information she can legitimately give him. All women in the novel are caught by the despotism of convention: whether they transgress the limits of decorum or they repress the flow of feeling, they are likely to be the victims of oppression or misunderstanding.

It is through the uncomfortable limits of sexual signals that the novel indirectly explores a profoundly important political question: when is it right to conceal or to reveal information; when is it right to speak out? Lady Catherine implicitly condemns Elizabeth for expressing 'opinions'. But these 'opinions' win hands down in open dispute about class, status, and independence when Darcy's aunt visits Longbourn. Withholding information does more harm in this novel than 'opinions'. Darcy, afraid to expose his family, does not reveal Wickham's seduction of his sister; similarly, Elizabeth and Jane decide not to damage his reputation by revealing his immorality. Kitty keeps Lydia's elopement secret. Mr Bennet, withholding even the most trivial social news from his family to exert his power over them, exemplifies the despotism exercised over information. He does not tell them that Mr Collins is arriving until breakfast-time on the day of his arrival, even though he has known of it for a month. Earlier, with a streak of meanness which makes him in so many ways an inadequate father, he had kept back from his family the news of his visit to Bingley. Conversely, Lydia reveals to Elizabeth the secret of Darcy's presence at her marriage. This is a crucial revelation, for it confirms Elizabeth's own perception of Darcy's transformation, and without this catalyst Elizabeth and Darcy would not have come so speedily, if at all, to their new understanding. The 'fallen' sister inadvertently enables the respectable upper-class marriage to take place.

The novel was written in a period when government repression was fierce, and the definition of sedition extraordinarily narrow. From John Wilkes's challenge to authority, to the treason trials of the late 1790s, and beyond that to the Hone trials of 1815, the question of what you could legitimately *say* and *know* was deeply at issue. What was subversive of the state, what were the limits of repression and censorship, and what belonged to the private and public domain were necessarily issues raised by revolutionary action and despotism alike. Even public records of parliamentary debates were not established until 1812 with Hansard.

This preoccupation with what can and cannot be known and said and the constraints governing expression begins to dominate the latter part of the novel in such a way that neither the first nor the second titles of the novel ultimately seem adequate to the text. At many points the novel frequently gives the impression that the words 'pride' and 'prejudice' have been interpolated to satisfy the demands of the 'new' title – Mary's dry and abstract generalisations, for instance, or Darcy's housekeeper's pride of and prejudice in favour of her master. There is a sketchy attempt to stress the positive aspects of pride in the later part of the novel: Elizabeth feels disinterested pride in Darcy's honourable and generous intervention on Lydia's behalf after the elopement, for example. But it is as if the text loses interest in this. Instead it is enthralled with the way news and information – and gossip – circulate in a local neighbourhood. Its anxieties increasingly surface as it comes to its conclusion.

The words 'neighbour' and 'neighbourhood' appear insistently as Jane and Elizabeth are about to leave the world of Longbourn and Meryton. The novel abounds in references to people (such as Mrs

Long, Miss King, and Mr Jones's shop boy) and events ('a private had been flogged' [p. 53]) we hear of but never see. Johnson defines 'neighbourhood' as 'Those that live within reach of communication'. He defines 'neighbour' as 'a word of civility' and offers one meaning as used in divinity with a theological resonance – 'one partaking of the same nature'. A neighbourhood can be narrow and must exclude as well as include, the poor falling uneasily within and outside its 'civility'. Mrs Bennet, with her definition of an ample neighbourhood as four and twenty families who dine at Longbourn, does not even know where Newcastle is, the destination of Wickham and Lydia. Local gossip and report precipitate Darcy's decision to remove Bingley from Netherfield and Lady Catherine's decision to arraign Elizabeth. It is the local nature of gossip networks which permits the unknown Wickham to deceive. On the other hand, the neighbourhood generates a supportive and energetic life. Despite Mr Bennet's scepticism about them, neighbours provide friendship and community.

The informality of Longbourn contrasts with the hierarchical neighbourhood of Rosings – with its palings carefully delimiting the landowner's property, and its neighbours who live beyond the Collins's style – and again with the Darcy seat – whose family does not visit the local town. These differences produce an almost sinister sense of a dissolving social organisation. Mrs Bennet seems to be clinging to an older definition of neighbourhood when she feels that it is a positive obligation for the tenant of Netherfield not to be an absentee. Her ability to enumerate so many possible dwellings for Lydia and Wickham in the locality suggests an emptying out of the community. At the same time, such interest discloses an appealing side to her: she has a warm sense of community. Misdirected though her sense of neighbourliness is, she is a better neighbour than her husband, just as she is sometimes a better parent. It is Darcy who brings relativism into the idea of neighbourhood, when he devalues 'strong local attachment' and forces Elizabeth to admit that 'The far and the near must be relative' in one of his few private conversations with her at Rosings (p. 159). This is another point in the novel where distance changes perspective. As Elizabeth points out, the rich man, Darcy, can travel where he likes.

What is a neighbourhood, a community? When supportive local networks of communication begin to atrophy, what takes their place? The book takes an almost fierce pleasure in the dispersal northwards of the Bennet sisters, whose social mobility leaves so many embarrassments behind, yet in departing they enter into another, less cohesive and more relativist world, the new world of both upper and middle classes. What kinds of cohesion, and what kinds of exchange of information, supersede neighbourhood bonding? There is a ruthless prescience about a changing perception of social organisation and relations which makes this truly a post-revolutionary text, a text fully of the Napoleonic Wars.

It is perhaps no accident that Uvedale Price, with his sharp sense of the shifting boundaries of our categories, was able to define one of the radical shifts in perception created by the Wars. He wrote a pamphlet about the necessity of exploiting neighbourhood forces and existing structures of local loyalty and allegiance for defence against an invasion by the French. The uniquely cohesive nature of British society was created by the 'gradations' of property from the highest to the middle ranks.[28] It is significant here that Elizabeth reminds Lady Catherine that, in spite of the Bennet family's connections with trade, she is a gentleman's daughter. For Price, such gentlemen would present a united front in war. In war, each neighbourhood would defend its own. He deprecated a centrally organised *national* army because it dispersed and weakened local bonds and atomised relationships. The presence of a national army, indeed, provokes a crisis of definition and communal identity for him which he is clearly attempting to avoid. But this crisis is exactly what is provoked by the arrival of the —shire Militia in Jane Austen's text. All the complexities and crises stem from its presence. The Militia, once local in function and provenance, were reorganised during the Napoleonic Wars to provide national defences.[29] Wickham moves from the Militia to the Regulars, the national standing army, on his marriage, as if to endorse that shifting allegiance which comes from both fragmentation and centralisation. This is a dispersal to which almost every character in the novel is subject, man or woman, high or low, subversive or reactionary.

Pride and Prejudice opens up questions of great complexity. It is hard to assign it to a fixed political category – Jacobin, anti-Jacobin, conservative, revolutionary. But one can say that the text asks demanding and radical questions – perhaps the more radical because they are indirect. The luckiest character in the novel crosses a narrow bridge to security, fulfilment, and virtually another class. But bridges declare that there are gaps and rifts to be crossed, and there may even be chasms which are impassable. The novel leaves these implications unexplored. But the ease of its reconciliation may have been what prompted Jane Austen's self-critical remarks about the novel's 'lightness'. Certainly it seems that *Pride and Prejudice* made the next novel, *Mansfield Park*, almost inevitable. For *Mansfield Park* picks up the questions of class privilege and power and how these are sustained. It explores the problems of social mobility in the poignant difficulties of Fanny Price. *Pride and Prejudice* leaves these problems before they become acute. That is why the assuaging and energising dreamwork of its comedy have no parallel in Jane Austen's other novels. But, no dreamer, she constructed a text which would challenge its dream.

From the Introduction to *Pride and Prejudice*, ed. Isobel Armstrong (Oxford, 1990), pp. vii–xxx.

NOTES

[Isobel Armstrong reminds us that despite the 'light, bright and sparkling' air of *Pride and Prejudice* it was written and rewritten across sixteen or seventeen very difficult years in Britain's history. Drafted as *First Impressions* in 1797 when the Terror of the French Revolution was at its height, it was published in the midst of the Napoleonic wars. Armstrong sees the bright surface of the novel and its conservative plot as providing a displaced representation of the anxieties provoked by the historical context, yet the narrative resolution is constantly questioned by the complex instabilities of the novel's key terms. The title's keywords had achieved rich moral and philosophical resonance in the work of David Hume for whom *pride* is an exaggerated self-esteem, a prejudice in favour of the self which subsumes *prejudice* towards others. Prejudice is a matter of partial knowledge, a perhaps necessary corollary of admitting that points of view must be partial, and is implicitly linked to the proliferating sciences of the visual through which the Enlightenment develops its obsessive project of objectively knowing the external world. Beginning with Newton's work to establish the science of optics, this project gives rise to the aesthetic theorisation of the sublime by Edmund Burke, then to the cultivation of the picturesque by Uvedale Price. Whereas optics lead supposedly to true understanding, and Burke's theories of the sublime and the beautiful imply finite and objective distinctions between dichotomous conditions, prejudice and the picturesque admit the perspective of an observer and are inherently dynamic and unstable. Prejudice and the picturesque imply that there is no truth position from which experience can be finally resolved, just as pride, in some ways a necessary quality of authority, proves itself mistaken in pre-judging the world. The expectation raised by Austen's title is that one will experience a tightly-controlled treatise in moral philosophy, a novel about clear antitheses (after the manner of *Sense and Sensibility*). But this implication is undermined by the progressive recognition that each term involves the other and no position allows either to be put to rest. Although the end of the novel provides romantic closure, the deeper implication is that this is merely an arbitrary moment of arrest before renewed instability. References are to the World's Classics edition of the novel (Oxford, 1990). Ed.]

1. Marilyn Butler, *Jane Austen and the War of Ideas* (Oxford, 1975; repr. with a new Introduction, 1987).

2. Franco Moretti, *The Way of the World: The Bildungsroman in European Culture* (London, 1987), pp. 1–73.

3. *Jane Austen's Letters to her Sister Cassandra and Others*, ed. R. W. Chapman (2nd edn, London, 1952; repr. 1979), pp. 299–300.

4. B. C. Southam, *Jane Austen's Literary Manuscripts: A Study of the Novelist's Development through the Surviving Papers* (London and New York, 1964), p. 58.

5. Tony Tanner (ed.), 'Introduction', *Pride and Prejudice* (Harmondsworth, 1972), p. 11.

6. Southam, *Jane Austen's Literary Manuscripts*, p. 60.

7. David Hume, *A Treatise of Human Nature* (1739), ed. A. D. Lindsay (London and New York, 1911; rev. 1956), vol. 2, bk. 2, 'Of the Passions', pp. 6–7.

8. Ibid., p. 8.

9. Samuel Johnson's *Dictionary* was first published in 1755.

10. Hume, 'Of the Passions', p. 13: 'these movements mutually assist each other, and the mind receives a double impulse from the relations both of its impressions and ideas!'

11. Hume, *Treatise*, see vol. 2, bk. 2, pt. 2.

12. Anna Laetitia Barbauld, 'On Prejudice', *Works*, with a Memoir by Lucy Aikin, 2 vols (London, 1825), vol. 2, pp. 321–37; p. 322.

13. Ibid., p. 322.

14. Ibid., p. 326. Interestingly, Mrs Barbauld insists that ideas of 'female honour and decorum' are not innate but culturally conditioned or 'imprest first as prejudice' (p. 330). The prejudice that girls should have husbands has 'imprest' itself on Lydia more strongly than ideas of decorum, the result of Mrs Bennet's anxious fears for the financial support of her daughters.

15. Hume, 'Of the Passions', p. 11.

16. Sir Isaac Newton, *Opticks or, a treatise of the reflexions, refractions, inflexions and Colours of Lights* (London, 1704), pt. 1, p. 10.

17. Ibid.

18. Sir Joshua Reynolds, 'Fourteenth Discourse', *Discourses, 1769–90* (London, 1842), p. 255.

19. Uvedale Price, *A Dialogue on the Distinct Characters of the Picturesque and the Beautiful. In answer to the Objections of Mr Knight: Prefaced by An Introductory Essay on Beauty; with Remarks on the Ideal of Sir Joshua Reynolds and Mr Burke upon that Subject* (London, 1801), pp. 130, 131.

20. See Walter John Hipple, *The Beautiful, The Sublime, and The Picturesque in Eighteenth-Century British Aesthetic Theory* (Carbondale, 1957), p. 241.

21. Uvedale Price's *Dialogue* was provoked by Payne Knight's refusal to consider the picturesque as an aesthetic category. The *Dialogue* is conducted by Hamilton, representing Price, Howard, representing Knight, and a sensible ignoramus, Seymour, who acts both as an intellectual fall guy and as an intelligent commentator. Knight's ideas of the beautiful – harmony between the extremes of the monotonous and the harsh – are best represented by Howard's discussion of the pictures in the gallery visited towards the end of the *Dialogue* (pp. 140–60).

22. Hipple, *The Beautiful*, p. 241: 'should our opinions be prescribed to us, and, like our places, be moulded into one form ...?' [Price].

23. The three participants in the *Dialogue* meet an old, tanned gypsy by a hovel at the start of their walk. The picturesque components of this scene, which is a touchstone for the category, are analysed in detail (pp. 130–2). The importance of time and the status of the ruin in eighteenth-century culture are discussed (pp. 183–91).

24. Price, *Dialogue*, pp. 136–8.

25. See Hipple, *The Beautiful*, p. 249: Price (*Dialogue*, p. 135), also makes a rustic bridge an important aspect of the picturesque.

26. Sir William Blackstone (*Commentaries on the Laws of England* [4 vols; 9th edn, rev. R. I. Burn, London, 1783], vol. 1, 449–50), comments on the rigidity of inheritance laws in England. Though the principle of 'liberty' is satisfied in the freedom to bestow property in any way one wishes, children should surely be granted a 'necessary subsistence'. Elsewhere (vol. 2, p. 114) he considers entail as a survival from the feudal system. Clearly the Bennet sisters suffer from a will 'prejudicial' to women. Despite the way in which she personalises the situation, Mrs Bennet is right to complain of it.

27. Mary Wollstonecraft, *A Vindication of the Rights of Woman* (1792), ed. Miriam Brody Kromnick (Harmondsworth, 1978), p. 97. Wollstonecraft produces what might be the scenario for *Pride and Prejudice*: 'Besides, nothing can be so *prejudicial* [my italics] to the

morals of the inhabitants of country towns as the occasional residence of a set of idle superficial young men, whose only occupation is gallantry, and whose polished manners render vice more dangerous, by concealing its deformity under gay ornamental drapery. An air of fashion ... is but a badge of slavery'.

28. Uvedale Price, *Thoughts on the Defence of Property. Addressed to the County of Hereford* (Hereford, 1797), p. 16.

29. See John Randle Western, *The English Militia in the Eighteenth Century. The Story of a Political Issue 1660–1802* (London and Toronto, 1965), for an account of military policy during the French wars. For a study of local organisation and military policy at a slightly later date in Hampshire, Jane Austen's county, see Ruscombe Foster, *The Politics of Country Power: Wellington and the Hampshire Gentlemen, 1820–1852* (Hemel Hempstead, 1989).

10

Irony and Authority

RACHEL M. BROWNSTEIN

It is a truth universally acknowledged that language is crucial in the give and take of pleasure and power: contemporary writers elaborate the point to get what measure of both they can for themselves. Jane Austen, before them, had interesting things to say on the subject. By her uses of the word 'power' she acknowledges the salient fact that there are different kinds: in *Pride and Prejudice*, for instance, Elizabeth says, 'It is not in my power to accept' an invitation (p. 211) shortly after observing, 'I do not know any body who seems more to enjoy the power of doing what he likes than Mr Darcy' (p. 183); Charlotte Lucas reflects at about the same time that 'all her friend's dislike [of Darcy] would vanish, if she could suppose him to be in her power' (p. 181). The degrees of power that people enjoy, over themselves and one another, and the drama of courtship as power play, are subjects of Austen's novels; playing with – and against – power is the act the novels engage in. By deploying words so as to point to the limits of definitive, assertive language, Jane Austen suggests a powerful and pleasurable relation that women in patriarchy may have to discursive authority.

The title page of *Sense and Sensibility*, the first novel Austen published, identified it as a work by 'A Lady'; *Pride and Prejudice* is signed 'By the Author of "Sense and Sensibility"', in other words by A Lady already published. The veiling signature insists on the dignity of femininity itself as 'Currer Bell,' 'George Eliot', 'Fanny Fern', or 'Mrs Humphry Ward' do not. It implies, as if modestly, that all ladies speak in the same voice – Austen was of course not the only one to write as one – which with pointedly feminine obliquity will avoid such blunt signifiers as proper names, and say precisely what one might expect it appropriately to say, and no more. 'A Lady' insists like a post-modern critic on an author's gender and class, indeed identifies the writer simply as a representative, perhaps only a function, of class and gender. It makes the titillating suggestion that sex is the subject, and also a promise that it will be avoided. (Austen obliges on both counts.) Finally, the signature indicates that the female is an accepted kind of author, probably one who will make herself delightful and useful without going so far as to set up as an authority. As Mary Ellmann wrote decades before the body became a theme of cultural critics, 'the male body lends credence to assertions while the female takes it away'.[1] Signing herself 'A Lady', even a published author promises to assert neither her (discreetly veiled) self nor any original idea of her own. This novelist will not, presumably, pit her literary capacity and performances against 'the abilities of the nine-hundredth abridger of the History of England, or of the man who collects and publishes in a volume some dozen lines of Milton, Pope, and Prior, with a paper from the Spectator, and a chapter from Sterne, [which] are eulogised by a thousand pens'; she does not claim authority, merely, slyly, 'genius, wit and taste' (*Northanger Abbey*, p. 37).

On the other hand, precisely by coming on as A Lady the author is assuming a certain kind of authority: as Mary Poovey has argued,[2] economic changes, together with anxieties about class and gender distinctions, created in eighteenth-century England the enthroned image of the Proper Lady, symbol of refinement and taste (and perhaps wit, if not genius) and with it, at considerable cost to themselves and their sex, some real power for ladies. It was largely limited to the drawing-room. Austen's writing as such A Lady, her mode of assuming ladylike authority in ladylike language, provokes the questions about her social and political allegiances that have divided critical authorities on the most respected woman writer in English. Jane Austen's awesome respectability has alienated some of her readers, and inspired wrong-headed enthusiasm in others. Does she want women's power confined to drawing-rooms? Does she sanction or mock the image of the authoritative proper lady, which confines as it defines feminine power?

As A Lady, Austen seems now to represent and speak for British civility, perhaps even civilisation, at its toniest. In *The Counterlife*, the American novelist Philip Roth introduces a representative traditional Austen fan, an Englishwoman who re-reads the novels each year because, she says 'The characters are so very good'. More explicitly, she continues, 'I'm very fond of Fanny Price, in *Mansfield Park*. When she goes back to Portsmouth after living down with the Bertrams in great style and grandeur, and she finds her own family and is so shocked by the squalor – people are very critical of her for that and say she's a snob, and maybe it's because I'm a snob myself – I suppose I am – but I find it very sympathetic. I think that's how one would behave, if one went back to a much lower standard of living.'[3] By 'good' Mrs Freshfield means that the characters are fastidious, and that the author is – that both dislike squalor, quite as she does. It is not fair to lump such a reader with the so-called Janeites; she is no idealiser of a gentle, genteel Jane; what she is is a Jane Austen snob. She imagines Jane Austen has the same standards of embattled gentility as she has, that like her Austen values those standards above everything. Readers of *Mansfield Park* will allow that Mrs Freshfield's confusion of standards *for* living with standards *of* living is something Jane Austen tempts one toward; the serious question is whether Austen is accountable for attracting snobs like her and encouraging them in snobbishness. I think she is. When we thrill to the way Mrs Bennet is dispatched as 'a woman of mean understanding, little information, and uncertain temper', or to the translucent, transcendent tact with which Mr Bennet tells his daughter Mary, in company, 'You have delighted us long enough' (p. 101), we respond with approval to a snob's ruthless high standards, and to her high-handedness. Austen's novels set us at a little, pleasant, critical distance from the actual, inelegant, disorderly world her letters reveal she herself lived in just as we do. Furthermore, the twentieth-century reader who, while not an authentic member of the English gentry, enjoys the sublime confidence of *Pride and Prejudice* – famously one of the world's impeccable masterpieces – can congratulate herself on her superior taste with a smugness very like Mrs Freshfield's. I suspect that even morally serious readers able to list the shortcomings of Sir Thomas and Lady Bertram, and prove Jane Austen knew they are no better than Fanny Price's Portsmouth parents, enjoy their own complicity with Austen's sure, exclusive Lady's tone.

This tone is, wonderfully, so authoritative as to enable Austen to put down titled ladies. Those of us who are not complacent about being snobs enjoy noting that titled ladies are not among the most admirable characters in the novels: that hypercorrected Lady Middleton and empty Lady Bertram are portrayed as patriarchy's mere creatures, and conventional Lady Russell and authoritarian Lady Catherine de Bourgh as its wrong-headed police. Nevertheless, it is as a lady – an untitled member of the gentry, 'a gentleman's daughter', which is how Elizabeth Bennet appropriates the term for herself – that Jane Austen condemns them. Austen carefully shows that Lady Catherine's manners are no more than her aspirations better than Mrs Bennet's. To mock Lady Catherine's 'authoritative manner' (p. 84) she reports in unexceptionably calm and decorous ladylike tones that, for instance, after dinner and cards at Rosings, 'the party ... gathered round the fire to hear Lady Catherine determine what weather they were to have on the morrow. From these instructions they were summoned by the arrival of the coach ...' (p. 166). Austen's special interest in exposing the pomposities of a great Lady or the pretensions of a couple of would-be ones – for example, the 'two elegant ladies' (p. 41) who are the Bingley sisters' maids – are signs, if we need them, that she signs herself with irony. There are ladies and ladies; 'A Lady', as a signature, claims to be generic and claims at the same time a certain classy distinction. Which claim is more correct? How are the claims related?

About being A Lady writing, which is to say about writing as a member of the group of women novelists, Austen's irony is even clearer, and also more complex. Her position on women's novels is spelled out in *Northanger Abbey*: they are more original than most of what's published, she declares. Even though their characters are very often stereotyped and their plots are commonly implausible, she says, they are both pleasurable and accurate, works 'in which the greatest powers of the mind are displayed, in which the most thorough knowledge of human nature, the happiest delineation of its varieties, the liveliest effusions of wit and humour are conveyed to the world in the best chosen language' (*Northanger Abbey*, p. 38). The emphasis falls tellingly on 'chosen language'. Choosing language, commenting on the stereotypes and formulae of novelists, and the language available for use in social life, is always Austen's subject. Of Emma's response to Mr Knightley's proposal, the narrator writes: 'What did she say? – Just what she ought, of course. A lady always does' (*Emma*, p. 431). Writing as A Lady, Austen savours the discrepancy between being a stable sign in her culture as well as a user and analyst of its signs.

A letter to her niece Fanny Knight suggests her relish of a woman writer's peculiar position and power. Fanny, evidently, had regaled her aunt by recounting an adventure rather wilder than a fictional

Austen heroine might have had, a visit to a gentleman's room. Intending to be charmed, indeed excited, there, poor Fanny had ended up disgusted, like Swift's gentleman in the lady's squalid dressing-room. Evidently she emerged with her sense of irony intact, and of this her aunt expressed approval: 'Your trying to excite your own feelings by a visit to his room amused me excessively. – The dirty Shaving Rag was exquisite! – Such a circumstance ought to be in print. Much too good to be lost' (*Letters*, p. 412). A cluster of characteristic Austen values come together here: an appreciation of telling details; a pleasure in telling them, and in hearing tell; a clear sense of the connections between saying and feeling, and social and emotional life; and seriousness about getting into print. Austen valued the novel because it told stories like Fanny's that focus on the ironic self-awareness of a rational creature absurdly caught in a lady's place, and because it could suggest some uses of language in ordinary life to make certain very important discriminations.

Her own language, with its ostentatious embrace and sly mockery of the tropes of fiction for women, depends on her readers' familiarity with that fiction – on their having the thorough, easy knowledge of them that enables one to recognise social or literary conventions as such, and to relish them. The reader she counts on will respond to a turn of standard plot as if to the anthem of an outgrown school, and treasure a collegial allusion to such matters as the 'tell-tale compression of the pages [that promises] … we are all hastening together to perfect felicity' (*Northanger Abbey*, p. 250) – all of us together, characters and narrator and readers assembled in the same linguistic craft. Austen presents herself as a daughter of the novelists who had formed her vision and her readers', and continued to inform it. Condescending, mocking, competitive, this attitude is also defensively and devotedly filial. Far from struggling in a Bloomian agon with awesome precursors she aims to overthrow, Austen keeps her mother and sister novelists always in mind to measure the ways she is like and yet unlike them.

Austen wrote first of all for her intimate family of 'great Novel-readers & not ashamed of being so' (*Letters*, p. 38), as she put it; Austen fans tend like a very close family to be clubby and even a little apologetic about a very personal taste (as opposed to a liking for George Herbert, say, or George Eliot). We relish a sense of the choosiness and the exclusiveness (the sad accident of there being only six novels enhances it) of our little community. The pronoun in the title of Lionel Trilling's last essay, 'Why We Read Jane Austen',[4] reveals something more than a magisterial critic's traditionalist, universalist attitude: the feeling that the culture we share with Jane Austen is beleaguered or not enough valued, that powerful people on the outside don't take it seriously, serves to bind us more tightly together, 'we' snobs like Mrs Freshfield, 'we' readers of women's novels, 'we' humanists in a dehumanising world, even 'we' wary students of how language determines our pleasures and power. Those others who take the truth to be whatever is universally acknowledged remain ever in the corner of Jane Austen's eye: by their limitations we measure our own sagacity, and also our snugness. As Katherine Mansfield remarked, 'every true admirer of the novels cherishes the happy thought that he alone – reading between the lines – has become the secret friend of their author'. Wayne Booth, quoting this in *The Rhetoric of Fiction*, adds – losing the connection with words on the page, but avoiding Mansfield's 'he' – that the Austen reader has an 'illusion of travelling intimately with a hardy little band of readers whose heads are screwed on tight and whose hearts are in the right place'.[5] The illusion depends on the way the confident, confidential tones of A Lady are deployed so as to mock the accents of authoritative patriarchal discourse in the universe that contains her universe and her fictions.

The literary tradition in which Jane Austen was placed and/or placed herself – the tradition of Jane West and Mary Brunton – was not the dominant tradition; one of the most arduous projects of feminist scholars has been to retrieve and re-evaluate eighteenth-century fiction by women. Everything Austen wrote about the novel (and perhaps everything in her novels too) indicates that she knew quite as well as we do that the genre she chose or was constrained to choose (rather as her heroines choose their husbands) was not universally esteemed – that Catherine Morland is representative if not accurate in her assumption that 'gentlemen read better books' (*Northanger Abbey*, p. 106), presumably works of greater heft and seriousness. Logically enough, while portraying authority figures and their discourse as in general not exemplary, Austen mocked women's novels most for their moralising. The maxims that articulate the attitude of patriarchal authority on sex and marriage, the main subject of such novels, are parodied in *Pride and Prejudice*: Elizabeth lifts up her eyes in amazement as her sister Mary moralises, after Lydia runs away, 'that loss of virtue in a female is irretrievable – that one false step involves her in endless ruin – that her reputation is no less brittle than it is beautiful' (*Pride and Prejudice*, p. 289). Pointedly, Austen does not write down: she will not preach like pedantic Mary. To laugh at him and them, she makes Mr Collins comically echo the stentorian tones of the 'learned doctors' who spell out the moral meanings of romantic actions in novels by, for instance, Charlotte Lennox and Frances Burney. In his final letter to Mr Bennet he warns 'my cousin Elizabeth, and yourself, of what evils you may incur, by a precipitate closure with [Darcy's] propos-als', and declares his amazement at the 'encouragement of vice' that occurred when Lydia and Wickham were received by her parents (pp. 363–4). Mr Bennet rightly observes that this clergyman's atti-tude is less than Christian, but he himself is a no more reliable authority than his heir. He is, as Elizabeth's meditations on his char-acter point out, considerably less than ineffectual, not only pathetic-ally hampered by the entail from disposing of his own patrimony, but worse than useless as a head of his household. Austen's shift from the explicit didacticism of her predecessors is signalled by the striking absence of an authoritarian father figure in the novel: Mr Gardiner, who has the tact to arrange some things, is a shadowy minor character. There is no one but the hero and heroine them-selves to discuss, at the end, what 'the moral' of their story might be (p. 381). Hapless Mr Bennet's comment on life itself meanwhile resonates: 'For what do we live, but to make sport for our neigh-bours, and laugh at them in our turn?' (p. 364). It is neither the moral of the whole novel nor one the whole novel repudiates.

Pride and Prejudice is about women's lives in relation to sexual roles and to marriage; therefore – that the connection is inevitable is Jane Austen's point – it is about power and independence and authority. The novel opens, seductively, in the authoritative mode of the Johnsonian essayist: 'It is a truth universally acknowledged that a single man in possession of a good fortune must be in want of a wife.' On the face of it this sentence has an authoritative ring: as surely, it is the paradigmatic Jane Austen sentence, which was famously and enigmatically praised by Virginia Woolf as 'a woman's sentence'. Confronted by the sentence suitable for men writers, Woolf declared, Austen 'laughed at it and devised a perfectly nat-ural, shapely sentence proper for her own use and never departed from it'.[6] The initiating philosophical-sounding premise of *Pride and Prejudice* laughs at authoritative sentence-making. As everyone has pointed out, it is full of logical holes: a truth universally acknowledged is probably less than true; the truth at issue here is not really that single men want girls (which 'in want of' does not mean anyway) but that poor girls need husbands. And, far from describing the real state of things in society, the novel's first sentence expresses a gossip's fantasy that women exchange or traffic in men. The sentence acknowledges, by putting it first, Mrs Bennet's view of things (or is it only what for her purposes Mrs Bennet acts as if she believes?): that rich men want to be supplied with (even poor) wives. We are encouraged to reflect that although this is not the case, it may be operatively true when people act as if it's true. The power of discourse to determine action is suggested.

The last sentences of Chapter 1, quite as authoritative as the first sentence is, complement it, by contrast. Far from entertaining Mrs Bennet's point of view, the narrator here speaks from above, and decisively detaches herself from the woman: 'she was a woman of mean understanding, little information, and uncertain temper. When she was discontented she fancied herself nervous. The business of her life was to get her daughters married; its solace was visiting and news.' These dismissive declaratives crackling with the briskness that charms snobs are very different from the meditative voice that pronounces the ironic, pseudo-philosophical first sentence. But the conclusion of the chapter resembles its commencement in one important regard, that is, in claiming distance and authority – the authority a lady in a drawing-room shares with a philosopher, a society epigrammatist shares with a judge. The reader is encouraged to reflect on the similarities and also the differences between ladies and philosophers, drawing-rooms and the arenas of real power. And the limits of any authoritative statement are suggested when we look more closely and discover that the impressive balance and antithesis of the final sentence is factitious: Mrs Bennet's solace, far from being a change from her business, is her mode of conducting that. 'News', the narrator's last word on this first chapter, a simple word rather elaborately kinder to Mrs Bennet than 'gossip' might be, nicely labels the subject of the chapter. The cap it puts on the chapter suggests that it was indeed substantive; but as Chapter 2 follows, the roundness and fullness the cap helps to emphasise begins to seem illusory. We find that the scene between Mr and Mrs Bennet was by no means as crucial and conclusive as we thought when it turns out that Mr Bennet visited Mr Bingley before his wife asked him to.

The first sentence and the first chapter of *Pride and Prejudice*, integral, finished units in their different, equally forceful ways, mime so as subtly to mock the certainties of authoritative discourse; in the plot of the novel, such discourse becomes a theme. Proud Mr Darcy sets the action going when he scrutinises Elizabeth Bennet and pronounces her 'tolerable, but not handsome enough to tempt *me*!'. For the feminist critic, that italicised pronoun evokes the sinister bar of the masculine 'I' that Virginia Woolf described, in *A Room of One's Own*, as a shadow disfiguring male texts: as Darcy goes on to declare his opinions on female accomplishments and related matters, his character as a pronouncer of judgements is amusingly sketched. The action that devolves from his comment on Elizabeth proves his authoritative statement was false and the first step toward its own undoing. To begin with, Elizabeth mocks by repeating the line, telling the story on him; 'she had a lively, playful disposition', the narrator explains, 'which delighted in any thing ridiculous' (p. 12). By talking so as to render him ridiculous she is deliberately manipulating her own psyche (rather in the manner of Fanny Knight visiting her gentleman's room). 'He has a very satirical eye', she tells Charlotte, 'and if I do not begin by being impertinent myself, I shall soon grow afraid of him' (p. 24). In other words, by repeating his words to others she is talking for – in effect to – herself, choosing and using language not to express feeling but to create it, to make herself feel powerful. Darcy will accurately observe, much later, that she finds 'great enjoyment in occasionally professing opinions which in fact are not [her] own' (p. 174). Lest we think she does this just to flirt, we find her, very much later in the novel, doing the same thing in the very private precincts of her own mind, as she thinks about the question of whether Bingley will propose to Jane. At the conclusion of that gentleman's visit to Longbourn, toward the novel's end, the narrator tells us that, 'Not a word passed between the sisters concerning Bingley; but Elizabeth went to bed in the happy belief that all must speedily be concluded, unless Mr Darcy returned within the stated time. Seriously, however, she felt tolerably persuaded that all this must have taken place with that gentleman's concurrence' (p. 346). Here again, talky Elizabeth is enjoying herself by professing – silently, but nevertheless as if to a drawing-room audience, in well-constructed, carefully timed sentences – an opinion that is not seriously – 'not in fact' – her own. The remarkable sentence that begins 'Seriously, however', as it remarks on the non-seriousness of the one that precedes it, raises interesting questions about the power of positive assertions – highly subversive questions about the seriousness of all definitive statements and sentences, in what is after all a tissue of words, a series of sentences. Austen invites us to consider that words and sentences might not be signs or containers of meaning after all: 'My dearest sister', Jane says once her affairs are settled and Elizabeth's are at issue, 'now *be* serious. I want to talk very seriously. Let me know every thing that I am to know, without delay. Will you tell me how long you have loved him?' Elizabeth answers, 'It has been coming on so gradually, that I hardly know when it began. But I believe I must date it from my first seeing his beautiful grounds at Pemberley.' Jane can tell she doesn't mean it: 'Another intreaty that she would be serious, however, produced the desired effect; and she soon satisfied Jane by her solemn assurances of attachment' (p. 373).

Elizabeth could tell herself Darcy might ruin her sister's happiness only because she knew he would not, being ready by now to have his friend marry Jane. As she also knows, he was long before conquered by her own 'lively' – he does not call them 'satirical' – eyes, 'bewitched' by her powers, so much so as to ask her to understand – she would have had to be either an impossibly rational creature or a very smug witch to do so – that he fell in love with her against his better judgement. But she does not say these things. Many chapters later, when they finally can both with dignity agree to marry, it is after a long talk which ends with Elizabeth biting her tongue: on the verge of making a caustic observation, she 'checked herself', for 'she remembered that he had yet to learn to be laughed at, and it was rather too early to begin' (p. 371). Since people are comical, quite as Mr Bennet says, dignity is precarious, and silence helps better than words to maintain it. Darcy will eventually be made to learn to laugh: in the novel's nearly penultimate paragraph, which begins to detail the bliss of the married life of the Darcys at Pemberley, we are told that Darcy's sister Georgiana ' at first ... listened with an astonishment bordering on alarm, at [Elizabeth's] lively, sportive, manner of talking to her brother. He, who had always inspired in herself a respect which almost overcame her affection, she now saw the object of open pleasantry. Her mind received knowledge which had never before fallen in her way. By Elizabeth's instructions she began to comprehend that a woman may take liberties with her husband, which a brother will not always allow in a sister more than ten years younger than himself' (p. 388). In the happy end Georgiana will take the place at Elizabeth's side of Jane, the more feeling sister with whom Elizabeth shared the sisterly mockery of men Jane never could engage in either. She will be the female confidante and foil – the other woman to talk to – that is necessary to the happiness of even the mistress of Pemberley. Both Darcys, then, will be instructed by Elizabeth happily ever after. In other words, just as the marriage plot comes to triumphant closure it is neatly undercut: female bonding and women's laughter are elements of this novel's happy end. One woman will make a man the subject of her pleasantries while another one listens and learns. This subtle subversion of the conventional romantic plot accords with the novel's attitude toward verbal tissues that appear to wrap things up once for all.

Like her heroine, Austen questions authoritative discourse through dialogue. Dialogue, Mary Ellmann wrote, 'might be defined as the prevention of monologue';[7] as such it is a critique of patriarchal absolutism in prose. There are many modes of dialogue in *Pride and Prejudice*, the first of which is the mode of ironic narrative. When Austen refers to the 'two elegant ladies' who wait on the Bingley sisters she means that these women absurdly pretend, like their mistresses, to elegance. Irony is an efficient mode: the description of the maids serves for the mistresses. Like an impatiently rude interlocutor, irony questions a statement as it is made; the single sentence becomes in effect two, assertion cum contradiction.

Literal dialogue between characters in the novel may also be a process of assertion and contradiction, sometimes of opinions, sometimes of the authority to state them. Although we tend to remember *Pride and Prejudice* as chock full of witty exchanges, some of the most interesting dialogue is between talk and the lack of it. There dialogue is as much the subject as the mode of discourse. The first chapter is a case in point: 'My dear Mr Bennet', his lady begins the action by saying to him one day, 'have you heard that Netherfield Park is let at last?', to which 'Mr Bennet replied that he had not'. The switch to indirect discourse signals the man's taciturnity; he is not quite responding to his wife. One is reminded of this marital lack of exchange when Elizabeth and Darcy talk together later: '"It is *your* turn to say something now, Mr Darcy – *I* talked about the dance, and *you* ought to make some kind of remark on the size of the room, or the number of couples." He smiled, and assured her that whatever she wished him to say should be said' (p. 19). Elizabeth is unlike her mother making deliberate, sophisticated conversation about conversing, but my point – aside from the small truths that voluble Elizabeth somewhat resembles her mother, that Austen's egoistic young people both tend to italicise pronouns – is that Darcy is hardly a Benedick to Elizabeth's

Beatrice, therefore that the real exchange is between talking and not talking, and that that is one way Austen suggests the limits of discursive authority.

In her Lady's voice, which combines an authoritative ring with flexible self-mocking undertones, Austen can comment with varying degrees of explicitness on the limits of rhetorical and human authority. Through self-reflexive irony she can keep her distance from the discourse of authority, the patriarchal mode of imposing oneself through language. Except for ladies in domestic and literary circumstances (drawing-rooms and fictions) circumscribed by the world of men, women have been denied such authority. By writing as A Lady and considering the circumstances that determine her persona – that is, by seeing it as a persona – Austen could simultaneously reflect and reflect on the power of authoritative language. When Elizabeth scrutinises her third-volume feelings about Darcy, she considers the fact that it is she who has the power to provoke the words that will change her life: 'She respected, she esteemed, she was grateful to him, she felt a real interest in his welfare; and she only wanted to know how far she wished that welfare to depend upon herself, and how far it would be for the happiness of both that she should employ the power which her fancy told her she still possessed, of bringing on the renewal of his addresses' (p. 266). The rhythms are authoritative, magisterial. The novel reader knows the heroine must wait, and we with her, for a second proposal it is not in her power to make – but meanwhile it seems that Elizabeth's struggle to turn fancy into knowledge is the significant action. The proposal, important though it is, will be a coda to the inner action of discriminating among thoughts and the words for them. Only if we ignore that sentence and its sisters can we read *Pride and Prejudice* as a mere romance. Which is not to gainsay the pleasure we take in the novelist's very romantically and conventionally 'uniting them', as she puts it, in the end – or, rather, in the Gardiners' having done so. Having been responsible for the mechanics of getting the couple together, Elizabeth's relatives are thrust forward in the novel's last sentence as the only legitimate claimants to agency. Does the emphasis fall on the fact that the hero and heroine are mere puppets of circumstances, or perhaps of the marriage plot? Are we meant to envy their prospect of happiness ever after in the paradise of Pemberley? Or to note with sly pleasure that these cultivated but rather dull middle-class Gardiners will be frequent guests at that monument to Lady Catherine's class? It is hard to decide, and this, I think, is what must be borne in mind when we write about Jane Austen, whose authoritative irony eludes, even mocks, our authoritative critical discourses.

From *Women's Studies*, 15 (1988), 57–69.

NOTES

[Rachel Brownstein extends Mary Poovey's conception of 'the Proper Lady' to notice that this ideology has implications for active class discrimination as well as gender discrimination. Writing as 'a Lady' allows Jane Austen to patronise anyone who is vulgar, whether aristocrat or bourgeois, by birth or by purchase. The ironic mockery extends from people to ideas and books, and situates Austen by presumption on a superior moral and intellectual ground. This assumption of superiority is, as I explained in the Introduction, what makes Austen such a useful writer to Modernist elitists. Having recognised this rather unpalatable aspect of Austen, Brownstein argues that it is this very same tendency to assume superiority that leads Austen to adopt patriarchal maxims, yet frequently to mock their absurdity. We are thus offered the paradox of a woman writer who adopts the male authoritative sentence in order to subvert it from within. Attentive readers of Jane Austen can therefore experience a radical ironic liberation from all manner of presumptious authority, however founded. Page references are to *The Novels of Jane Austen*, 3rd edn, ed. R. W. Chapman, 5 vols (Oxford, 1933), and to *Jane Austen's Letters*, collected and edited by R. W. Chapman (Oxford, 1979). Ed.]

1. Mary Ellman, *Thinking about Women* (New York, 1968), p. 148.

2. Mary Poovey, *The Proper Lady and the Woman Writer* (Chicago, 1984).

3. Philip Roth, *The Counterlife* (New York, 1986), p. 270.

4. Lionel Trilling, 'Why we read Jane Austen', *The Times Literary Supplement*, 5 March 1976.

5. Wayne Booth, *The Rhetoric of Fiction* (Chicago, 1966), p. 266.

6. Virginia Woolf, *A Room of One's Own* (New York and London, 1957), p. 80.

7. Mary Ellman, *Thinking about Women*, p. xii.

11

Can this Marriage be Saved: Jane Austen Makes Sense of an Ending

KAREN NEWMAN

> 'You agree with me in not liking Corinne, then?'
> 'I didn't finish the book,' said Maggie. 'As soon as I came to the blond-haired young lady reading in the park, I shut it up and determined to read no further. I foresaw that the light-complexioned girl would win away all the love from Corinne and make her miserable. I'm determined to read no more books where the blond-haired women carry away all the happiness. If you could give me some story now, where the dark woman triumphs, it would restore the balance.'
> (George Eliot, *The Mill on the Floss*)

Despite Maggie Tulliver's plea for novels in which the dark woman triumphs, many feminists have not been kind in their judgement of such plots. Marriage, almost inevitably the narrative event that constitutes a happy ending, represents in their view submission to a masculine narrative imperative that has traditionally allotted women love and men the world. Ironically, perhaps, such readers have preferred novels that show the destructive effects of patriarchal oppression, for they complain that Austen's endings, her happily-ever-after marriages, represent a decline in her protagonists: 'as in much women's fiction, the end, the reward, of women's apprentice-ship to life is marriage ... marriage which requires [Elizabeth Bennet] to dwindle by degrees into a wife.'[1]

The question I want to address is, can this marriage be saved? That question poses a larger and more theoretical question about how we read endings generally. In his foreword to a recent number of *Nineteenth-Century Fiction* devoted to endings, Alexander Welsh suggests that 'endings are critical points for analysis in all examinations of plot; quite literally, any action is defined by its ending'.[2] Many readers of Austen have taken just this attitude toward her endings. Either the critic reads an Austen novel as a romantic love story in which social and economic realities of nineteenth-century women's lives are exposed but undermined by comedy, irony, and most tellingly marriage, or she reads marriage as a metaphor for self-knowledge, the overcoming of egoism and the mark of psychic development: in Austen's *Emma*, for example, marriage 'is most significant as a social ritual which ratifies a transformation in Emma herself ... [just as] the union of Jane Eyre and Rochester ... takes its meaning from the heroine's own psychic growth'.[3] Neither approach seems satisfactory, for both ignore important aspects of these texts and their historical context. The event, marriage, does after all refer to a real social institution that, in the nineteenth century particularly, robbed women of their human rights.[4] The most cursory look at the legal and cultural history of women makes it clear that these narrative events reflect the social and legal limitations that women of the eighteenth and nineteenth centuries faced and that in turn reflect the way a patriarchal society has manipulated biological roles for its own advantage. To read marriage as metaphor is not a sufficient answer.

Nor can we accept the feminist judgement that Austen's endings undermine her critique of social and economic forces and their effects on women.[5] The assumptions of such a reading bear scrutiny, for they read the novel as an object to be consumed by the dominant culture. As D. A. Miller observes in his recent book on narrative closure, 'once the ending is enshrined as an all-embracing cause in which the elements of a narrative find their ultimate justification, it is difficult for analysis to assert anything short of total coherence'.[6] By reading an Austen novel as a unity with romantic marriage as its final statement, we impose a resolution on her work that makes it conform to the very expectations for women and novels that Austen's irony constantly undermines. Such a habit of reading, which, as Welsh puts it, defines any action by its ending, falls prey to a teleological prejudice that contemporary criticism has called into question. As critics and feminists, we must refuse the *effect* of her endings; instead of simply accepting the text as it presents itself, we must investigate the contradictory, disparate elements from which it is made: the psychological paradigms, the raw materials of ideology and of women's place in culture. An Austen novel and indeed any fashioned work of art conceals and diverts attention from the visible seams where these contradictory materials are joined; the critic's task is to analyse how this diversion takes place, to investigate *how* the text produces its meaning and effect.[7]

If instead of assuming that endings define the action of a novel (an enterprise we would never even attempt in reading poetry) we assume that our sense of an ending is a function of the principles of structure by which the novel is generated or according to which one element follows another, in the case of Austen our sense of closure is markedly different from the one a teleological reading provides. Austen exposes the fundamental discrepancy in her society between its avowed ideology of love and its implicit economic motivation. But her response to this conflict is more complex than the simple juxtaposition of the languages of love and money so often remarked by her critics since Dorothy Van Ghent and Mark Schorer in the early fifties.[8] Her consistent use of economic language to talk about human relations and her many portraits of unsatisfactory marriages prevent us from dismissing her novels as romantic love stories in which Austen succumbs uncritically to the 'rewards' her culture allotted women. Even more important, however, are the unresolved contradictions between romantic and materialist notions of marriage and human relationships that govern the production of meaning in her texts.[9] Austen's novels provide us with rival versions of a single set of facts that coexist without final reconciliation or resolution, and the text displays these gaps or disjunctions on the levels of both plot and sentence.

Nancy Miller has called attention to the usefulness of formalist approaches, particularly the work of Gérard Genette, for reading women's fiction.[10] In his essay 'Vraisemblance et Motivation', Genette defined *vraisemblance* in a literary text as action that conforms to the maxims, presuppositions, or received opinions of the public or society: 'Real or assumed, this opinion is pretty much what today would be called ideology, that is to say, a body of maxims and prejudices which constitute both a vision of the world and a system of values.'[11]

For Genette, texts solve the problem of *vraisemblance* in three ways. In the first kind of text, 'the relationship between a plausible narrative and the system of plausibility to which it subjects itself ... is essentially mute'. Such works conform to the 'tacit contract between a work and its public', and this silence indicates the text's conformity to the dominant ideology. The second kind of text is liberated from ideology, but is also silent because it refuses to justify the 'motives and maxims of the actions'. The silence of the first text is a function of what Genette calls 'plausible narrative'; that of the second, a function of arbitrary narrative'. It is only in the third type of narrative that these silences are voiced in what Genette calls the 'endless chatting' of the Balzacian novel. Balzac presents the reader with an 'artificial plausibility' in which authorial commentary justifies the plot by inventing the missing maxims. I would like to suggest that Jane Austen's novels represent a variant of this third type. *Pride and Prejudice* begins with a maxim on which the ensuing narrative is based – that 'it is a truth universally acknowledged that a single man in possession of a good fortune must be in want of a wife'.[12] What is the relation of this maxim to the novel and its context? Neither of the young men in possession of a fortune in the novel seems in want of a wife; on the contrary, it is the young women without property – the Bennets, Charlotte Lucas – who are in need of spouses, and not the reverse. The maxim, then, on which the novel is based does not justify the story; its function is not *vraisemblance* but exposure, for it serves as a continual ironic reminder of the discrepancy or gap between social convention and economic necessity.

In *Emma*, maxims serve a somewhat different function. Early in the novel, in talking to Harriet of that lady's farmer suitor, Robert Martin, the heroine announces that 'The yeomanry are precisely the order of people with whom I feel I can have nothing to do'.[13] This maxim does not function for everyone of Emma's rank and social class but is designed to expose her own snobbery and class prejudice. Knightley has 'to do' not only with Robert Martin, but also with William Larkin; the Westons dine with the Coles. The maxim serves to expose the contradiction between Emma's ideas of herself and her class and the actual social relations the novel portrays.

Genette argues that the maxims and generalisations that an author makes are all determined by the *telos* – in this case marriage. In Austen's case, however, the generalisation that opens *Pride and Prejudice* in no way explains or justifies the ultimate ending of the novel, for it is not the young men who are in want of spouses, but all those without property. In this novel, then, Austen creates a deliberate disjunction between received opinion and social reality.

Her epigrammatic maxims, instead of being designed to justify ends, or simply to create irony, are designed to expose the contradiction between their own pretence of causality and the real economic basis for action in the novel.

There are abundant examples in Austen's novels of her ironic juxtaposition of incongruous elements to satirise a character. One of my favourites is, not surprisingly, a conversational tidbit of Mrs Bennet's. After lamenting the defection of Bingley and the treachery of the Lucases in gaining Mr Collins, she says to her sister-in-law, Mrs Gardiner, 'your coming just at this time is the greatest of comforts, and I am very glad to hear what you tell us of long sleeves' (p. 178). The wonderful parallel juxtaposition of 'comfort' and 'long sleeves', both of which fall at the end of their respective independent clauses, and the superlative 'greatest' expose marvellously Mrs Bennet's characteristic exaggeration of trivialities and corresponding diminution of real values. But there are other moments in the text when Austen's irony does not serve so simple a purpose.

In chapter 3 Austen finally provides us with a description of the Netherfield party that has been the subject of such interest and anxiety in the neighbourhood:

> Mr Bingley was good looking and gentlemanlike; he had a pleasant countenance and easy and unaffected manners; his sisters were fine women with an air of decided fashion. His brother-in-law, Mr Hurst, merely looked the gentleman; but his friend Mr Darcy drew the attention of the room by his fine, tall person, handsome features, noble mien; and the report which was in general circulation within five minutes after his entrance, of his having ten thousand a year. The gentlemen pronounced him to be a fine figure of a man, the ladies declared he was much handsomer than Mr Bingley.
>
> (p. 58)

Here Austen's irony is not directed at a fool but at society, and she does not exclude Elizabeth or Jane Bennet, those characters whom we regard as admirable. On the contrary, she emphasises that the report was in *general* circulation and uses the generic *ladies* and *gentlemen*. This passage details the way in which wealth determines judgement, not only of character, but also even of appearance. Each member of the Netherfield party, though seemingly rated according to his or her 'natural' attributes, is actually rated according to his fortune – Darcy, Bingley, the sisters, Mr Hurst.[14] Austen's point here is clearly the way in which wealth determines point of view.

Traditionally Elizabeth is excluded from this judgement, but as Sir Walter Scott long ago noticed, Elizabeth's change of heart toward Darcy happens at Pemberley in response to his property. I do not mean to denigrate Elizabeth – she is a superior individual, and what impresses her about Pemberley is not simply its wealth but also the taste and judgement it implies.[15] Scott was, of course, wrong in reducing Elizabeth's change of heart to crass materialist motives, but not, I think, entirely, for a close examination of Elizabeth's relation to property reveals a deliberate intention on Austen's part to show us not simply a moral development, Elizabeth's sense that she had not known herself and had misread others in her prejudice, but a growing recognition of her 'interest'.[16]

Austen is at pains from early in the novel to show us Elizabeth's response to Darcy's wealth. When she is at Netherfield nursing her sister, Austen unfolds a scene in which Elizabeth overhears a conversation between Darcy and Miss Bingley about his property in Derbyshire. The function of the scene is not simply to introduce and describe Darcy's property or to show Miss Bingley's clear interest in it; its function is explained by the description of Elizabeth's behaviour that follows the conversation:

> Elizabeth was so much caught by what passed, as to leave her very little attention for her book, and soon laying it wholly aside, she drew near the cardtable and stationed herself between Mr Bingley and his eldest sister, to observe the game.
>
> (p. 84)

Clearly the motivation for Elizabeth's action is not the ironic one given by the narrator, 'to observe the game', but to hear more on the subject of Darcy's estate. Elizabeth was so much *caught* by what passed. Later, when she seeks to discover from Wickham the reason for Darcy's reaction to meeting him, Elizabeth says to him tellingly, unwilling, we are told, to let the subject drop, 'he is a man of very large property in Derbyshire, I understand' (p. 121). In her revealing conversation with Mrs Gardiner about Wickham's affection, she says that 'he is the most agreeable man I ever saw – and if he becomes really attached to me – I believe it will be better that he should not. I see the imprudence of it – Oh, that abominable Mr Darcy' (p. 181). On a syntactic level, Darcy here literally blocks her affections for the impecunious Wickham! Austen voices through Elizabeth herself the fundamental contradiction of the novel: 'What is the difference in matrimonial affairs between the mercenary and the prudent motive? Where does discretion end and avarice begin?' (p. 188). No one, particularly no woman who is economically dependent, not *even* Elizabeth, whom we admire, is unmoved by property. We should remember that only the ignorant and imprudent Lydia marries 'for love', and then a man whom Darcy has paid to tie the knot.

A close reading of *Pride and Prejudice* reveals the contours of the patriarchal ideology from which Austen's novels emerge and in which women are at the mercy of male control of the means of production. Should we say, as Judith Lowder Newton does, that the range and complexity of the Marxist-feminist problematic the novel poses is blocked or repressed by the fantasy-wish-fulfilment structure of the boy-meets-girl-leads-to-marriage convention? I don't think so, for I think the constant alternation between the fairy tale structure and the materialist language that pervades the novel emphasises rather than represses or obscures what Terry Eagleton terms the 'fault lines' of nineteenth-century English society.[17]

Let us return briefly to the sentence quoted earlier describing Darcy at the ball: 'but his friend Mr Darcy drew the attention of the room by his fine, tall person, handsome features, noble mien; and the report which was in general circulation within five minutes after his entrance, of his having ten thousand a year' (p. 58). Austen juxtaposes the 'Prince Charming' description of Darcy – his fine, tall person, handsome features, noble mien – with the final attribute of the series that reports his having ten thousand a year. The juxtaposition of these two classes represents the two conflicting and independent perspectives that function in the novel – love and money. The tension created by this contrast in which neither perspective is subordinated to the other reveals what the French critic Pierre Macherey would call the 'not said' or silence of the novel – the true place of women in a materialist culture in which men control money: this silence 'is the juxtaposition and conflict of several meanings which produces the radical otherness which shapes the work; this conflict is not resolved or absorbed, but simply displayed'.[18] The happy ending of an Austen novel gives it an apparent unity that is false, for meaning is produced not so much by resolution, but by means of oppositions and contradictions, by the incompatibility of several meanings.

Such an understanding of Austen's art explains the extremes of critical thinking her novels have generated – the claims, such as Marilyn Butler's on the one hand, that Austen's books 'belong decisively to one class of novels, the conservative', which criticises indi-

vidualism and the unconventional, or those of Van Ghent and more
recently Nina Auerbach and Susan Morgan, who read her novels as
revolutionary, romantic, or both.[19] Butler is convincing in her claim
that Austen works out of the anti-Jacobin tradition, but to conclude
that her novels are therefore conservative is problematic. To justify
such claims, Butler is forced to infer that the meaning of *Pride and
Prejudice* 'is not precisely or not sufficiently written into the text'
and worse, that *Persuasion* is 'muddle'.[20] And however many times
we are told that 'Austen's subject is perception' or that *Persuasion*
is about the self imperilled by change and time, we still recognise in
Austen's work principles of proportion and social integration quite
unromantic and unrevolutionary.[21]

If, instead of taking a partisan view, we admit that culture is not
a harmonious and unified whole in which political and social beliefs
and institutions are at one with aesthetic productions, whether anti-
Jacobin or romantic, we are in a better position to understand
Austen's art and its relation to ideology. In his 'Letter on Art in
Reply to André Daspre', Althusser proposes that art makes us 'see'
or 'perceive' 'the ideology from which it is born, in which it bathes,
from which it detaches itself as art, and to which it alludes'.[22] Art is
not a reflection of ideology because this act of seeing, the 'view'
that art provides, presupposes 'an internal distanciation from the
very ideology from which such novels [Balzac's] emerged'.[23] We are
not required, therefore, to argue that Austen abandoned a conservative political position in order to claim that her novels criticise the
patriarchal ideology from which they emerged, for her personal
political views are only one component of the content of her work.

Instead we must recognise that Austen's artistic achievement in
rendering the inner life of her characters, of Elizabeth, Emma, and
Anne, wins our sympathy regardless of the ultimate 'lessons' these
heroines may learn. Our sympathy with their inner lives may even
conflict with the author's critical intentions, just as Austen's irony
in treating her romantic endings contradicts their conventional
claims for the happily-ever-after. These contradictions are not artistic failures or 'muddle'; they allow us a view, from a critical distance, of English society and the position of women in the first
decades of the nineteenth century.

Oppositions are also evident in the ironic ambiguity of Austen's
diction. For example, Johnson defines 'to fix' as (1) to make fast,
firm or stable; (2) to settle, to establish invariably; (3) to direct
without variation; (4) to deprive of volatility; (5) to pierce, to

transfix; and finally, (6) to withhold from motion. Austen plays on the polysemous nature of 'fix' at various, often significant, moments in her text. The novel's opening maxim, we learn in the second paragraph, 'is so well fixed in the minds of the surrounding families' that a single man 'is considered as the rightful property of some one or other of their daughters' (p. 51). The second meaning of 'fix' occurs so frequently in the novel as not to require example, but those senses concerned with motionlessness deserve quotation: Charlotte judges Jane's composure with Bingley disadvantageous because 'If a woman conceals her affection with the same skill from the object of it, she may lose the opportunity of fixing him' (p. 68). Here the entomologist's eye and pin seem fixed on that 'single man in possession of a good fortune'. In the plot of *Pride and Prejudice*, women try to fix men, but it is women who are 'fixed' in all of Johnson's senses of the word. When Elizabeth stands before Darcy's portrait at Pemberley, she does not fix her eyes on him; instead we find an oddly subjectless clause that inscribes Elizabeth in a scopic economy and highlights her position in a patriarchy:

> Every idea that had been brought forward by the housekeeper was favourable to his character, and as she stood before the canvas, on which he was represented, and fixed his eyes upon herself, she thought of his regard with a deeper sentiment of gratitude than it had ever raised before.
>
> (p. 272)

Here the syntax leads us to expect Elizabeth as the subject of 'fixed', but we are brought up short by the possessive pronoun 'his'. It is Darcy's 'regard' that fixes Elizabeth.

The multiple meanings of words in Austen's prose are means for exposing the social contradictions that are the subject of her novels. Johnson defines 'amiable' as (1) 'pleasing or lovely' and (2) 'pretending or shewing love'. When Elizabeth thanks Charlotte Lucas for listening to Mr Collins and thus sparing Elizabeth herself, Charlotte

> assured her friend of her satisfaction in being useful, and that it amply repaid her for the little sacrifice of her time. This was very amiable, but Charlotte's kindness extended farther than Elizabeth had any conception of; – its object was nothing less, than to secure her from any return of Mr Collins's addresses, by engaging them towards herself. Such was Miss Lucas's scheme.
>
> (p. 162)

As her emphasis on Charlotte's scheming suggests, Austen intends both meanings of 'amiable' to work on the reader in this passage. Two chapters later the narrator remarks: 'After a week spent in professions of love and schemes of felicity, Mr Collins was called from his amiable Charlotte' (p. 177). The adjective with its contradictory meanings, here linked with other similarly ambiguous words – 'schemes', 'professions' – becomes almost an epithet for Charlotte, perhaps even for courtship itself, in this section of the novel.

'Prudent', like 'amiable', also has conflicting meanings in *Pride and Prejudice*. In its original sense, *prudentia* was one of the cardinal virtues in pagan and Christian ethics. Prudence was the practical wisdom of moral conduct, but as Glenn Hatfield has pointed out in his discussion of the word in Fielding, in the eighteenth century the term was debased by custom and usage to mean cunning or deceit making for the appearance of virtue.[24] In *Pride and Prejudice* Elizabeth puzzles over the meaning of prudence in matrimonial affairs. Jane deems Charlotte prudent when she endeavours to soften Elizabeth's condemnation of her friend's match with the boorish Mr Collins, but Elizabeth counters 'that selfishness is not prudence' (p. 174).[25] Soon afterward, Mrs Gardiner warns her of the imprudence of a match with Wickham. Elizabeth admits to her aunt, 'I see the imprudence of it' (p. 181). When Wickham begins courting the heiress Miss King, the narrator comments:

> Elizabeth, less clear-sighted perhaps in his case than Charlotte's, did not quarrel with him for his wish of independence. Nothing, on the contrary, could be more natural .... she was ready to allow it a wise and desirable measure for both, and could very sincerely wish him happy.
>
> (p. 186)

The *perhaps* that follows 'less clear-sighted' undermines the force of this judgement. We wonder, is Elizabeth really clear-sighted in her condemnation of Charlotte, or is the novel as much about her learning the complexities of 'prudence' as those of 'pride' and 'prejudice'?[26]

Though the meaning of imprudence may be clear enough, prudence in matrimonial affairs is more complex.[27] Charlotte is prudent, and, as the quotation above suggests, scheming in her pursuit of Mr Collins. Yet the narrator's report of what are admittedly Charlotte's reflections on her choice do not betray Elizabeth's prejudice:

A
Without thinking highly either of men
B
or matrimony, marriage had always been
C
her object; it was the only honourable
provision for well educated young women
A
of small fortune, and however uncertain of
B
giving happiness, must be their pleasantest preservative from want.

(p. 163)

The careful eighteenth-century balance of clauses in this passage emphasises the conflicting forces women encounter in culture. The negative clause that begins the passage is contrasted with the contradictory 'marriage had always been her object', just as the negative clause of the final lines is juxtaposed with the opposed sentiment expressed in the final clause to give us the following scheme: A/B C A/B.[28] The realistic Charlotte has no romantic illusions about marriage, but she nevertheless deems it the best alternative for 'well educated young women of small fortune' in her society. The unresolvable conflicts inherent in her situation are expressed in the characteristic Austenian balance the novelist inherits from the Augustans. In Jane Austen, prudence is not only the practical wisdom of moral conduct; it is also what we might define as acting in one's own interest in accordance with virtue, but with a realistic appraisal of the limits and difficulties life presents. When she visits Charlotte, Elizabeth is compelled, we recall, to meditate 'upon Charlotte's degree of contentment, to understand her address in guiding, and composure in bearing with her husband, and to acknowledge that it was all done very well' (p. 193).

That this technique of exploiting the connotations or variations in meaning of key words is central to Austen's irony and meaning is evident in the titles of her novels. In those with paired words, this opposition is clear, but even in the late novel *Persuasion* variation in meaning is important.[29] Johnson's dictionary defines 'persuade' as (1) 'to bring to any particular opinion' and (2) 'to influence by argument'. So in *Persuasion* Anne Elliott 'was persuaded to believe the engagement a wrong thing – indiscreet, improper, hardly capable of success, and not deserving it' by Lady Russell's influence on her pliant will.[30] Now that Anne is more mature, however, even after considering every argument against her engagement to Wentworth,

> She was persuaded that under every disadvantage of disapprobation at home, and every anxiety attending his profession, of all their probable fears, delays and disappointment, she should yet have been a happier woman in maintaining the engagement than she had been in the sacrifice of it.

If we turn to the endings themselves, we find an ironic self-consciousness that emphasises the contradiction between the sentimentality of Austen's comic conclusions and the realism of her view of marriage and of women's plight.[31] Darcy's second proposal is prompted by Elizabeth's thanking him, despite her aunt's admonitions of secrecy, for his part in effecting the marriage of Lydia and Wickham. In chapter 60, after they are united and reflecting on the past, Elizabeth exclaims: 'what becomes of the moral, if our comfort springs from a breach of promise' (p. 389). Here Austen subverts the traditional sentimental ending with a moral. Though often brought about by ironic reversals or miraculous coincidences from which moral lessons can be drawn, reconciliations in eighteenth- and nineteenth-century fiction are not usually dependent on a breach of promise! Darcy counters with his vision by claiming that it was not Elizabeth's breach of promise but Lady Catherine's interference that led him to hazard a second proposal.

In Austen's novels, our conventional expectations are often met but at the same time undermined by self-consciousness and parody. Wickham and Lydia are not punished with misery and unhappiness, but live tolerably well given their weaknesses and extravagance; Miss Bingley has no change of heart when acquainted with her brother's happiness – her congratulations 'were all that was affectionate and insincere' (p. 391). But perhaps no detail in the final pages better suggests Austen's ironic treatment of her own happy endings than Mr Bennet's brusque letter to Mr Collins: 'I must trouble you once more for congratulations. Elizabeth will soon be the wife of Mr Darcy. Console Lady Catherine as well as you can. But, if I were you, I would stand by the nephew. He has more to give' (p. 390).

In *Emma* the heroine despairs over her father's anxiety about her marriage. We are told 'she could not proceed' (p. 380). Austen pointedly observes that no 'sudden illumination' or 'wonderful changes' in Mr Woodhouse's character made the marriage possible;

instead a pilfering of poultry yards so frightened the old man that Emma's marriage became desirable (pp. 380–1). So also in *Persuasion* she consistently undercuts our expectation of a reconciliation between Anne and Wentworth. The so-called autumnal descriptions of Anne's faded beauty and the overheard conversations between the Musgroves and Wentworth serve to contradict our usual expectations for a comic ending of matrimonial reunion. Austen's comic conclusions neither undermine her heroines by making them dwindle into wives nor institute what has been called a virtual 'ideological paradise';[32] they reveal the gap between sentimental ideals and novelistic conventions on the one hand, and the social realities of sexist prejudice, hypocrisy, and avarice on the other.

Austen's novels show us women confronting the limitations imposed by late eighteenth- and nineteenth-century English society. Instead of assuming, as critics so often have, that Austen's respect for limits grows out of eighteenth-century philosophical thought and the conservative anti-Jacobin sentiments of the 1790s we might attribute a part at least of her strong sense of boundaries to her experience of women's limited horizons and opportunities for action.[33] If Jane Austen had not written with a deep sense of those limitations, she would have written utopian fantasy, not novels. What is positive and pleasurable about Austen's or Brontë's novels is that their heroines live powerfully within the limits imposed by ideology. In doing so, they redefine what we think of as power, helping us to avoid the trap that traditional male definitions of power present, arguing that a woman's freedom is not simply a freedom to parody male models of action. These novels of the past and their endings are valuable because they do not assume that what men do is what every human being wants to do. As I suggested earlier, the marriages that solve the narrative problem created by an independent female protagonist are strategies for arriving at solutions that ideology precludes. In *Pride and Prejudice*, everything about Elizabeth – her poverty, her inferior social position, the behaviour of her family, her initial preference for Wickham, and her refusal of Darcy's first offer of marriage – all these things ideologically should lead if not to death, at best to genteel poverty and spinsterhood. Instead Austen has her marry despite her violations of these accepted norms of female behaviour, and in so doing, she distorts the very historical and economic realities of marriage that her novel so forcefully depicts. Brontë does similar things both in *Jane Eyre* and *Villette*. In *Jane Eyre*, traditional critics call Bertha, the madwomen in the attic, a gothic romantic holdover from Brontë's childhood fantasies of Angria; feminists, however, interpret Bertha as the incarnation of Jane's repressed rage and sexual desire. In terms of narrative, this element of the plot, then, is a device for expressing what cannot be articulated; Bertha is a literary device for circumventing the ideological strictures that prevent Brontë from writing openly about Jane's sexuality.[34]

The literary text's mode of resolving a particular ideological conflict may also produce conflicts on levels of the text other than that of plot, as in Austen's sentence describing Darcy in which the two clauses mediate our understanding of love and money in the novel. A novel's value, then, or indeed the value of any work of art for feminists, is determined not by its progressive picture of woman or by any exhortation to change a sexist society, but rather by its articulation of the conflict, or what is sometimes called the problematic, posed by a sexist ideology, in the background but nevertheless dominant, in which female consciousness is foregrounded. Austen's novels in fact suggest that space, time, and human relations – what we might call ideology – are understandable and controllable, that power is in self-mastery, internal not external. Brontë, on the other hand, implies that circumstances should and can be overcome; her heroines, in fact, change them.

So Austen, as students notice and puzzle over, is both reactionary and revolutionary. She takes women's exclusion from political power and action as she finds it. In the nineteenth century she clearly looked backward, and her sense of order represents in part at least a reaction to the social and political upheaval caused by the revolutions in France and America. But she is also revolutionary in her determination to change our ideal of what power is by arguing that women cannot be excused from power by the limits society imposes on them. She in fact argues that those who succeed are larger than their circumstances, that they control their fate and exercise real power, and from such characters and actions come the claims for Austen's kinship with the Romantics. In *Persuasion*, Wentworth seems to have the power of choice over Anne. He has all the advantages of male power and privilege – travel, the opportunity to make his fortune, the power to choose a wife – but he must return to the limits of the neighbourhood of Kellynch Hall and finally wait for Anne to choose him, for her words to pierce his soul. 'Only Anne', as Austen introduces her, to whom no one listened and whom no one heard (p. 11). Austen is in this sense revolutionary – she redefines our traditional assumptions about the nature of power.

The feminist critic's rejection of Austen's endings is all too easily subsumed by the old complaints about the smallness of her art, the claims that it is limited because she ignored or even fought against currents of thought released by the French revolution, or in the case of the feminist critic, by Wollstonecraft and the early movements for women's rights. No criticism of Austen's art more effectively reveals the dangers of what has been called 'phallocentric' criticism, which privileges the traditional male domains of action and modes of reading, for as the London-based Marxist Feminist Literature Collective points out:

> Austen's refusal to write about anything she didn't know is as under-mining to the patriarchal hegemony as Wollstonecraft's demand for a widening of women's choices: the very narrowness of her novels gave them a subversive dimension of which she herself was unaware, and which has been registered in critics' bewilderment at what status to accord them.[35]

I would quarrel with this statement only in its assertion that Austen was unaware of the subversive dimension of her novels, for how can we know?

In closing I want to consider briefly the problem of specificity in women's writing. Feminist critics have been preoccupied with dis-covering 'what, if anything, makes women's writing different from men's'.[36] The most common answer is that women's lives and experi-ences differ from men's, and that the difference is inscribed in their writing – in imagery, and more important, in content. This judge-ment is ironically consonant with the traditional rejection of Austen's small world, her 'little bit (two inches wide) of Ivory', though the feminist critic usually, but not always, recognises the value of the women's world Austen portrays. Alternatively feminists have hypothesised a feminine or female consciousness different from the masculine that produces a specifically feminine or female style. Both approaches have met criticism from those who point out that male writing often manifests a content or style elsewhere termed feminine or female. Rather than attempt to label particular features of style or units of content as feminine, we would be better served by recognising common strategies among women and men who are, for whatever reason, excluded or alienated from traditional patriar-chal power structures. In Austen's case, irony and parody are subversive strategies that undermine the male hegemony her novels portray and reveal the romantic and materialist contradictions of which her plots and characters are made.

The French feminist psychoanalyst Luce Irigaray claims that women's writing is impossible because men control language. Women's access to language, to the Word, is determined by the cultural constructions of patriarchal power.[37] Their only recourse, according to Irigaray, is mimesis, imitation of male forms, but imitation that is self-conscious or reflexive, what we might call imitation with a difference. Parody is that literary form which most openly declares its status as imitation, its difference.[38] We might say, then, that Austen's parody, particularly her parodic endings, is her means of interrogating patriarchal plots and power. The marriages that end her novels can only be saved by reading them not as statements of romantic harmony or escape, but in the context in which she placed them. Far from acquiescing to women's traditional role in culture, Austen's parodic conclusions measure the distance between novelistic conventions with their culturally coded sentiments and the social realities of patriarchal power.

From *Journal of English Literary History*, 50 (1983), 693–708.

NOTES

[Karen Newman takes her point of departure by questioning the reading of Austen's novels as if all their meanings were determined by their endings. She points up the need for critics, and especially feminists, to observe the contradictions that exist between differing aspects of the text and not assume that because the novels are generically obliged to produce a conservative closure at the end, all meaning is thereby rendered retrospectively less radical than it was. This strategy of reading is especially important with Austen since her novels expose fundamental discrepancies between the ideology of love and marriage and its implicit economic motivation. Newman suggests that we might need to read Austen's representation of Elizabeth Bennet's love for Darcy as more consciously economic than fits with modern tastes. The romance plot does not conceal economic motivations, rather it is articulated with those motivations in a manner that reveals how desire is mobilised by need. Here Newman adopts the theory of Louis Althusser and Pierre Macherey which invites us to see the literary text as establishing an internal distance from the ideology with which it is inspired. To read Austen correctly requires an acute attention to the contemporary significations of key words (a feature noted by Isobel Armstrong in this volume) because

Austen frequently employs words whose shifts in sense (here, for example, *prudence*) are determined by recent changes in relations between money, power, class and values. Austen, like Shakespeare, is a philological writer, whose work sparks where the word in one person's mouth is not the same in another person's ear. When one is aware of this difference one recognises that Austen's writing opens a possible disbelief around what it appears to propound. The wish-fulfilment fantasy of *Pride and Prejudice* requires that we hold in opposition the desired satisfaction and the ironic knowledge that conventional utterances, beliefs and fictions are misleading representations of their actual psychological and economic motives and conditions. References to Jane Austen's *Pride and Prejudice* are to the Penguin edition, ed. Tony Tanner (Harmondsworth, 1972). Ed.]

1. See Judith Lowder Newton, 'Pride and Prejudice: Power, Fantasy, and Subversion in Jane Austen', *Feminist Studies*, 4 (Fall, 1978), 41; and her more recent *Women, Power, and Subversion* (Athens, Ga., 1981), pp. 55ff. [reprinted in this volume Ed.] see also Nina Auerbach's discussion of 'equivocal' female power and Elizabeth's acquiescence to Darcy in *Communities of Women* (Cambridge, 1978), pp. 38ff.; and Sandra M. Gilbert and Susan Gubar, *The Madwoman in the Attic: the Woman Writer and the Nineteenth-Century Literary Imagination* (New Haven, 1979), pp. 154ff.

2. Alexander Welsh, Foreword, *Narrative Endings, Nineteenth-Century Fiction*, 33 (1978), 1; see also D. A. Miller's discussion of the 'common assumption of an a priori determination of means by the ends' in twentieth-century narratology in *Narrative and its Discontents* (Princeton, 1981), pp. xiiff.

3. Ruth Yeazell, 'Fictional Heroines and Feminist Critics', *Novel*, 8 (1974), 34.

4. For a survey of the legal and social aspects of marriage and their impact on women in the eighteenth and nineteenth centuries, see Patricia Thomson, *The Victorian Heroine: A Changing Ideal* (London, 1956); Duncan Crow, *The Victorian Woman* (London, 1971); Francoise Basch, *Relative Creatures*, trans. Anthony Rudolf (New York, 1974); and Jenni Calder, *Women and Marriage in Victorian Fiction* (New York, 1976).

5. Newton, 'Pride and Prejudice', pp. 27–42; Gilbert and Gubar, *Madwoman in the Attic*, pp. 154ff.

6. Miller, *Narrative and its Discontents*, p. xiii.

7. My discussion of the critical enterprise owes a great deal to Pierre Macherey's *Pour une théorie de la production littéraire* (Paris, 1971).

8. Mark Schorer, 'Fiction and the "Matrix of Analogy"', *Kenyon Review*, 11 (1949), 539–60; Dorothy Van Ghent, *The English Novel* (New

York, 1953); and David Daiches, who calls Austen a 'Marxist before Marx' in 'Jane Austen, Karl Marx and the Aristocratic Dance', *American Scholar*, 17 (1948), 289–98.

9. For an interesting discussion of contradiction in literary texts, see Rosalind Coward and John Ellis, *Language and Materialism* (London, 1977), pp. 87ff.

10. Nancy K. Miller, 'Emphasis Added: Plots and Plausibilities in Women's Fiction', *PMLA*, 97 (1981), 36–48; my remarks on maxims are based on Miller's discussion.

11. Gérard Genette, 'Vraisemblance et Motivation', in *Figures*, II (Paris, 1969), 71–99; translated by Nancy Miller, 'Emphasis Added', pp. 38–9.

12. *Pride and Prejudice*, p. 51.

13. Jane Austen, *Emma*, ed. R. W. Chapman (Cambridge, 1957), p. 20. All references are to this edition.

14. In an essay on *Persuasion*, Gene Ruoff points out that at the end of *Pride and Prejudice*, the worth of each character is represented by his or her 'proximity and access to Pemberley' ('Anne Elliott's Dowry: Reflections on the Ending of *Persuasion*', *The Wordsworth Circle*, 7 [1976], 343).

15. See Tanner's introduction to the Penguin edition of *Pride and Prejudice* (Harmondsworth, 1972) in which he points out that 'the grounds, the house, the portrait, all bespeak the man – they represent a visible extension of his inner qualities, his true style' (p. 24).

16. Remember that late in the novel in response to Jane's question, 'tell me how long you have loved him', Elizabeth says, 'I believe I must date it from my first seeing his beautiful grounds at Pemberley' (p. 382). This sentence is followed by 'another entreaty that she should be serious', but Austen's point is clear enough – no one is immune.

17. Terry Eagleton, *Criticism and Ideology* (New York, 1978) discusses the way in which novels display the 'fault lines' of a particular period or culture. His Marxist perspective is useful to any feminist analysis of literary texts.

18. Macherey, trans. Geoffrey Wall, *A Theory of Literary Production* (London, 1978), p. 84. See also Wolfgang Iser's discussion of indeterminacy in *The Implied Reader* (Baltimore, 1974), pp. 29–56.

19. Marilyn Butler, *Jane Austen and the War of Ideas* (Oxford, 1976), p. 3. For recent examples of the opposing point of view, see Nina Auerbach's 'O Brave New World: Evolution and Revolution in *Persuasion*', *Journal of English History*, 39 (1972), 112–28; and Susan Morgan, *In the Meantime* (Chicago, 1980).

20. Butler, *Jane Austen*, p. 215, p. 290.

21. Morgan, *In the Meantime*, p. 10, and William A. Walling, 'The glorious Anxiety of Motion: Jane Austen's *Persuasion*', *The Wordsworth Circle*, 8 (1976), 333–41.

22. Louis Althusser, *Lenin and Philosophy and Other Essays*, trans. Ben Brewster (New York, 1971), p. 222.

23. Althusser, ibid., pp. 222–3.

24. Glenn W. Hatfield, *Henry Fielding and the Language of Irony* (Chicago, 1968), pp. 177–96.

25. See Morgan, who takes Elizabeth's view (*In the Meantime*, pp. 92–7). She condemns Charlotte Lucas to the 'immoral' company of Isabella Thorpe, Mary Crawford, and Lucy Steele, a singularly ungenerous judgement that distorts the test and ignores both Austen's ironic commentary on Elizabeth's very different judgement of Wickham's engagement and Elizabeth's own changed opinion of Charlotte's situation later during her visit with her friend.

26. Butler sees Elizabeth's conflicting attitudes toward Charlotte and Wickham as 'pointlessly inconsistent' (*Jane Austen*, p. 214). She ignores Austen's emphatic critique of the double standard that condoned such behaviour for a man who must, after all, head a household, but condemned a woman who makes similar choices as mercenary.

27. Hatfield claims that Austen insists only on the 'original' meaning of the word *prudence* rather than on its increasingly common meaning in eighteenth-century usage, 'deceit' or 'cunning' (*Henry Fielding*, p. 196); however, attention to the various uses of the word in her novel suggests that Austen, like Fielding, plays with the conflicting meanings of the term.

28. For a discussion of style as meaning and of eighteenth-century parallelism and antithesis generally, see W. K. Wimsatt, Jr, *The Prose Style of Samuel Johnson* (New Haven, 1941).

29. Lloyd W. Brown, *Bits of Ivory* (Baton Rouge, 1973) presents an interesting discussion of Austen's ambiguous diction in terms of eighteenth-century philosophical and moral writings (pp. 15–51). See also K. C. Phillips, *Jane Austen* (Chicago, 1973); and most recently, Janice Bowman Swanson, 'Toward a Rhetoric of Self: the Art of *Persuasion*', *Nineteenth-Century Fiction*, 36 (1981), 1–21.

30. Jane Austen, *Persuasion* (New York, 1964), p. 31. All references are to this edition.

31. See also Brown's discussion of Austen's narrative conclusions, *Bits of Ivory*, pp. 223–35.

32. For Miller in *Narrative and its Discontents*, Austen's fiction enacts a perpetual double bind between 'its tendency to disown at an ideological level what it embraces at a constructional one', that is, the moral lapses, blindness, or waywardness of her heroines. Despite the richness of his reading of Austen, he fails to see that the 'coincidence of truth with closure in Jane Austen's novels' is undermined by her ironic play with the conventions of the female plot (pp. 46–54).

33. For a detailed and scholarly discussion of Austen's place on the philosophical and political map of the late eighteenth and early nineteenth centuries, see Butler, *Jane Austen*, and Tanner's introduction, *Pride and Prejudice*, pp. 42–45.

34. Marxist Feminist Literature Collective, 'Women's Writing: *Jane Eyre, Shirley, Villette, Aurora Leigh*', *Ideology and Consciousness* (Spring, 1978) 34–5. Nancy Miller argues that the fantasy and extravagance of the plot in women's fiction is linked to their unsatisfied ambitious wishes or desires often concealed in seemingly erotic longing ('Emphasis Added', pp. 40–1); see also Gilbert and Gubar, *Madwoman in the Attic*, pp. 336ff.

35. 'Women's Writing', p. 31.

36. Annette Kolodny, 'Some Notes on Defining a Feminist Literary Criticism', *Critical Inquiry*, 2 (1975), 78.

37. *Ce sexe qui n'en est pas un* (Paris, 1977), pp. 134ff.

38. See Froma I. Zeitlin's interesting discussion of parody and mimesis in 'Travesties of Gender and Genre in Aristophanes', *Thesmophoriazousae*', *Critical Inquiry*, 8 (1981), 311ff.

Further Reading

The following brief reading list covers a range of topics and includes works from which I would have liked to select had there been space in the volume. I have collected them into categories as a rough guide to approach. In some cases this is a very arbitrary process: the concerns of most feminist approaches are deeply historical, the concerns of many historical approaches are feminist. Labels are useful, but only as labels. The best advice always is to judge what is written, not what the category is.

BIOGRAPHY AND THE SOCIAL CONTEXT

There are now a number of differently useful biographies of Jane Austen. Since the documentary traces that Jane Austen might have left for history were erased by her sister Cassandra and other members of her family, her biographers have to resort to reading the life and social context in and out of the historical record and the novels themselves. There is arguable good in all of them. They are:

John Halperin, *The Life of Jane Austen* (Brighton: Harvester, 1984).
Park Honan, *Jane Austen: Her Life* (London: Weidenfeld and Nicholson, 1987).
Oliver McDonagh, *Jane Austen* (New Haven: Yale University Press, 1991).

On the relationship between Austen and her socio-political context, apart from works mentioned in the Introduction to this volume, see:

D. D. Devlin, *Jane Austen and Education* (London: Macmillan, 1975).
Warren Roberts, *Jane Austen and the French Revolution* (London: Macmillan, 1979).
Igor Webb, *From Custom to Capital: the English Novel and the Industrial Revolution* (Ithaca, NY: Cornell University Press, 1981).

FEMINIST STUDIES

Nancy Armstrong, *Desire and Domestic Fiction: A Political History of the Novel* (New York: Oxford University Press, 1987).
Nina Auerbach, *Communities of Women: an Idea in Fiction* (Cambridge, MA: Harvard University Press, 1978).

Rachel M. Brownstein, *Becoming a Heroine: Reading about Women in Novels* (Harmondsworth: Penguin, 1984).

Mary Evans, *Jane Austen and the State* (London: Tavistock Publications, 1987).

Claudia L. Johnson, *Jane Austen: Women, Politics and the Novel* (Chicago: Chicago University Press, 1988).

Claudia L. Johnson, 'A Sweet Face as White as Death', *Novel: A Forum on Fiction*, 22 (1989), 159–74.

Margaret Kirkham, *Jane Austen: Feminism and Fiction* (Brighton: Harvester, 1983).

Ellen Moers, *Literary Women* (London: W. H. Allen, 1977).

Laura G. Mooneyham, *Romance, Language and Education in the Novels of Jane Austen* (London: Macmillan, 1988).

Lillian S. Robinson, *Sex, Class and Culture* (New York: Methuen, 1986).

Patricia Meyer Spacks, 'Austen's Laughter', *Women's Studies*, 15 (1988), 71–85.

Patricia Spacks, *The Female Imagination* (New York, 1975).

Janet Todd, *Women's Friendship* (London: Allen & Unwin, 1976).

Janet Todd, 'Jane Austen, Politics and Sensibility', in Susan Sellers and Linda Hutcheon (eds), *Feminist Criticism: Theory and Practice* (London: Harvester Wheatsheaf), pp. 71–87.

LANGUAGE

The most important aspect of Jane Austen's works is obviously her language. Without its irony, why would one read her novels? Yet the very stuff of her art is difficult to ascertain. Helpful contributions can be found in:

Ann Banfield, *Unspeakable Sentences: Narration and Representation in the Language of Fiction* (London: Routledge, 1982).

Zelda Boyd, 'Jane Austen's "must": the Will and the World,' *Nineteenth-Century Fiction*, 39 (1984), 127–43.

J. F. Burrows, *Computation in Criticism: A Study of Jane Austen's Novels and an Experiment in Method* (Oxford: Clarendon Press, 1987).

C. Finch and P. Bowen, 'The Tittle-Tattle of Highbury – Gossip and the Free Indirect Style in *Emma*', *Representations*, 31 (1990), 1–18.

Louise Flavin, '*Mansfield Park*: Free Indirect Discourse and the Psychological Novel', *Studies in the Novel*, 19 (1987), 137–57.

Jan B. Gordon, 'A-filiative Families and Subversive Reproduction – Gossip in Jane Austen', *Genre*, 21 (1988), 5–46.

Jane Nardin, *Those Elegant Decorums: The Concept of Propriety in Jane Austen's Novels* (Albany: University of New York Press, 1973).

Norman Page, *The Language of Jane Austen* (New York: Barnes & Noble, 1972).

Roy Pascal, *The Dual Voice: Free Indirect Speech and its Functioning in the 19th Century European Novel* (Manchester: Manchester University Press, 1977).

LANDSCAPE STUDIES

As the essays by Alistair Duckworth and Isobel Armstrong in the present volume make clear, Jane Austen was profoundly engaged with the political aesthetics of landscape gardening and its conjoint concern, estate improvement. The following essays explore this most important aspect of her work:

B. M. Benedict, 'Jane Austen's *Sense and Sensibility*: the Politics of Point of View', *Philological Quarterly*, 69 (1990), 453–70.
Rosemarie Bodenheimer, 'Looking at the Landscape in Jane Austen', *Studies in English Literature*, 21 (1981), 605–23.
John Dixon Hunt, 'Sense and Sensibility in the Landscape Designs of Humphry Repton', *Studies in Burke and His Time*, 19 (1978), 3–28.

IDEATIONAL AND LITERARY CONTEXT

Philip Drew, 'Jane Austen and Bishop Butler', *Nineteenth-Century Fiction*, 35 (1980), 127–49.
W. Galperin, 'Byron, Austen and the Revolution of Irony', *Criticism*, 32 (1990), 51–80.
Claudia L. Johnson, 'The "Twilight of Probability": Uncertainty and Hope in *Sense and Sensibility*', *Philological Quarterly*, 62 (1983), 171–86.
Claudia L. Johnson, 'The Operations of Time, and the Changes of the Human Mind: Jane Austen and Dr Johnson Again', *Modern Language Quarterly*, 44 (1983), 23–38.
Robert Scholes, 'Dr Johnson and Jane Austen', *Philological Quarterly*, 54 (1975), 380–90.
Janet Todd, *Sensibility: An Introduction* (London: Methuen, 1986).

OTHERS

All groupings create a category of the excluded. These are some that seriously merit attention:

Derek Brewer, *Symbolic Stories: Traditional Narratives of the Family Drama in English Literature* (London: Longman, 1988).
Lennard Davis, *Resisting Novels* (London: Methuen, 1987).
Franco Moretti, *The Way of the World: the Bildungsroman in European Culture* (London: Verso, 1987).
Meier Sternberg, *Expositional Modes and Temporal Ordering in Fiction* (Baltimore: Johns Hopkins Press, 1978).
Tony Tanner, *Jane Austen* (London: Macmillan, 1986).

BIBLIOGRAPHY

For those who wish to explore criticism written before 1980, David Gilson provides a useful guide in his *A Bibliography of Jane Austen* (Oxford: Oxford University Press, 1982).

Notes on Contributors

Isabel Armstrong is Professor of English at Birkbeck College, University of London. She is the author of *Language as Living Form in Nineteenth Century Poetry* (Brighton, 1982), *Mansfield Park: Penguin Critical Studies* (Harmondsworth, 1988), *New Feminist Discourses: Critical Essays on Theories and Texts* (London, 1992).

Julia Prewitt Brown is Professor of English at Providence College, Rhode Island. She is the author of *Jane Austen's Novels* (Boston, 1979).

Rachel Brownstein is Professor of English in the Graduate School of the City University of New York. She is the author of *Becoming a Heroine: Reading about Women in Novels* (New York, 1982).

Marilyn Butler is King Edward VII Professor of English at the University of Cambridge. She is author of *Maria Edgeworth, a Literary Biography* (Cambridge, 1972), *Peacock Displayed: A Satirist in his Social Context* (London, 1979), *Romantics, Rebels and Reactionaries* (Oxford, 1981), *Paine, Godwin and the Revolution Controversy* (Cambridge, 1984) and, as editor with Janet Todd, *The Works of Mary Wollstonecraft* (London, 1989–).

Alistair Duckworth is Professor of English at the University of Florida, Gainesville. He is the author of *The Improvement of the Estate* (Baltimore, 1971).

Angela Leighton is Senior Lecturer in English at the University of Hull. She is author of *Shelley and the Sublime: An Interpretation of the Major Poems* (Cambridge, 1984), *Elizabeth Barrett Browning* (Brighton, 1986), and *Victorian Women Poets: Writing Against the Heart* (Harvester, 1992).

D. A. Miller is Professor of English at Harvard University, Cambridge, Mass. He is the author of *The Novel and the Police* (Berkeley, 1988).

Karen Newman is Professor of English at Brown University, Providence, Rhode Island. She is the author of *Shakespeare's Rhetoric of Comic Character: Dramatic Convention in Classical and Renaissance Comedy* (New York, 1985) and *Fashioning Femininity and English Renaissance Drama* (Chicago, 1991).

Judith Lowder Newton is Professor of English at La Salle University, Philadelphia. She is the author of *Feminist Criticism and Social Change: Sex, Class and Race in Literature and Culture* (New York, 1985).

Mary Poovey is Professor of English at the Johns Hopkins University, Baltimore. She is the author of *Uneven Developments: the Ideological Work of Gender in Mid-Victorian England* (London, 1989).

Index